the
spanish
treasure
fleets

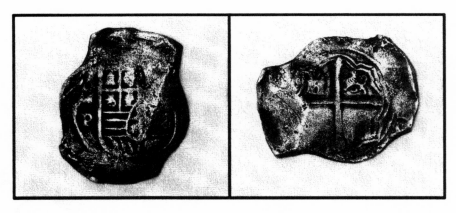

Evidence that an integrated global economy existed more than 300 years ago. *This silver peso, from the Mexico City mint, was one of millions of crude coins, known as cobs, that the Spanish produced in the colonial mints and then sent to Europe via the treasure fleets. Many of these coins ended up in the Netherlands as commercial profits or war booty. The Dutch, the greatest global traders of the seventeenth century, then used this form of currency, highly regarded because of its high silver content, to purchase goods in the Far East. On a voyage to Asia in 1656, the Dutch trading vessel* Vergulde Draeck (Golden Dragon), *carrying thousands of coins, including the one pictured here, sank off western Australia. Sports divers found the wreck in 1963, and in the 1970s professional marine archaeologists painstakingly surveyed the site and salvaged much of what remained of the cargo. (Photo from the author's collection)*

the spanish treasure fleets

Timothy R. Walton

Pineapple Press, Inc.
Sarasota, Florida

Inquiries should be addressed to:
Pineapple Press, Inc.
P.O. Box 3889
Sarasota, Florida 34230

www.pineapplepress.com

Library of Congress Cataloging-in-Publication data
Walton, Timothy R., 1948–
    Spanish treasure fleets / Timothy R. Walton
      p.   cm.
    Includes bibliographical references(p.   ) and index.
    ISBN 1-56164-049-2 (alk. paper)—ISBN 1-56164-261-4 (pbk. : alk. paper)
    1. Latin America—History—To 1830. 2. Gold mines and mining—Latin America—
History. 3. Silver mines and mining—Latin America—History. 4. Spain—Commerce—
History. 5. Merchant marine—Spain—History. 6. Money—Political aspects—History. 7.
Power (Social sciences)—Economic aspects—History. 8. Commerce—History.
I. Title.
F1411.W35   1994
980'.013—dc20   93-46419

First Edition
10   9   8   7   6   5   4   3   2

Design and composition by Cynthia Keenan
Printed in the United States of America

contents

maps and Illustrations

Maps

Illustrations

Diver's dream, archaeologist's nightmare. Page 212.
Divers at work on wreck sites. Page 214.
Coins recovered from Spanish wrecks. Pages 218-219.

All photographs of coins are actual size.

preface

his is a book about money. It looks at money as an economic and political institution that motivates people, shapes nations, and provides part of the historical record of our past. The story that unfolds in the following pages involves some of the most fundamental of human pursuits — the interwoven quests for wealth and power. There are many case studies of what individuals and nations do to acquire money and how they have used and abused great wealth once it has come into their possession. One of the most instructive examples illuminating these issues is the story of the struggle to control the mineral wealth of Latin America.

Five hundred years ago, Columbus sailed to the New World and claimed it for Spain. His voyages opened up a new era in history in which the previously isolated regions of the globe became linked into a single political and economic system. As a result, events in Madrid, London, and Amsterdam had repercussions in Manila, Mexico City, and New York. It is an era we are still living in, with oil and coffee as today's widely traded international commodities instead of the silks and spices of the sixteenth century. In our time, the American dollar is an international currency that is crucial for making the international system work. Four hundred years ago, it was the precious metals of the Indies that performed a similar function. For 300 years, the Spanish treasure fleets kept gold and silver moving throughout the world, and the ships, cargoes, and sailors of the treasure fleets helped create the foundations of the modern political and economic system. This book is the story of how those fleets performed their function.

My hobby of coin collecting originally prompted me to research the story of the Spanish treasure fleets. Like most collectors, I spend a certain amount of time wondering where my coins traveled before they reached me. There are some Spanish colonial coins in my collection, and it's hard to hold in your hand a Spanish piece of eight, minted in Mexico but bearing chopmarks indicating that it circulated in China, without asking yourself what tales it would tell if it could talk. Such a coin is concrete proof that a worldwide financial and trading system has functioned for centuries.

As I began to read about the mines, mints, and galleons of the Spanish Empire, the outlines of a fascinating maritime epic covering 300 years emerged. It was not too surprising to find that Christopher Columbus and Sir Francis Drake had played important parts in this saga, but it was unexpected to find that Sir Isaac Newton and Thomas Jefferson had also been involved. As I read more, it became clear that although a great deal of information is available about the diffusion of gold and silver from the Americas throughout the world, no one has pulled the whole story together and placed it into the economic, strategic, and diplomatic context of its time. That is what I have tried to do in this book.

To tell the story of the treasure fleets, I have concentrated on trying to find answers to several interrelated questions:

- What steps did the Spanish take to produce maximum output from the gold and silver mines and assure the political and economic value of what they produced?
- How much treasure resulted from these methods of production and how did the Spanish transport it to Europe?
- What were the main threats to the treasure fleets, and how successful were Spanish plans for protection?
- What happened to the large amounts of gold and silver carried by the treasure fleets, including what was lost in wars and shipwrecks?
- What role did precious metals from the Americas play in the budget of the Spanish government and the international financial system?

To find answers to these questions, I began to read books on the treasure fleets and related subjects and to jot down notes.

As my research continued, I found that many of my other interests and experiences helped get me involved in writing the story of the Spanish treasure fleets. For example, I served in the United States Navy and sailed some of the same routes taken by the Spanish treasure fleets. I have retained an interest in maritime and strategic matters ever since, and my years in the Navy helped me understand some of the problems, such as weather and distance, that Spanish sailors had to cope with.

As I accumulated information, I fell into the habits that have come from my academic training as a historian at the University of Virginia and my current job as an analyst for the Central Intelligence Agency. I was determined to find the main pieces of the story and put them together into a coherent whole. In time, it became clear that the operation of the treasure fleets was a major undercurrent to much of the world's history from the sixteenth to the eighteenth century.

Looking back from the perspective of centuries, the importance of the story of the treasure fleets emerges clearly. It should not be forgotten, however, that, at the time, individual events were shrouded in confusion and uncertainty and it was not always apparent that there was an intelligible pattern of development. The passage of time gives us an understanding of the past, but it also creates distortion by imposing an order that was not then present. It is useful to recall, from time to time, how dimly most individuals in the past understood the wisdom or relevance of what they were doing and how much, or how little, impact they would have on our world today.

Because of the demands of a full-time job and a shortage of funds (only a very limited part of the treasures of the Indies have found their way into my hands), I was unable to do research in the archives in Seville, Spain, which is the great storehouse of the records of the treasure fleets. Instead, I have drawn on the many writers who have presented various aspects of the story of the treasure fleets. A list of the works I consulted is provided in the recommendations for further reading. This approach has meant drawing on a variety of experts, such as academics, nonacademic historians, numismatists, and treasure hunters. Although they employ different techniques, all these writers liberally used intelligence, persistence, and imagination; and they have my gratitude and respect. I have tried to summarize judiciously a long and complicated story, but I am aware that specialists in the various periods and fields might fault me for slighting their specialty. Those who desire more details on particular aspects are invited to consult the works cited.

This book would not have been possible without access to major libraries. In this regard, I am particularly lucky to live near Washington, D.C., and to be able to visit the unrivaled library resources in the area. I consulted the collections at the Library of Congress, George Washington University, George Mason University, American University, and Georgetown University. In addition, the Fairfax County Public Library not only has one of the largest public library collections in the country but also acquired many books for me through interlibrary loans. I would like to extend many thanks to those who maintain these great collections and who provided me with cheerful and competent assistance.

I owe a special debt of gratitude to the numerous people who helped me turn a manuscript into a book. This is especially the case for two individuals who reviewed the draft and brought me back to reality on some issues that had become distorted during the years spent in libraries and in front of a word processor. Dr. Frank Sedwick meticulously went over the text and brought his great numismatic and historical knowledge to bear on various points. Robert F. Marx also made a number of valuable suggestions on how to improve the manuscript and provided invaluable assistance in locating many of the illustrations. June Cussen and the people at Pineapple Press were consistently helpful and understanding about the many editorial questions that came up during production. Finally, the staff at Editorial Experts Inc., of Alexandria, Virginia, were very patient and skillful in working with me to produce the graphics. Naturally, I take final responsibility for the accuracy, relevance, and completeness of the work that follows.

A Note on Currency Values

In a book in which money plays such a central role, it is only natural to wonder what the money is worth; that is to say, how much the coins of the past could purchase today. Although this is a simple and reasonable question, it does not have a satisfactory answer.

To begin with, economic structures have changed so much over 500 years that comparisons of value are virtually meaningless. There is nothing that has retained the same value over all those years and thus could function as a standard by which we can measure relative value, especially in monetary terms. A common possession of known value in the sixteenth century, such as a horse or a sword, has much less of a role in the modern economy, and its value is harder to determine in twentieth-century terms. Similarly, a common and inexpensive product of today's industrialized society, such as a wristwatch, would have fetched a much greater relative price several centuries ago. The value of most things, in relation to each other and in relation to money, are constantly changing and are simply not comparable over long periods of time.

Another difficulty is that there are different ways to judge the values of the coins that served as a standard of value, a medium of exchange, and a store of wealth during the time period under examination. One way is to look at their purchasing power; but as we have seen, values of objects, and thus the value of coins used to purchase those objects, change over time. Another way is to consider the present intrinsic value of the coins; but in many cases, their numismatic value is now far more than their old purchasing power or the current price of the gold and silver in the coins. Therefore, assigning value to old coins based on their current intrinsic value would give a distorted picture of what they were worth centuries ago.

One deceptively simple solution often employed is just to render the monetary amounts as they are given in the historical sources of the period. Although this provides an accurate measure of any particular financial transaction, it also produces a confusing array of crowns, *ducats*, *florins*, *escudos*, and potentially dozens more denominations. This does not provide much of a sense of what the historical monetary amounts are worth in relation to each other, not to mention what they would be worth today.

Before the reader gives up completely in frustration and confusion over how to determine the value of the treasure carried by the Spanish fleets, let me point out that the Spanish themselves provided a fairly reasonable answer. There was one factor that remained nearly constant in all the flux in economic matters over hundreds of years: the coins with the denomination of 8 *reales*, the famous pieces of eight, which came to be called pesos. The Spanish turned much of the silver they mined in the New World into pesos. These large silver coins were more widely circulated than their more valuable counterparts made from gold, and they became the models for the American silver dollar. Over the 300-year history of the Spanish treasure fleets, the silver content of those pesos declined by only about 5 percent.

Although it is not totally satisfactory to measure value by the amount of precious metal in coins, because the value of silver changed over time, the peso does provide a convenient accounting device that makes it possible to make rough comparisons of monetary amounts over vast amounts of space and time. For example, 10,000 pesos in Mexico City in 1550 has about the same silver content as 10,000 pesos in Manila in 1750 (but not the same purchasing power). Although inflation eroded the peso's purchasing power, throughout the period from the sixteenth to the eighteenth century, it was worth a considerable amount. An approximate idea of its value can be derived from the fact that in Columbus's time, the richest aristocrat in Spain earned over 80,000 pesos a year from his estates, while at the opposite end of the social scale, a typical poor laborer earned about 25 pesos annually.

Therefore, I have chosen to express all the monetary values in this book in pesos. In many cases, this was the original way of denominating the amount. In the remaining instances, I have converted other currencies into pesos at the exchange rate prevailing at the time. The amounts are usually rounded off, since they are provided to give an approximation of orders of magnitude rather than precise values. Because silver's value and other economic factors are still constantly changing, I have not assigned a modern purchasing power to the peso.

"There is no way of getting away from a treasure . . .
once it fastens itself upon our mind."

—Joseph Conrad

the
spanish
treasure
fleets

1. conquest, 1492–1544

n the last half of the fifteenth century, the age of the Renaissance, Europe was emerging from a troubled period that had lasted for more than 100 years and had included disasters such as the Black Death, the Hundred Years' War between France and England, and the loss of the great Christian metropolis of Constantinople to the Ottoman Turks. At this time, Europe was hardly any more developed, in political and economic terms, than other areas of the world. Indeed, Europe suffered somewhat in contrast to the dynamic expansion of the Turks and the size, wealth, and antiquity of Chinese civilization. Europeans were unable to make similar achievements because of internal divisions, shortage of resources, and pressure from powerful neighbors.

Forces were at work, however, that would soon make Europe the dominant continent. The pace of economic growth was picking up, and new techniques and inventions were enabling Europeans to travel great distances and impose their will throughout the planet. Politically, the areas along the western coast of the continent were coalescing into nation states, which would prove to be formidable institutions for organizing human effort. Personal ambition, national interest, and religious faith all contributed to Europe's drive to reach out to the rest of the world, but interwoven with all these other motives was the pursuit of wealth, especially in the form of precious metals.

Background to Conquest

The story of what would eventually become a worldwide imperial system linked by the treasure fleets begins in fifteenth-century Spain, but the realm King Ferdinand and Queen Isabella ruled was an unlikely seat of empire. It was an arid land, where most men made a hard living through farming or sheep herding. Other areas of Europe had more advantages and seemed more likely to become great imperial powers. The Low Countries and Italy, for example, had more developed commercial economies. Portugal had already taken the lead in searching out opportunities overseas. France, with some 15 million people, had more than twice the population of Spain. Spain did have important resources, however, including long-range ships, brave and skillful fighting men, and a sound currency. These turned out to be key elements in building the system of treasure fleets.

Spain under Ferdinand and Isabella was really two kingdoms, each with its own distinctive traditions, interests, and outlook. Ferdinand's Aragon, which included extensive provinces in Italy, was a major naval and commercial power in the Mediterranean, where the weather was usually mild and the distances to be traveled were relatively short. These factors had produced a distinctive approach to trade and war at sea.

The main warship for the Aragonese, as it had been for Mediterranean peoples since the days of the ancient Greeks, was the galley. Galleys could be used under many different conditions because their lateen sails, which were large triangular pieces of canvas hanging from long booms, enabled the ship to move forward even when the wind was not dead astern. When the wind died or when short bursts of speed and maneuverability were needed in combat, the galley had dozens of oars to push it forward. Because it was long, thin, and light, the galley could move quickly; but the disadvantage of its design was limited firepower. Such a ship could carry only a handful of the new cannon, which had been developed in the late medieval period. Moreover, it was only practical to place these cannon in the bow. The main striking force of the galley came from two factors: its ability to ram another vessel and the large contingent of soldiers on board who could cross over, once the galley made contact with an enemy ship, and overwhelm the opponent through hand-to-hand combat.

Because of its large crew and small cargo space, the galley was not suitable for extended voyages, and during wars this type of ship was usually used in conjunction with armies rather than as a wide-ranging, separate naval force. The Aragonese and other Mediterranean traders did not use the galley for long-distance trade either, except to carry luxuries with a small volume relative to their value, such as spices. For long-distance shipping of bulk goods, such as grain or wool, Mediterranean merchants used large, solid, pot-bellied ships called roundships, which depended solely on sails for propulsion and could be operated by only a small crew.

In the fifteenth century, in one of the great breakthroughs in seaborne transportation, shipbuilders in Spain and Portugal combined characteristics of the galley and the roundship, along with elements drawn from the sturdy merchant ships used in the rougher seas of northern Europe, to create a new ship type known as the caravel. Caravels were small ships, with a carrying capacity of about 100 tons or less of cargo and a crew of a few dozen men. But the caravel, which was solidly built and used a combination of square and lateen sails, had a much greater range than the galley. It was the basic vessel for the voyages of exploration that established the seaborne links between the continents in the late fifteenth and early sixteenth centuries.

One of the caravel's most important attributes was that it could carry a dozen or more cannon along its sides. Fifteenth-century shipboard guns were usually made of wrought iron and could handle only a small charge and projectile. Although they were not powerful enough to sink another ship, these early cannon could do serious damage to enemy personnel who were above deck outside the protective shell of the hull.[1]

In contrast to Aragon, Queen Isabella's Castile was mainly a land-based power. Castile had borne the brunt of the 700-year struggle to push the Muslims out of Spain, and as a result, its traditions were predominantly aristocratic and military. Unlike their more commercially oriented neighbors in Aragon, the Castilian leadership thought of advancement in terms of honor, glory, and conquest. After an austere life in a poor country, Castilian soldiers were used to danger and self-sacrifice. They were also crusaders, imbued with an exalted sense of mission. In the late fifteenth century, this potent mix of attitudes and experience made the Castilian infantry probably the best military men in Europe. These formidable fighting men had proven their value in driving the Moors out of Spain and keeping the French out of Italy. Whenever the fighting in Europe eased, one of the Spanish monarchs' main assets was the large number of proud, unemployed soldiers looking for wealth and glory.

It was the militant and aristocratic Castilians who conquered the New World, and their traditions and values had a powerful influence on the nature of the Spanish Empire. Castile's inclination was to seize the wealth of the New World rather than acquire it through trade. Although Castile did not have a great maritime tradition, it did have extensive coastlines, good harbors on the Atlantic Ocean, and experience in establishing overseas colonies in the Canary Islands.[2]

As Spain began to look outward in the late fifteenth century, it could also take advantage of developments taking place throughout Europe during the Renaissance. Although the pious Spanish were not interested in the secularism of the Renaissance, they were avid participants in other current trends. Not only in Spain, but also in England, France, and Portugal, states were becoming better organized and more powerful, so more resources could be effectively applied to problems. The enhanced capabilities of these more cohesive states fostered enterprise and national cohesion but also produced ambition and fear, especially among rulers. As a result, the international political arena became a more violent and dangerous environment.

In all these states, the form of government was monarchy, so domestic politics revolved around the efforts of the monarchs to impose their will on the other elements of society — the aristocracy, the merchant class, and the church. Monarchs also had to keep a wary eye on events outside their borders. Typically, they sought to strengthen their international position through conquest and marriage. One other thing that would help the emerging monarchs fulfill their ambitions was money, and they all craved it.

There were also improvements in ways of handling business as the medieval world gave way to the modern one, and here, too, much of the focus was on getting control of money. New means of financing, such as bills of exchange and international banks, enabled firms to expand their operations. Moreover, businessmen were learning to spread the risks of commerce by forming ad hoc partnerships. Opportunities for trade were expanding, not only because mariners were improving ship designs, but also because they were enhancing their navigational skills with better instruments and mathematics. The result of all these developments was an expansion of trade among the countries of Europe, particularly in bulky basic commodities like wool and grain, which led to a continuing search for even more opportunities for growth and profits in other products.[3]

One of the restraints on the tremendous amount of political and economic energy building up in Europe in the late fifteenth century was a shortage of reliable currency. For an economy to operate with any system more complex than barter, there had to be a standard of value, a medium of exchange, and a store of wealth. Around 600 B.C., the Greeks had invented coins, which were specific amounts of precious metals whose weight and purity were guaranteed by the government, to fulfill these functions.

In the centuries that followed, Europeans came to believe that precious metals had intrinsic value and were unique sources of economic potency. Both gold and silver were attractive in appearance and relatively rare, they were easy to work into convenient shapes such as ingots or coins, they could be readily

Sixteenth-century mariner's astrolabe. *From the fifteenth to the sixteenth century, mariners used instruments like this to estimate their position at sea. There are small holes in the two metal plates on the revolving indicator. By rotating the indicator so that the sun shines through both holes, a navigator obtains a reading of his approximate latitude along the rim. The astrolabe can also be used to make mathematical calculations, to measure the height of distant objects, and to tell the time of day. This example, which is now in the National Maritime Museum in Greenwich, England, was found in Ireland in the nineteenth century. It may have come from one of the many ships of the Spanish Armada that ran aground on the western coast of Ireland in 1588. In the eighteenth century, the astrolabe was superseded by the more accurate sextant, which is still in use. (Photo courtesy of Robert F. Marx)*

subdivided, and they did not deteriorate during storage or shipment. Coins were an important way to promote commerce; and as long as there was faith in the quality of metallic currency, there was no need to delay transactions by checking the content of each coin.

By the fifteenth century, the fundamental economic role of gold and silver was an unquestioned principle in Europe. As a result, Europeans craved the precious metals, especially in the form of coins, because they believed that this form of currency was virtually the only reliable money and had the almost magical ability to be exchanged for any commodity, anywhere, at any time.

The two precious metals played somewhat different roles in Europe's economy at the time of the Renaissance. Monarchs and merchants preferred gold for large political and commercial transactions because of its high value per unit. But Europe had few gold mines and did not produce enough to support an expanding international economy. Much of the gold used in Europe came from the Songhai Empire in West Africa. The Africans, who did not use gold for currency, were glad to trade it for practical goods from Europe like cloth, salt, and horses. In the late fifteenth century, the Portuguese had already established control over the flow of gold from Africa, and the gold trade was one of their great assets in the struggle among the emerging states.

Silver, on the other hand, was of only secondary importance in international trade but was widely used in the domestic economies of the European states. In contrast to the situation in the gold trade, there were indigenous sources of silver in Europe, mainly in the lands of the Holy Roman Empire. A powerful banking family in Augsburg, the Fuggers, controlled much of the production of silver in central Europe. Silver was relatively scarce compared to gold in the last half of the fifteenth century. This meant higher silver prices, which stimulated production and helped make the Fuggers one of the wealthiest families of the time. During the period from 1460 to 1530, silver production in central Europe increased 500 percent; and by the latter date, the mines in the region were producing nearly 100 tons of silver a year. To make the German silver as useful as possible, it was minted into high-quality coins called *talers*, which became a standard currency in central Europe. In the Low Countries, they called *talers* "*daalders*," and in English they came to be known as "dollars."[4]

Ferdinand and Isabella were well aware of the economic problems and opportunities of their time, and they were determined to promote the wealth and security of their realms through a firm and responsible exercise of royal authority. Although Castile and Aragon remained separate political and economic systems, with their own laws and institutions, the two monarchs carried out a number of economic reforms which strengthened royal government and laid the foundation for imperial expansion.

One of their most important undertakings was to restore the reliability of Spain's coinage. Ferdinand and Isabella abandoned the shortsighted approach of their predecessors, who had reaped profits by reducing the amount of gold and silver in coins produced at royal mints. In time, it became known that the intrinsic value of the coins was less than the value assigned to them by the government, and the result had been confusion and inflation.

In 1497, the king and queen ordered the mints to issue only coins with a high content of precious metals. The basic silver coin was the 8-*reales* piece, which was modeled on the *taler*, weighed about 0.9 troy ounce (or slightly more than 27 grams), and was 93 percent silver. This was a somewhat higher silver content than most European coins of the time, which meant that the new coins were widely accepted, and the Spanish economy had a firm foundation. Spanish gold coinage was more diverse and was variously denominated as *excelentes, castellanos*, and *ducats*.[5]

The only other form of international money available in Europe to supplement gold and silver was the bill of exchange. Shipping precious metals over long distances was expensive, risky, and time-consuming; and in the late Medieval period, Italian merchants had devised the bill of exchange as an alternative way to transfer funds. A bill of exchange was a promise to pay an individual a specific amount of specie at a stipulated time and place. Although it could be arranged between two merchants who trusted each other, it was much more common for merchants who had good connections to provide the service, for a fee, to a wider circle of people in business and politics who needed to move money safely and quickly over long distances. Rather than redeem each bill in cash, merchants tended to accumulate them, match their debts against what others owed them, and then pay only the relatively small balances that remained in cash.

The matching of bills of exchange and settlement of balances in cash was usually accomplished at the periodic fairs held by merchants in such centers of trade as Medina del Campo, in Spain, and Lyon, in France. These fairs became the main financial markets of Europe in the late medieval era. Although an increasing number of bills of exchange circulated in Europe, there were restrictions on their effectiveness. They were used only among a small number of international merchants and financiers, and the broad mass of the population had no access to this supplementary form of money. Moreover, bills of exchange were not honored by merchants in the Far East, the source of many of the goods Europeans purchased through intercontinental trade.[6]

The World Outside Europe
In the late fifteenth century, Europe's increasingly sophisticated, money-based

economy was largely isolated from the rest of the world, except for the neighboring Muslim lands. Political contacts, such as embassies or alliances, with the distant civilizations of the Western Hemisphere, the Far East, and Africa south of the Sahara were virtually unknown. Moreover, there was only a minute amount of trade, and it had only limited economic, political, or social impact.

One of the few examples of international commerce was the trade in spices from Asia, which had been going on since Roman times. Spices were avidly sought after as flavorings and preservatives because the European diet was fairly boring and there was no other known way to keep meat from spoiling. Spices and other Asian products, such as silk, were expensive, however, because of the many middlemen involved in the trade. Only the small upper crust of European society could afford such costly luxuries.

Most of the population in Europe, however, was too poor to participate in such long-distance trade or even in a money economy. The vast majority of people lived in self-sufficient villages and handled most of their business and obligations through barter or personal service.

As European traders began to break out of their isolation in the late fifteenth century and establish contact with other continents, they found that the European idea that gold and silver had intrinsic value and could be used for coinage was not a universal one. Moreover, Europeans soon realized that there was a striking imbalance between the areas where commerce was advanced and there was a need for precious metals, such as Europe and China, and the areas which had important stocks of gold and silver but little or no local interest in using them for monetary purposes, such the Western Hemisphere and Africa. Anyone who could manipulate this imbalance to his own advantage would reap great profits.

The Muslim world, immediately adjacent to Christian Europe, was both a challenge and an opportunity for European kings and merchants. Fired by their religion and an impressive record of military victories, Muslim states, especially the Ottoman Turks, were severing traditional trade routes to Asia and pressing against the borders of Europe. Despite their political and religious differences, however, the Christian and Muslim cultures shared some common ideas about money and commerce. Muslims were familiar with the concept of using precious metals for money because the Greeks had spread the use of coins throughout Europe, the Middle East, North Africa, and as far away as India.

The Muslims were also avid traders and were more than ready to make a profit by selling spices and other Asian luxuries to Italian merchants for gold and silver. Their conquests had given the Muslims influence or control in a wide swath of territory from ports of the eastern Mediterranean to areas where spices were grown in India and the Spice Islands of southeast Asia. Although commercial activity was extensive in the Muslim world, military-minded rulers tended to over-tax trade and thus to limit its growth. This created opportunities for Western merchants.

A Portuguese expedition to India in 1497-1499, under Vasco da Gama, was the first European success in establishing direct contact with the sources of spices in Asia. This enabled Lisbon merchants to divert more of the vast profits of the luxury trade into their own hands. Portuguese traders could cut out the middlemen by going directly to India, but they could not change one fundamental problem of commerce with Asia: the unfavorable balance of trade. The harsh reality was that Europe produced little that the Asians would accept in exchange for their silks and spices. One of the things da Gama and those who followed him learned, however, was that the producers of spices in Asia, like the Muslim merchants along the eastern shore of the Mediterranean, would gladly trade their products for silver and gold. Therefore, the only way for trade with the East to grow and prosper was for the Europeans to find large and reliable sources of gold and silver, and to acquire the precious metals as cheaply as possible.[7]

Beyond the Muslim world lay China, an exotic realm with its own unique approach to money and commerce. China was the source of other luxury products, such as porcelain and silk, that were in demand in intercontinental trade. Like Westerners, the Chinese believed that precious metals, especially silver, had intrinsic value, but they did not use them as currency. Coins had been in use in China since about 200 B.C., but they were usually made of bronze; and because these coins, which foreigners called cash, had little intrinsic value, they were only convenient for small transactions.

Another problem with the cash coins was that the Ming dynasty, which governed China at the dawn of the modern era, never minted enough of the small denomination coins, and there were many counterfeits in circulation. For large transfers and as a store of wealth, the Chinese did not coin silver, which was in short supply, but instead used ingots in a wide variety of sizes, known as *sycee*, which were exchanged on the basis of the market price of silver contained in each ingot. This meant that the Chinese used precious metals as a commodity that could shift in price, as opposed to the European concept that gold and silver, in the form of coins, had a stable value guaranteed by the government.

For large transactions, the Chinese had paper money that could be redeemed in precious metals, and they found paper currency particularly useful because of the low value of their coins. China's experiment with paper money had been disappointing, however, because in the fourteenth century the government gave in to the temptation to issue excessive amounts of paper currency, and thus undermined its value. With insufficient low-denomination bronze coins, no silver currency, and discredited paper money, China's monetary system was in disarray by the sixteenth century, and the Chinese had a strong need for a dependable form of money.

Although the lack of a reliable currency was a hindrance to trade, this problem was not a high priority for the government, whose values were shaped by scholars and landowners. China's mandarins believed that commerce was unproductive and parasitical. They sought to control trade rather than to promote it by solving economic problems, such as the shortage of reliable currency.[8]

China did have some opportunities to change its views of money and commerce through more contact with the outside world, but it turned its back on these openings. The Mings' policy toward foreign trade was a revealing example. In addition to its large population and sophisticated culture, China had many of the elements that the West would later use to establish command of the seas, including large seagoing vessels, well-established maritime trade routes, cannon and gunpowder, and the magnetic compass.

Between 1405 and 1433, seven expeditions, under Admiral Zheng He, traveled south to the Spice Islands and as far west as Africa in search of opportunities to collect tribute. The Chinese fleets were made up of as many as 60 large junks, armed with cannon, along with dozens of smaller support vessels. Tens of thousands of sailors, merchants, and officials were aboard these junks.

But the Ming mandarins who ran China never followed up on these voyages, which in a way were abortive treasure fleets launched from Asia rather than from Europe. Although some Chinese, especially the merchants, yearned for contact with the outside world, Chinese officials in Beijing were jealous of Zheng He and sincerely believed that their country was self-sufficient. Moreover, China's scholar-officials feared that an active maritime policy would be expensive, disruptive of traditional values, and a distraction from the wars against the barbarian tribes pushing down against the northern frontier. The mandarins prevailed, and the policy China adopted was to control strictly any foreign trade, with the goal of keeping it to a minimum.[9]

Because most early European expeditions to Asia did not penetrate as far as China, and the Chinese were no longer reaching outward, the Middle Kingdom remained largely aloof from the world economy during the late fifteenth and early sixteenth centuries. During these years, China participated in international trade only on a small scale, and even then only through intermediaries. Although this rejection of intercontinental trade originated in China's strong sense of superiority, in time it became a potential source of weakness. For instance, Chinese conservatism kept them from making more use of the military technology available to them, such as cannons and gunpowder. Reluctance to change also kept the Chinese government from taking steps to reform the currency. Such complacency would become a dangerous luxury when China came into closer contact with the outside world.

In the late fifteenth century, the remainder of the world was as removed as China, or even more so, from intercontinental trade and the concept of using precious metals as money. In Africa south of the Sahara, most of the commerce among the indigenous peoples was still conducted by barter, and Africans viewed gold as having little intrinsic value except for their limited trade with outsiders. In Central and South America, the Aztec and Inca civilizations believed that gold and silver were of divine origin and used them for religious and decorative purposes. The Incas referred to gold as the sweat of the sun and to silver as tears of the moon. Although they valued the precious metals, the Aztecs and Incas did not employ them for monetary purposes. Elsewhere, in North America, inner Asia, the Pacific Islands, and Australia, the mining and use of gold and silver were hardly known.

Europe Reaches Out to the World

Christopher Columbus found himself at the focal point of many of the great political and economic movements of his time. He approached Ferdinand and Isabella with his scheme for finding an alternate route to the Far East and opening up a new source of wealth at just the time the Spanish monarchs, who were completing the conquest of the last Muslim state in Western Europe, were in a position to take on new challenges. In many ways, the idea of finding an alternative pathway to the riches of the Far East was just an extension of the reconquest of Spain. What Columbus was offering was a solution to two of the greatest problems of the time: the shortage of precious metals and Muslim control of the trade routes to the East. His self-confidence came from his years of working with the Genoese and the Portuguese, which had given him a familiarity with improvements in ships and navigation and an awareness of the critical economic importance of precious metals, in particular, gold.

Columbus appears to have been obsessed with gold, and the craving for it helped mold his mission in the New World. From the very beginning, the effort to gain control of the mineral wealth of the New World inspired greed, violence, tragedy, and disappointment. In his reports of his voyages to Ferdinand and Isabella, he referred to the search for gold constantly. On his second day in the New World, October 13, 1492, he noted in his log, "I have been very attentive and have tried to find out if there is any gold here." The urgency of his quest for gold continued to run through many of the log entries covering his first days in the New World: "There are many things that I will probably never know because I cannot stay long enough to see everything. I must move on to discover others and to find gold." (October 17) "It is true, however, that should I find gold or spices in abundance, I would delay my return to Spain until I have gathered as much as possible." (October 19) "I am not going to waste any more time looking for this king or lord, since I know there is no gold mine here ... I must move on and discover many lands, until I come across a very profitable one." (October 23) Later he expressed the judgment that "Gold is most excellent; of gold there is formed treasure.... Whoever has it may do what he wishes in this world and come to bring souls into paradise." Much to Columbus' delight, the natives in the New World did have gold, and they were willing to trade it for the trinkets he offered.

Ferdinand and Isabella had promised Columbus that he would be the governor of any lands he claimed in their name. One of his first uses of this authority was to turn away from trade as a means to acquire precious metals and impose a tribute, payable in gold, on the native inhabitants. The first census taken in the New World was Columbus' accounting of how many people would be paying the tribute.[10]

Columbus focused his attention on Hispaniola, the only island where he was able to find gold in any quantity, and he founded his first settlement there. In 1494, when it became clear that his new colony could not survive on local supplies, Columbus sent ships back to Spain for food and other necessities. Included in the return cargo was over 40,000 pesos' worth of gold, and the 1494 fleet was the first of the treasure fleets from the Indies.

Within a few years the Spanish had bartered away or seized all the natives' gold ornaments, and Columbus had to keep up production by adopting a program of forced labor to pan for gold under Spanish supervision in the streams of Hispaniola. He paid the Spanish settlers a set wage, regardless of how much gold they forced the natives to produce.[11]

Despite all his efforts to find gold, Columbus' tenure as governor turned out to be a disappointment. Even though he called his new realm "the Indies," there was no new route to the Far East; and the golden tribute exacted from the "Indians" turned out to be meager. As a result of these and other problems, Ferdinand and Isabella removed Columbus from his post as governor, although they allowed him to continue his explorations.

Columbus' immediate successor was a special commissioner, Francisco de Bobadilla, who encouraged production of gold by permitting Spanish prospectors to keep a percentage of what they found rather than working for wages, as they had under Columbus. By 1502 Bobadilla had gathered over 300,000 pesos' worth of gold, and he prepared a fleet of 30 ships to return to Spain in triumph. Half the gold was for the royal treasury and half for private individuals.

Columbus, who was in the area for his last voyage of discovery, drew on the vast knowledge of weather conditions he had gained from his explorations and warned of the probability of a hurricane. Bobadilla paid no heed and sailed for home. Before the fleet had gone very far, a hurricane did indeed strike, and Bobadilla, along with most of the ships, crews, and treasure, were lost at sea just off the eastern coast of Hispaniola.[12]

The effort to produce gold by panning and mining in the islands continued, but with diminishing returns. Vigorous extraction exhausted the gold deposits, which were never very extensive to begin with, and forced labor and disease killed off most of the native workers. Production peaked in the second decade of the sixteenth century at about 400,000 pesos' worth a year and then began to decline. In the meantime, expeditions traveling further west across the Caribbean had returned with gold ornaments and tales of rich civilizations, and the colonists' attention began to shift to the mainland.[13]

Other Spanish voyages of exploration after Columbus expanded the Spanish Empire even further. The most spectacular of these journeys was Ferdinand Magellan's expedition of 1519-1521, the first to circumnavigate the globe. This impressive achievement was a mixture of tragedy and short-term futility: natives in the Philippines killed Magellan, and the Spanish government did not immediately follow up by sending settlers or traders across the Pacific.

Another intrepid traveler, Amerigo Vespucci, sailed with several Spanish expeditions to South America and was among the first to claim that the lands Columbus had explored were not the fringes of Asia but a New World. Vespucci's arguments were so convincing that people began to refer to the new discoveries as America in his honor.

The *Conquistadores*

The nature of the Spanish conquests in the Western Hemisphere and the heritage passed on to future generations were due in large measure to the mindset of men known as the *conquistadores*, or conquerors. They were violent men, often veterans of the wars against the French, the Italians, and the Muslims in southern Spain. Most of them came from poor, provincial families, and they believed that their swords were probably the only way they could carve out a pathway up the rigid social hierarchy of the time. Gold was the key to their dreams, and they had little or no thought of using diplomacy, reasoned argument, or trade to get it.

Vasco Núñez de Balboa led the first of the great expeditions on the mainland of the New World. In 1513, he and a small band of adventurers crossed the Isthmus of Panama and became the first Europeans to see the Pacific Ocean from the east. Balboa claimed the ocean and all lands that bordered on it for the

Gold figure from Panama. Natives in what is now Panama cast this representation of an alligator, which is about 5.5 inches (14 centimeters) long, out of an alloy of gold and copper. Columbus explored this area during his fourth and final voyage to the Caribbean, in 1502-1504, and called it Veragua. He was so impressed with the amount of gold he saw there that he claimed the region as his personal fief, and his descendants still hold the title of Duke of Veragua. (Transparency No. 2067(2). Courtesy Department of Library Services, American Museum of Natural History)

King of Spain. The natives of Panama had gold ornaments, but when the Spanish inquired about the source of the gold, the Indians asserted that there were no mines in the area. Balboa refused to believe them and tortured several native chiefs to death in an effort to get them to reveal the origins of the gold. The natives had been right, however; there were no gold mines of any consequence in Panama. Balboa himself was soon the victim of a judicial murder at the hands of his rivals, but his expedition had opened up a vast new area for conquest.[14]

In Cuba, the governor appointed Hernán Cortés to prepare to investigate the tales of rich civilizations to the west and to lead a small army of several hundred men there. In 1519, Cortés was so impatient that he left for the mainland without authorization. He founded the city of Veracruz as a base and began preparing to push inland. Two days after Cortés's arrival, the local Aztec governor paid a visit to the strangers' camp. He presented gifts, including gold ornaments, and asked Cortés where he came from and what his purpose was. Cortés replied, in a classic statement of the mentality of the *conquistadores*, that he and his companions "suffered from a disease of the heart that can only be cured by gold." Cortés was careful to dispatch immediately a share of the Aztec gifts to Charles V, who had recently succeeded Ferdinand as king, to show that he could deliver gold and to remove any doubts about his right to conduct an expedition that technically was illegal.

The golden presents were proof of the wealth of the mainland, and they provided all the motivation Cortés needed to march on to the Aztec capital, Tenochtitlán. Cortés was able to advance quickly on the capital city by making skillful use of alliances with other tribes, who resented the harsh rule of the Aztecs. It was also to Cortés's advantage that although the number of Spaniards under his command was small, they were ruthless and skilled fighters with weapons such as steel swords and pikes, cannon, and horses that confused and frightened the natives. Cortés also had a psychological advantage because of the Aztec legend that Quetzalcoatl, a white-skinned god who had bestowed the gifts of civilization on the tribe, would return in the early sixteenth century to reclaim the gold and silver he had hidden in the hills outside Tenochtitlán. The Aztecs believed that the Quetzalcoatl's arrival would herald the end of the Aztec Empire.

One of Cortés's most crucial early moves was to make the Aztec ruler, Moctezuma, his prisoner. Moctezuma had little choice but to acknowledge Spanish sovereignty; and because he did not share the Spanish worship of precious metals, he readily agreed to pay tribute. In obedience to Moctezuma's orders, the Aztecs turned over large amounts of gold and much smaller quantities of silver to the Spanish. Cortés's men melted down the cruder gold objects into bullion worth over 250,000 pesos and kept intact the finer pieces with artistic value, whose worth the Spanish estimated at another 700,000 pesos.

Cortés had overplayed his hand, however, and the natives soon rebelled against the Spanish. Moctezuma died during the fighting, depriving the Spanish of his value as a shield. In one bloody and confused night, Cortés evacuated the capital but lost much of the treasure.

Having seen the wealth and vulnerability of the Aztecs, Cortés was determined to conquer them. He forged a successful alliance with disaffected local tribes, subverted an expedition sent from Cuba to arrest him, and again marched on Tenochtitlán. This time he decided to starve the city methodically into submission and to destroy it in the process. For the decisive phase of the campaign he had less than a thousand soldiers at his disposal.

Aztec gold ornament. *Only a handful of the gold and silver objects that Cortés sent back to Spain were not melted down. The only other way to find out about the artwork of native goldsmiths in the Western Hemisphere is to recover items from tombs or hoards that the Spanish did not find. This example, now in the American Museum of Natural History in New York, was worn in a perforation made in an Aztec warrior's lower lip. For centuries, farmers or treasure hunters occasionally stumbled across caches of such ornaments. Until the twentieth century, most people considered the bullion value of pre-Columbian art to be far more important than the artistic worth, and native gold work usually went into the melting pot. (Negative No. 2A 2978, Photo by Boltin. Courtesy Department of Library Services, American Museum of Natural History)*

When Cortés and his men subdued the capital for the second and final time in 1521, they found only some 200,000 pesos' worth of gold in the ruins. Cortés was convinced there should have been more, and he tortured Cuauhtémoc, the last Aztec ruler, in an effort to find the location of the remaining Aztec treasure. Cuauhtémoc claimed his people had thrown the gold into the lake that surrounded the city. Although the Spanish recovered some gold from the waters around Tenochtitlán, they were disappointed at what they believed was a meager return on their efforts during the conquest. Cortés renamed the mainland New Spain, and the new capital of the colony, Mexico City, soon rose over the ruins of Tenochtitlán.[15]

The wealth Cortés began sending back to Europe caused a sensation. Albrecht Durer, a German artist whose father had been a goldsmith, had a good eye for skilled craftsmanship in the use of precious metals. When he saw some of the figurines Moctezuma sent Charles V as gifts, he exclaimed: "Never in all my life have I seen things that delighted my heart as much as these. For I saw among them amazing artistic objects, and I marvelled at the subtle ingenuity of the people of those distant lands." One of Charles V's courtiers marveled, "I am astonished to see workmanship excel the substance.... I never saw anything whose beauty might so allure the eye of man."

But those who rated the aesthetic worth above the monetary value were a tiny minority. What really excited Europeans was the existence of a new source of hard currency, and word spread quickly about the large amounts of gold and silver coming from New Spain. From the beginning of sustained contact between the two continents, an important component of the European concept of the New World was its potential as a vast storehouse of wealth in the form of precious metals.[16]

The French were the first among Spain's rivals to make a concerted effort to seize the wealth being brought back by the early treasure fleets. Rather than trying to search the vast and largely unknown waters of the Atlantic, the initial French strategy was to lie in wait off the Spanish ports, where they knew treasure ships would have to appear sooner or later. In 1522, French privateers, private ships that attacked shipping with the encouragement of the French government, seized some of the ships carrying back the first booty from the fall of the Aztec Empire. In the five years after the defeat of the Aztecs, the French strategy bore considerable fruit, and only about 220,000 pesos' worth of precious metals got through the swarms of privateers.

Because of the French attacks, Spanish authorities began to take the first steps to organize the defense of the treasure fleets. The government assembled a protective fleet of warships in 1522 and sent it out into the Atlantic to escort homeward-bound merchant ships carrying the treasure. In order to pay for the escort fleet, Spanish officials levied a new tax, the *averia*, which was a percentage of the value of the cargo. From 1526 on, the government also insisted that Spanish ships going to the New World travel in convoys.[17]

Because they wanted to maximize the flow of precious metals from the colonies, officials in the mother country were reluctant to send coins to New Spain, and this hindered economic development. In 1535, the government responded to pleas from the colonists and authorized the establishment of a mint in Mexico City. This was the first mint in the New World. The coins from the Mexico City mint were meant both for local use and for shipment to Spain on the treasure fleets. Silver production at this time was limited, however, and the

One of the earliest coins minted in the Western Hemisphere. This is a 4-reales piece made in Mexico City during the reign of Charles V. Charles's mother, Juana, who was kept in seclusion because she was mad, was technically his co-ruler, and her name also appears on the coinage. Colonial coins had designs that were different from coins minted in Spain. On the obverse was the coat of arms of Castile and on the reverse was Emperor Charles's emblem, the pillars of Hercules, and his motto, the Latin phrase "Plus Ultra," or more beyond. The pillars of Hercules, Gibraltar and its sister mountain on the south side of the strait, marked the gateway to the seas that connected all the continents. These pillars were the distinctive mark of colonial coins and were meant to symbolize Spanish preeminence in the world. The exact year of mintage was not indicated on these early coins. (Photo from the author's collection)

highest denomination coin produced was 4 *reales.*

Like many other government functions at the time, such as tax collecting and even manning and equipping the army and navy, the mints were not operated directly by the crown. Instead, private individuals agreed through *asientos,* or contracts, to provide a service for the government in return for cash or privileges. In the case of the colonial mints, individuals paid a fee to the government in return for a lease to operate the mint for their lifetimes.[18]

Two years after the founding of the mint at Mexico City, Charles consolidated the various kinds of gold currency of his empire and ordered gold coin to be denominated only in *escudos.* The largest gold coin was the 8-*escudo* piece, which was the same weight as the silver peso, about 0.9 troy ounce (27 grams), and was 92 percent gold. Large-scale minting of *escudos* did not actually begin until after Charles died. From then on, the system of gold coins denominated in *escudos* and silver coins denominated in *reales* continued in Spain for the next 300 years, with one *escudo* equalling 16 *reales* for most of the time. Initially, however, gold coins were not manufactured in the colonial mints, and all gold was shipped to Europe as bullion.

Within a few years, most of the readily available gold of the Aztecs had been gathered up and dispatched to Europe. A colony could not be maintained for long on only plunder, however, and many of the *conquistadores* in New Spain settled into a dull routine of administering the newly conquered territory.

Most settled down on large estates, where they made a good living by raising grain and cattle. Some were not satisfied with such a settled life, however, and continued to search for the sources of the Aztec treasure. Although the settlers did not have much luck in finding gold mines, they did discover a few silver deposits. This was not enough to satisfy the more adventurous spirits, who soon became excited about rumors that there were other wealthy empires to the south waiting to be conquered.

In 1531, after several false starts, Francisco Pizarro, who had been a member of Balboa's expedition to the Pacific, landed on the coast of Peru, which was alleged to be rich in gold. He had less than 200 men with him. The tiny army marched inland, and within a few months they made their way to the camp of Atahualpa, the ruler of the Inca Empire. Pizarro had studied Cortés's methods, and his first move was to seize Atahualpa.

The Inca ruler quickly came to appreciate the newcomers' lust for gold, and he promised that, if the Spanish would release him, he would give orders to fill his cell with gold up to a mark on the wall and to load another nearby room twice over with silver. The Spanish, noting that the cell measured 22 feet by 17 feet and Atahualpa's mark was nine feet from the floor, quickly agreed to his offer. For months, Indian laborers hauled in gold and silver while the Spanish watched in amazement. Most of the ransom was made up of utensils and ornaments, because, like the Aztecs, the Incas used precious metals primarily for artistic or religious purposes rather than for money.

In the end, the ransom came to over 6.5 tons of gold and about 13 tons of silver. Pizarro's clerks calculated that the gold was worth well over 2 million pesos and the silver another 350,000. After the Spanish moved on and looted the Inca capital of Cuzco, where palaces and temples were sheathed in precious metals, they gathered another 1 million pesos in gold and 1.5 million in silver. When a priest urged Pizarro to put more effort into converting the natives to Christianity, he retorted, "I have not come for any such reasons. I have come to take their gold away from them."

Pizarro reneged on his part of the bargain with Atahualpa by killing the Inca ruler to keep him from becoming a rallying point for resistance. The conqueror of Peru then turned to organizing the colony and founded the city of Lima to serve as the capital.

By the mid-1530s, when the Peruvian treasure was arriving in Spain in earnest, the treasure fleets were carrying an average of over 1 million pesos per year. At last, the Spanish dream of vast wealth won by the sword had come true. Such large amounts of treasure caused a sensation in Spain, and Charles V was delighted, because 25 percent or more of the total came into the royal treasury through various taxes. The emperor was unimpressed, however, with the few

Inca silver figurine. This representation of a llama, the Incas' main domestic animal, is just over nine inches (25 centimeters) long. Llamas were a symbol of prosperity, and this figurine was probably intended as a devotional object to be left in some sacred place. Unlike the Aztec treasure, where a few items remained intact, not a single item of Atahualpa's ransom survived the melting pot. In the 1530s, most of the cargo on the treasure fleets was bullion made by melting down such objects. (Negative No. 330026. Courtesy Department of Library Services, American Museum of Natural History)

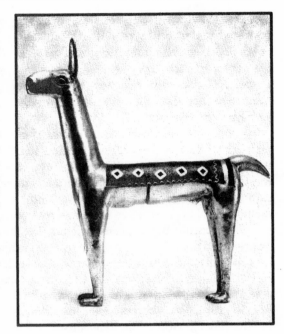

artistic objects made of precious metals saved from the melting pot as curiosities, and he ordered them all to be melted down with the rest of the gold and silver.[19]

The *conquistadores* in Peru soon began fighting among themselves over the huge treasure of the Incas; and, ironically, the violence soon provided a lesson in what constituted a "precious" metal. What the bickering *conquistadores* really needed was iron to make weapons and armor, but no iron ore had been found in Peru. So, despite its softness, they had to use the one metal that was readily available, silver, to make military equipment. Without a developed market economy, which Peru did not yet have, the silver was useless as a financial tool. Only when precious metals were shipped to Europe, or when the rest of the world outside Europe was molded into a commercial and financial system that operated on European terms, would the gold and silver of the New World be able to work the magic the *conquistadores* hoped for and transmute itself into power, possessions, and status.

In the meantime, the fighting over the wealth of Peru continued. Pizarro himself was killed in the struggle, and he never got to enjoy the wealth he had seized from the Incas. The turmoil went on for 15 years, and the disorder made it impossible to exploit fully the mineral wealth of Peru.[20]

The last of the great *conquistadores* was Gonzalo Jiménez de Quesada. He conquered New Granada, which is now Colombia plus parts of Venezuela and Ecuador, for Spain. Quesada was different from the other *conquistadores* in that he was a lawyer by training, but he was hardly less ruthless and greedy than the soldiers who headed the other ventures. Quesada began the conquest of New Granada in 1536 with a force of over 500 men. The Muisca people, who occupied the area, did not have large cities or elaborate architecture like the Aztecs and Incas, but they did have what Quesada and his men were looking for: gold.

In a three-year campaign, Quesada conquered the Muiscas and gathered up nearly a ton of gold, worth over 400,000 pesos, as booty. In what had now become the accepted *conquistador* style, Quesada sealed his conquest by founding a capital city, which he called Santa Fé de Bogotá. Despite the fact that Quesada successfully fended off rival claimants to the new colony and lawsuits claiming that he had cheated the government in accounting for the loot, Charles V refused to confirm Quesada as governor of the land he had conquered. Instead, Quesada, along with other Spaniards, became involved in the search for still more rich kingdoms to conquer.[21]

Vast reaches of the interior of North and South America remained unexplored in the mid-sixteenth century, and this fact gave rise to rumors of more wealth waiting for those who had the skill and determination to find it. The natives, desperate to do anything that would get the rapacious conquerors to move on, seemed to support these stories with their talk of golden realms just beyond the next mountain. Both Pizarro and Quesada had brothers who heard a mixture of fact and fancy about wealthy civilizations in the interior and believed this was an opportunity to make their own fortunes.

According to one popular tale in circulation, the ruler of a land high in the mountains was so rich that periodically he made a sacrifice to a local goddess by covering himself in gold dust and then bathing in a lake. The ruler and the land became known as *El Dorado*, the Gilded One. Gonzalo Pizarro spent two years trying to find *El Dorado* but ended up stranded in the upper reaches of the Amazon River. In desperation, he sent one of his lieutenants, Francisco de Orellana, and a small party down the river to find food. Orellana made it all the way to the Atlantic Ocean, and his men were the first Europeans to descend the length of the river and cross the continent.

Hernán Peréz de Quesada focused his search on Lake Guatavita, which filled the top of a dormant volcano deep in the mountains. Although he found some gold ornaments along the shore, Peréz de Quesada was never able to figure out a way to drain the lake.

In North America, there were similar fruitless expeditions, with Francisco

Vásquez de Coronado exploring the southwest section of the vast northern continent and Hernando de Soto scouring the southeast.[22]

The flow of treasure from the Indies continued to be an irresistible target for the French. They expanded their naval operations deep into the Atlantic in the 1530s, as the ocean became better known and the Spanish increased their security measures in home waters. French privateers captured nine ships in 1537, for example, and only about 1 million pesos arrived in Spain that year. The French also occasionally made raids on some of the chief cities in the Caribbean, including a successful attack on Cartagena, the main port of New Granada, in 1544.

The Spanish responded with a further tightening up of their defensive measures, with special attention to providing protection on the broad Atlantic. In 1537, for the first time, authorities in Spain sent a fleet of royal warships all the way to the Caribbean to escort the treasure fleets back to Spain. Six years later, after war with France broke out again, royal officials ordered all ships transiting to and from the Indies to travel in semiannual fleets that would be escorted by warships. Despite some losses, this system of convoys enabled the Spanish to bring home sizable amounts of treasure; and by the early 1540s receipts were averaging nearly 2 million pesos a year.[23]

The New World's Impact in Europe

Although the Spanish monarchs profited handsomely from their conquests in the Western Hemisphere, the Spanish Empire was not founded as a result of royal plans or initiatives. Instead, the crown approved the proposals or actions of private individuals, such as Cortés and Pizarro. In most cases, except for Columbus and Magellan, the government did not even provide financial assistance. If these private projects failed, the crown lost nothing; if they succeeded, the explorers and the monarch would share the profits.

Though disappointed by the initial results of colonization under Columbus, which did not bring great wealth or a path to the Orient, Ferdinand and Isabella moved quickly to obtain international agreements that would sanctify their claims to the Indies. In 1493, they persuaded Pope Alexander VI, a Spaniard who was indebted to them, to issue a series of papal bulls that adjudicated conflicting Spanish and Portuguese colonial claims by giving each a zone for their exclusive development. A year later, by the Treaty of Tordesillas, Spain and Portugal confirmed the concept of a dividing line and moved it somewhat to the west. The agreed boundary between the two empires bestowed most of the Western Hemisphere, except for Brazil, on Spain, while leaving the eastward route to Asia for Portugal.

For centuries to come, as the struggle to control the mineral wealth of the

Indies intensified, the Spanish would insist that, based on the work of their explorers and these documents, they had a lawful monopoly on the riches of the Indies. The papal bulls and the Treaty of Tordesillas were the first in a long series of attempts to regulate the affairs of the wider world, including the flow of precious metals, through diplomacy in Europe.[24]

It soon became clear, however, that the fate of the Indies and its treasures could not be decided by signing papers in Europe. Naturally, Spain's rivals, the English and French, refused to recognize the validity of the division of the world between Spain and Portugal. The English sent a Venetian, John Cabot, to investigate the potential of North America in 1497 and 1498. Giovanni de Verrazano, on behalf of the French king, made the first exploration down extensive stretches of the coast of North America in 1524. Ten years later, Jacques Cartier, also an agent of the French government, made the first of two trips to what would become Canada. The Spanish did not respond to these violations of their claimed monopoly because the voyages were far from the centers of wealth to the south and did not result in permanent settlements.

Charles V, first of the Habsburg monarchs of Spain and its empire overseas, had an overwhelming position in European politics that was a triumph of a family policy of political marriages. In 1516, he inherited the thrones of Castile and Aragon (including Naples and Sicily) from his maternal grandparents. The Low Countries, Franche-Comté in eastern France, Austria, and a scattering of lands in southern Germany came into his possession from his paternal grand-parents. Charles used his skills as a warrior, diplomat, and administrator to expand his realm even further. He arranged his election as Holy Roman Emperor in 1519, which gave him a loose authority over most of central Europe. Within a few more years, he had conquered Milan and made an alliance with Genoa, which gave him control of much of Italy.

By the 1530s, when the emperor surveyed the continent of Europe, only France, the British Isles, Portugal, Scandinavia, and Poland remained outside his authority; Russia was distant and virtually unknown, and the Balkans were part of the Ottoman Empire. Charles's motto, "*Plus Ultra*," implied that he believed there were no limits to his potential possessions or authority, and the conquest of the lands and wealth of the New World appeared to confirm these extravagant claims. No ruler since Charlemagne had dominated so much of Europe, and no one anywhere in the world had ever commanded such a large empire overseas.

Charles's realm was large and rich but also scattered and diverse, with little or no common ties of kinship, language, or geography. His holdings and areas over which he had influence included the most economically valuable part of Europe: the great commercial center of Antwerp, textile and armaments

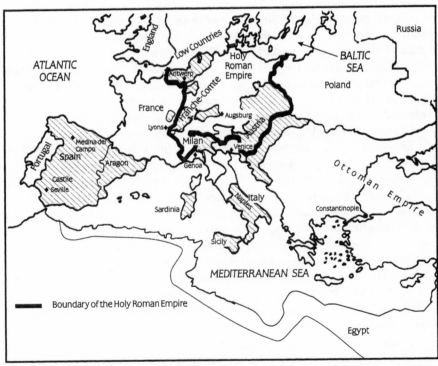

Map 1. The European Realm of Emperor Charles V in 1535

manufacturing regions in the Low Countries and northern Italy, the silver mines of southern Germany, and the wealthy banking centers of Augsburg and Genoa. He made no attempt to enforce a coherent policy for economic development for his entire empire, however, and he maintained local privileges, such as Castile's monopoly of the Indies trade, rather than make them available to the whole empire.

The strategic linchpin of the entire Habsburg system was northern Italy, which was easily accessible by sea and also commanded land routes west into France, north to the Netherlands and Germany, and east to Austria and the frontier with the Turks. Retaining control of this vital area of northern Italy became one of the chief goals of Charles and his successors, and one of the greatest drains on the wealth coming from the Indies.[25]

Charles V's vast array of power generated a formidable array of enemies. Habsburg lands surrounded France, and because of the needs of self-defense and their own ambitions, the French kings became Charles' greatest rivals in Europe. Charles also had to defend his possessions against the Turkish advance in the Mediterranean and the Balkans. Finally, with the coming of the Reformation in Germany, Charles became the chief guardian of the Catholic faith.

Charles V's many responsibilities meant that he was almost constantly at war and always in need of large amounts of money. His requirement for a large income was further exacerbated by the fact that the quickening pace of economic activity in the sixteenth century, combined with the flow of precious metals from the mines in Germany and the plunder of the New World, were causing inflation and reducing the purchasing power of royal revenues. Charles and his officials found themselves on a treadmill — the more they conquered and spent, the more money they needed to keep the system going.

Charles's main source of income was tax receipts, especially from Castile. Castile, with its colonies in the New World, was vital to Charles's imperial system because it was the only one of his realms that produced a sizable financial surplus. Through great efforts, he was able to increase the income of the Spanish crown from about 1.5 million pesos annually in the 1520s to over 2.5 million pesos by the 1550s. During this same period, his revenue from the Indies increased from 50,000 pesos a year to over 400,000. Although the amounts brought by the treasure fleets from the New World were only a limited percentage of Charles V's overall income, they were more useful than taxes because they were ready cash under the unquestioned control of the emperor.[26]

Both taxes and treasure were erratic sources of income, however, and Charles depended on the great banking houses of Genoa, Augsburg, and Antwerp to provide a larger and more even flow of money through loans. To finance his election as Holy Roman Emperor, for example, Charles V had

Emperor Charles V by Titian. *Charles was constantly on the move, personally conducting the functions of his exalted office in the many regions in Europe where he ruled. In addition to such peaceful chores as dispensing justice and conducting diplomatic negotiations, he also led his troops in battle. The strain of such a vigorous life shows in this portrait, done late in his life, which is now in the Alte Pinakothek in Munich. Charles viewed his authority though the prism of tradition and dealt with each of the areas he ruled through its own laws and customs rather than trying to establish a new and uniform system for the empire as a whole. (Photo courtesy of North Wind Picture Archives.)*

borrowed the equivalent of over 1 million pesos from a consortium of German bankers led by the Fuggers. The security he offered was gold from the New World. Thus, from the beginning, the wealth of the Indies and Charles's political ambitions were closely linked.

The crown raised other funds to pay its obligations in a variety of ways, including two kinds of borrowing: short-term loans and long-term bonds that worked like annuities. Arranging the short-term loans, like so many of the functions of government in the sixteenth century, was done through *asientos*. The *asiento* loans usually came from foreigners, with bankers from Germany and the Netherlands providing most of the money. In 1536, the Fuggers made a typical *asiento* for a loan, in which they provided 135,000 pesos in return for 14 percent interest and the first claim on the cargo of the next treasure fleet. Annuity bonds, or *juros*, had been used by the Spanish government to raise money since the time of Ferdinand and Isabella. *Juros* paid a lower interest rate than *asientos*—10 percent—and Charles V later lowered the rate to 7 percent in an effort to cut expenses. Even with the lower rate of return, the *juros* were popular, and many Spaniards and foreign investors considered them a safer investment than commercial or industrial enterprises.[27]

The bankers were also useful to Charles V because they could securely make transfers of money wherever it was needed throughout Charles's extensive domains. In the mid-sixteenth century, the commercial and financial capital of Europe was Antwerp, and this city provided the mechanisms through which the treasure of the New World flowed into the European economy. Spain itself had long sent wool and silver to Antwerp in return for textiles. Provinces near Antwerp also produced some of the best cannon and firearms in Europe, and they had customers all over the continent. In addition, Antwerp served as a broker for the grain and naval stores, such as timber, flax for sails, and hemp for rope, that came from the Baltic. Because of the need to import goods both for its own needs and for the colonies in the Indies, Spain had a negative trade balance and had to export gold and silver to make up the difference. The large amount of commercial activity carried out in Antwerp created a large pool of capital that Charles increasingly called upon for political purposes.

Through repayment of loans to bankers, as well as through wars and trade, the wealth of the New World spread throughout Europe. As a Venetian ambassador noted, "This gold that comes from the Indies does on Spain as rain does on a roof — it pours on her and it flows away." Much of the fuel for the massive financial engine that kept Charles's empire going came from the steady stream of New World gold and silver, and in time, the financial system of Europe became closely intertwined with the size and timing of the treasure fleets from the Indies. Large and regular shipments of precious metals kept international finance on an even keel; any interruption of the flow made it difficult to make payments and could create a financial panic.[28]

There never seemed to be enough money for Charles's government, and his expenditures always exceeded his income. As a result, the royal share from the treasure fleets was usually pledged to bankers years in advance of its receipt. In 1523, Charles was in desperate financial condition because the bankers would not loan him enough cash for his war with France, and he used more extreme measures to raise money by seizing private funds from the treasure fleets. The hapless private individuals who had shipped their wealth on Spanish ships were compensated with *juros*. By the end of his reign, in 1556, Charles owed over 25 million pesos to bankers, two-thirds of his budget went to finance his debts, and his annual payments on the debt exceeded receipts from the New World.[29]

The Administration of the Indies
The main Spanish tool for controlling the flow of wealth from the New World was the imperial bureaucracy, and the administrative machinery grew as the empire increased in size and wealth. Originally, a few court officials and a small staff of clerks in Seville, the main port for arrivals and departures, handled most colonial matters. Ferdinand and Isabella hoped to operate the trade of the Indies as a royal monopoly, as was done in Portugal. In time, however, it became clear that the commerce of the Atlantic was too large to be handled by such limited means, and the government resigned itself to supervising the work of private entrepreneurs.

In 1503, the Spanish government established the *Casa de Contratación*, or House of Trade, which had its headquarters in Seville and functioned as a many-faceted ministry of colonial trade for nearly three centuries. The *Casa* enforced the royal decrees concerning trade with the Indies, including regulations on ships, cargo, and passengers. Its responsibilities also included collecting customs duties and the royal share of the gold and silver. Moreover, *Casa* officials operated as a court that had both civil and criminal jurisdiction over the fleets. Finally, the *Casa* included a maritime academy that maintained charts of the New World and licensed navigators. Vespucci was the first head of this academy.[30]

The government ordered that all colonial trade should pass through Seville, and there were both advantages and disadvantages to this arrangement. Seville was the largest and wealthiest port along the Atlantic coast of Spain, and by the 1530s it had a population of about 55,000. From the point of view of the royal officials, it was easier to control both inbound and outbound commerce if it passed through a single city. Unlike ports in northern Spain or the Mediterra-

Shipbuilding in Seville. *Seville was not only an administrative and commercial hub of the Spanish colonies but also an important industrial center. Many of the vessels used in the treasure fleets were made in shipyards in and around Seville. Ships were the largest and most complex machines of the time, but virtually all the work of constructing them was done by hand. Another important center of Spanish shipbuilding was in the Basque country in the north. (Photo courtesy of the Hispanic Society of America)*

nean, Seville had an advantage because it was close to the currents and winds that carried ships westward across the Atlantic. Seville also was in the middle of a fertile area that produced the grain, wine, and olive oil that was in demand in the colonies. The city was more than 50 miles up the Guadalquivir River, and thus safe from surprise attack by hostile naval forces. On the other hand, the long river trip was difficult and time-consuming for ships, and a treacherous sand bar at the mouth of the river was the scene of many wrecks. All in all, though, the advantages outweighed the disadvantages, and colonial trade made Seville a boom town. Because of its special role as link to the New World, it was always full of exotic goods and people, and a local poet described it as "not a city but a world." Seville quickly gained an unsavory reputation for vice and ostentatious display, but it put its indelible stamp on the New World. All Spanish settlers and officials passed through Seville; and the city's red tile roofs, whitewashed walls, flower-decked wrought-iron balconies, and shaded courtyards were soon being duplicated in dozens of towns in the colonies.[31]

The main organization for managing the crown's revenues, including the income from the Indies, was the Council of Finance, which Charles V set up in 1523. The Council had jurisdiction only in Spain, however, and there was no central treasury or imperial bank to coordinate the finances of Charles's many possessions. In the early sixteenth century, the crown derived income from a wide variety of sources besides the treasure fleets, including sales taxes, customs receipts, grants from the church and the Cortes (a weak representative body with no real legislative power), rent from the monarch's large landholdings, and the sale of offices and titles. One of the many weaknesses of the Spanish financial system was the fact that two of the largest sources of wealth in Spain, the aristocracy and the church, were exempt from most taxes. This meant that the heaviest fiscal burden fell on those who were politically weak and least able to bear it, the poor.[32]

The Council of the Indies, established in 1524, was responsible for managing the Spanish empire in the New World. This Council and its small staff remained with the royal court, which had no permanent home in the early sixteenth century and moved around with the monarch on his travels. There was no separation of powers in the kingdom of Spain; in the name of the monarch, the Council exercised control over courts, taxation and expenditures, the church, military and naval forces, and economic policy. The Council made all important appointments and settled all disputes.

The Council's vast responsibilities, its sincere desire to be thorough, and its methods of deliberation meant that the most striking characteristic of Spanish administration was the slow pace of decision making. Members of the Council requested reports from the colonies on every conceivable topic, then wrote their own commentaries on them and passed the dossiers among themselves for further comments and questions. The system was made even more complex by the fact that the jurisdictions of the various councils often overlapped. At some point in the deliberations, the ever fatter files were forwarded to the monarch. He might make a decision, or he might request further information or analysis, and the process of study and deliberation would continue. As a result, the administration of the colonies was soon awash in a sea of paper.

Once the conquest of the Indies was complete, the Council of the Indies sent royal viceroys to the New World to act as personal representatives of the monarch and exert control over the unruly *conquistadores*. Spain's monarchs were trying to impose their will at home, and they had no desire to create an independent aristocracy in the New World. The first viceroy, Antonio de Mendoza, went to New Spain in 1535 and distinguished himself by establishing

spanish treasure fleets

European institutions such as a mint and a printing press. Viceroys did not rule alone, however, and the crown's authority in the Indies was wielded through a partnership with the church and an extensive colonial bureaucracy. In dramatic contrast to the brash and risky methods of the period of conquest, the colonial administration preferred to work in a manner that stressed paperwork, order, and routine. Given the vast distances involved and the limited means of communication, there were few alternatives.

This was the administrative heritage of the treasure fleets, whose operations would be guided by such bureaucratic procedures. Sometimes this was a source of strength, because everyone knew exactly what they should be doing. But at other times it resulted in weakness, because those who ran the fleets could be slow to respond to changing conditions.

Colonial government's slow pace was made even worse by institutional rivalries inherent in the system. A viceroy's influence was limited not only by his temporary tenure, but also by the power of the permanent officials of the royal judiciary, who were lawyers sent out from Spain. The viceroy and the law courts, as upholders of royal authority, were in turn restricted by the power of the town councils, manned by the local oligarchs. There were other checks to avoid the concentration of too much power, such as audits of officials after their time in office. Another technique was the use of special missions, which authorities in Spain sent out from time to time for specific investigations and which had full authority to take remedial action in the name of the crown.[33]

The last of the major components of the administrative machinery of Spain's maritime lifelines was the *Consulado*, or merchants' guild, founded in Seville in 1543. The main purpose of the *Consulado* was to settle civil disputes among the merchants, a useful service that took some of the load off the *Casa*. The *Consulado* also provided advice on commercial matters to the government, arranged marine insurance, assisted in the collection of taxes and, from time to time, made loans to the royal government. Many members of the *Consulado* were Genoese, who provided investment funds, knowledge of business techniques, and valuable international connections. Before long, the *Consulado* became a powerful lobby in defense of the merchants' interests.[34]

All this administrative machinery functioned in accordance with a view of colonial affairs and a set of economic assumptions that, in time, came to be known as mercantilism. The fundamental premise of mercantilism was that the economy of a country should be carefully managed by the government in order to maximize national power and independence. Colonies were an important part of the drive for state power, because they were a source of goods that could not be produced in the mother country and they provided protected markets on the mother country's terms. Mercantilists assumed that the amount of wealth in the world was finite and that there would be fierce international competition to control shares of that wealth. The central goal of a mercantilist state economy was to amass precious metals, which authorities believed had intrinsic value and could readily be turned into resources for trade and war. In a mercantilist system, successful operation of the treasure fleets would be one of the government's highest priorities.

Mercantilism reflected the worldview of the soldiers, lawyers, and officials who manned the bureaucracy rather than merchants or bankers who actually conducted Spain's commerce. But mercantilist measures could be turned to the businessmen's advantage, so they did not challenge the system. The results of the mercantilist outlook were policies such as the Seville monopoly and a ban on exporting bullion. Although mercantilism was severely criticized by later liberal theorists, the emphasis on bullion made some sense in an age when precious metals were the main form of money. Moreover, a rigid system of controls was probably the only viable way to dispose of high-priced Spanish goods.[35]

After Columbus opened transatlantic communications, the financial, diplomatic, and strategic situation in Western Europe was completely transformed. Spain leapt into the front ranks of the powers as a result of developments in which chance rather than calculation or planning played a large role, such as the acquisition of a source of vast wealth in the Indies and the deaths and dynastic marriages that brought Charles V to the throne. Unlike the Portuguese, whose empire was basically a system of trading posts, the Spanish sent tens of thousands of settlers to live in the colonies. These colonists enhanced Spanish control; and Spain's impact on the language, religion, politics, and economy of the New World is still obvious today. Spain's conquest of the Indies was not only a military confrontation but also a clash of value systems, with the different views of precious metals held by the Spanish and the natives being only one example.

Many factors held the new Spanish Empire together in the sixteenth century. Spain, the mother country, was prosperous and dynamic, it had a strong army and navy, and the monarchs were active and competent. After the tumultuous era of the *conquistadores*, in which few leaders in the colonies lived long enough to enjoy their booty, the royal government began to impose bureaucratic controls on the flow of wealth from the new colonies. Although it was not fully integrated, the Spanish Empire made a certain amount of economic sense, and it provided a vital service by funneling additional precious metals into the European economy. In addition, the huge size of the empire meant that it would be difficult for anyone else to duplicate the work of the *conquistadores* and conquer it quickly.

Size was also a disadvantage, however. Because the empire had been conquered so quickly and easily, Spain had not built up enough of the machinery of empire, especially in economic terms, to control effectively such a vast enterprise. Spanish resources were stretched thin to manage the empire, and from the very beginning one consequence was that foreigners, such as Columbus and the other Genoese, played a prominent role. Another consequence was that from the earliest days foreigners, especially the French, were able to seize significant quantities of the wealth coming from the New World. The limited resources available, compared to the vast task of running the empire, meant that the commercial and naval strategy of the empire was basically conservative and concerned with holding onto what Spain already held. Combined with Spanish methods of administration, which stressed routine and habit, this strategy meant there was a danger that the empire might be slow to adapt to changing circumstances. Having a viable maritime strategy, which began to happen under Charles V, was absolutely crucial for retaining control of his possessions, because Spain was more dependent than previous empires on long and vulnerable maritime lifelines. Could Spain answer this challenge?

The new importance of the Atlantic also opened opportunities for the other powers. France was first to take advantage of this situation and attack Spanish interests, but those efforts were only sporadic. England, on the other hand, had been transformed by the opening of the North Atlantic from a country on the fringes of Europe to a potentially great power commanding Europe's seaborne communications with the wider world. As soon as the English realized the advantages of their position and focused their resources on sea power, they would be in a position to challenge Spain's position.

2. consolidation, 1545–1579

he Spanish had acquired a huge empire with amazingly little expenditure of time, planning, or effort. Their methods of exploiting the empire were also haphazard, and during the period of conquest they had concentrated on extracting wealth by looting gold and silver objects from the natives. It soon became clear, however, that this was a shortsighted policy. The Spanish realized that to exploit the riches of the New World fully, they would have to devote more effort to long-term management of their colonies. In order to unlock the vast potential wealth of the empire, which they thought of primarily in terms of precious metals, a number of problems would have to be solved. These included finding abundant sources of gold and silver, extracting and processing the maximum amount of precious metals, and arranging secure methods of transfer to Spain.

Mining the Precious Metals
In 1545, a native accidentally discovered silver ore on a mountainside in Peru and transformed the nature of the Spanish Empire in the New World. From that point on, mining rather than pillage was to become the main method of deriving precious metals from the Indies, and the focus shifted from gold to silver. The mountain was called Potosí, and it contained the richest silver deposits yet

discovered in the world, with some of the veins of ore near the surface containing 50 percent pure silver. Initially, the continuing civil war among the *conquistadores* delayed the development of this vast wealth. Then during the tenure of Francisco de Toledo, who served as viceroy of Peru from 1569 to 1581, the Spanish established a system for processing the silver as efficiently as possible using the technology of the time.

Potosí's location created a variety of problems for those who wished to tap its riches. The mountain was located at a high elevation and on the far side of the mountains from the coast and the capital at Lima. As a result, everything for the operation of the mines had to be painstakingly hauled over many miles of mountain trails. It could, for example, take as long as two and one half months for goods or messages from the capital of Lima to reach Potosí. Toledo's most pressing problem, however, was the lack of strong backs in the immediate vicinity of Potosí. He hoped to avoid taking advantage of the natives, but the government expected him to produce the maximum amount of silver possible.

In order to get the manpower for heavy mining work, Toledo set up a system of forced labor, called the *mita*, under which the colonial authorities required one seventh of the adult males to work in the mines for shifts of six months or more. Although the government provided food for the miners and paid a wage of 1 *real* a day, the natives usually had little money left after they paid their taxes. The tunnels into the mountain, where the natives worked, were dark, stuffy, noisy, and dangerous. One Spanish observer called the mine "a mouth of hell, into which a great mass of people enter every year and are sacrificed by the greed of the Spaniards to their 'god.'"

To refine the ore more efficiently, Toledo encouraged use of the chemical process of mercury amalgamation, which German mining engineers had brought to the New World in the 1550s. The mercury, along with other chemical additives, was mixed with water and crushed silver ore in large open reservoirs until a paste formed. Over a period of six to eight weeks the mixture was occasionally stirred, and gradually, through a natural chemical reaction, the silver adhered to the mercury. When the paste was mixed with more water, the heavy amalgam of mercury and silver sank to the bottom of the reservoir and the lighter impurities could be skimmed off. The final step was to drain the water and heat the amalgam, which burned off the mercury and left very pure silver.

Because mercury was essential for efficient, large-scale silver production, authorities operated the system of procuring and selling it as a government monopoly. Profits from the trade in mercury were an important source of royal revenue, and control of mercury served as a useful way to monitor output and prevent fraud. If the mine owners did not report production proportional to the quantity of mercury they had purchased, the authorities suspected they were

Processing silver ore at Potosí. In the foreground is one of the open-air compounds where workers crushed the ore and mixed it with water, mercury, and other chemicals. The city of Potosí lies at the foot of the mountain. Off in the distance looms the fabled cerro rico *or "rich hill" itself, riddled with mine shafts. (Photo courtesy of the Hispanic Society of America)*

holding back silver from the legal system for processing ore.

Mercury mines were quite rare. But in 1563, by a great coincidence, the Spanish discovered a mercury mine at Huancavélica, about 700 miles (1,100 kilometers) north of Potosí. Forced labor was also used at Huancavélica, where a Spanish official claimed that he never knew a native laborer who could survive more than three years of exposure to the hard work and mercury poisoning. Another Spaniard lamented that "sending them to such work is sending them to die." But the mercury was too essential for the Spanish to linger over such sentiments. By a further stroke of luck, the only other mercury mines of any importance in the world were at Almadén, Spain, and Idria, in the province of Slovenia, both of which were areas under Habsburg control.[1]

By Spanish law, all subsurface minerals belonged to the monarch, but the royal bureaucracy usually did not extract precious metals itself. In return for a percentage of production, traditionally one fifth and known as the *quinto*, the king allowed private individuals to operate the mines. Under Toledo's system,

Spanish silver ingot. *Spanish officials shipped bullion from the Indies in ingots like this. Decipher the markings as follows:*
- *The Roman numerals indicate the fineness of the silver (2376 parts pure silver on a scale from 0 to 2400) and the tally number for the ship's manifest (18).*
- *The Arabic numerals show the weight.*
- *The stamps prove the tax has been paid.*

the regulations stipulated that the operators of the mines should take all the silver they processed to royal assay offices, so that officials could determine if it met minimum standards of purity. If it was acceptable, the silver was cast into ingots weighing an average of 60 to 70 troy pounds (22 to 26 kilograms). Officials deducted the *quinto* for the king and stamped the remaining bars to indicate that the royal taxes had been paid. Only then could private individuals legally hold the silver in the colonies or ship it to Spain.[2]

In 1572, Toledo also established a mint at Potosí, where the workers

- *The other letters are the personal signs of the assayer, shipper, and owners.*
*The notch on the right was where the assayer took a "bite" to determine the purity. This bar
weighs 72 pounds (about 32.5 kilograms) and would have been worth over 1,000 pesos.
Robert F. Marx recovered this example from the* Nuestra Señora de las Maravillas, *which
sank in the Bahamas in the mid-seventeenth century. (Photo courtesy of Robert F. Marx)*

produced crude coins known as cobs. Although the origin of the word "cob" is
unclear, it may have come from *cabo de barra*, or end of the bar. Mint workers
hammered the silver into a thin bar, cut off chunks roughly equivalent to the
weight of the coins, and then trimmed and stamped the coins by hand. The mint
at Potosi used neither skilled labor nor elaborate machinery, and the emphasis
was on maximum levels of production and high silver content rather than
artistry.

These irregularly shaped coins had a drawback, because some of their silver could easily be shaved off without detection. Nonetheless, they provided a convenient means to ship the silver so it could be quickly and accurately divided up and paid out soon after it arrived. Although the Spanish shipped some silver in the form of ingots, these cob-type coins made up the bulk of the cargoes of the treasure fleets. After the crude cobs reached Europe, mint officials in Spain and elsewhere melted many of them down and restruck the silver into better-quality coins.[3]

Toledo's tenure as viceroy was a great success, from the Spanish point of view, and the basic elements of his techniques for methodical exploitation of the mineral wealth of Peru would be employed for over two centuries. The results spoke for themselves, as royal income from the Peruvian mines increased from 20,000 pesos in 1570 to almost 2 million in 1579. Potosí became a great boom town with a population of about 120,000, the largest Spanish-speaking city in the world. The city's motto, on its coat of arms, summed up the crown's attitude:

I am rich Potosí
Treasure of the world
The king of all mountains
And the envy of all kings.[4]

Early peso from the Potosí mint. With the increasing flow of silver to the mint at Potosí, the large 8-reales piece, known in the Indies as the peso, soon became the mainstay of production. Unlike the earlier coins from Mexico City, with their distinctive pillar motif, the Peruvian ones had a cross on the reverse, which made them very similar to the coins minted in Spain at the time. The colonial peso weighed roughly 1 Spanish ounce (about 27.5 grams) and was 93 percent pure silver, the same weight and purity as the Spanish coins of 8 reales. Like its Spanish counterpart, the peso quickly became a much-sought-after coin. These crude pesos were an eloquent symbol of the Spanish attitude toward management of the wealth of the New World, which emphasized getting large quantities of silver, in an easy-to-use form, to Spain as quickly as possible, regardless of other considerations. (Photo from the author's collection)

In 1546, just a year after the discovery of the silver deposits at Potosí, a small party of soldiers and priests traveled through the desert of central New Spain, looking for signs of precious metals and natives who might be converted. Near a place called Zacatecas, 300 miles (475 kilometers) northwest of Mexico City, the Spanish tried to strike up friendships with the Indians by giving them trinkets. The explorers were elated when, in return, the Indians gave them pieces of silver ore. Once word of the presence of silver spread, settlers poured into the area and soon opened a number of rich mines.

The Spanish quickly organized the mining and processing of silver in New Spain along lines similar to the techniques used in Peru. New Spain's mines were also in a remote area, and all supplies and labor had to brought in from outside, with trips taking as much as two or three months. Royal authorities in New Spain also used their management of the mercury supply and the assay offices to retain control of production.

Moreover, procedures at the Mexico City mint also became similar to those in Peru. The flood of silver depressed standards, and the mint churned out cob-type coins, especially pieces of eight, as quickly as possible. The Mexico City mint also adopted the shield and cross patterns used in Spain and Peru for its product, so that all coins of the Spanish Empire became similar in appearance.

There were several ways, however, in which silver mining in New Spain was different from the methods used in Peru. For one thing, there was no great single mining center in New Spain equivalent to Potosí in Peru. Zacatecas became the most productive of the early mines, but there were also rich ores at Guanajuato and other locations. Another difference was that output from the northern mines lagged behind that of Peru. As a result, in New Spain, royal authorities levied only a 10 percent tax, instead of 20 percent, to encourage production.[5]

The third great source of precious metals in the New World was in New Granada, where the Spanish had discovered gold deep in the interior in 1537. Most of the gold produced in New Granada came from panning along streams. Because the natives soon died out, the Spanish imported slaves from Africa to provide the necessary labor. The volume of gold produced in New Granada was nowhere near the amounts of silver coming from Peru and New Spain, but its higher value per ounce meant that it provided a significant contribution to the overall production of precious metals in the colonies. In the sixteenth century there was no mint in New Granada, and local authorities shipped the gold back to Spain as bullion.[6]

As a result of the discoveries of gold and silver deposits in the 1530s and 1540s, and the processing techniques the government instituted, the Spanish colonies in America became the world's greatest source of precious metals. Although the eastbound fleets carried other colonial products, such as hides and dyestuffs, most of the cargo was made up of precious metals. By the 1570s the colonies were sending a total of about 5 million pesos' worth of precious metals a year to Spain, which far surpassed what was available from the traditional sources in Germany and Africa. Over 95 percent of the total, by weight, was silver, although gold's higher price meant that it accounted for as much as one-third of the total value of the cargoes during this period.[7]

The more methodical exploitation of the wealth of the Indies in the late sixteenth century clearly showed that mining was more productive than plunder. Nonetheless, a few people still followed the dream of *El Dorado*, believing in an undiscovered and rich kingdom ripe for the picking by anyone who had the energy and ruthlessness to find it.

In 1560, an expedition to go in search of *El Dorado* was launched from Peru. After several months of fruitless searching, one of the officers, Lope de Aguirre, seized control, in the belief that he could be more effective at finding the elusive golden kingdom. Aguirre spent more months roaming the jungle, and somewhere along the way he apparently went mad and decided to take over Peru and make it his personal kingdom. Aguirre forced his men to renounce King Philip II and proclaimed one of the soldiers as "Prince of Peru." The search for gold eventually degenerated into squabbling among the Spaniards, along with torture, murder, and pillage inflicted on the natives. In response, colonial authorities declared Aguirre and his men to be outlaws. In a final spasm of violence, Aguirre killed his daughter and was then shot by his own men as the local militia closed in to arrest him. The *conquistador* mentality had reached its *reductio ad absurdum* with Aguirre, and his greed and brutality had gained him nothing. Quesada and some others continued to search for *El Dorado* on into the 1570s, but there were only a dwindling few who believed there was still gold in the Indies that could be gained by the sword.[8]

The Organization of the Treasure Fleets

The man who profited most from the great mining boom that started in the Indies in the mid-sixteenth century was Philip II, who became King of Spain in 1556, after his father, Charles V, retired. Philip did not assume all his father's titles and responsibilities, however; his uncle, Ferdinand I, received the Austrian provinces and later became Holy Roman Emperor. Philip's share of the inheritance was Spain, much of Italy, the Low Countries, and the colonies in the Indies. For a few years, he was married to Queen Mary of England, and as her king-consort had hopes of dominating that country as well.

Although Philip's responsibilities were less than those of his father, he still

King Philip II of Spain. *This painting, by Lucas de Heere and now in the Prado Museum in Madrid, shows Philip, who ruled Spain for 42 years, in his prime. In his youth, Philip followed his father's example and traveled widely in his dominions. But as the years went on, Philip, uncomfortable with personal contacts beyond his family and a close circle of advisers, became more of a recluse. He preferred to work in the Escorial Palace, outside Madrid, where he could pore over paperwork, consult priests for spiritual advice, ponder the tombs of his ancestors, and relax with his impressive collection of books and art. (Photo courtesy of Robert F. Marx)*

faced a number of major problems that constantly competed for attention and resources. The number and intensity of his problems, his personal sense of responsibility, and his proclivity for hard work meant that Philip paid close attention to every detail of the management of his vast empire. One of his chief concerns was to maintain control of the flow of wealth from the New World. He was particularly alarmed after the French plundered and burned Havana in 1555, and the merchants' *Consulado* of Seville cried out for action. Philip, in consultation with the officials of the Council of the Indies and the *Casa de Contratación*, examined the situation and concluded that an overhaul of the system of the treasure fleets was necessary.[9]

One of the key figures in Philip's renovation of the fleet system was the Spanish naval hero, Pedro Menéndez de Avilés. Unlike many of the men who held posts in the Spanish colonial bureaucracy, Menéndez had actually served in the treasure fleets. In 1555, he led a fleet of treasure ships safely home after the French sacking of Havana, and in the years that followed, Menéndez made a name for himself as a successful commander of other treasure fleets. Menéndez was not part of the clique of wealthy merchants who dominated the Seville commercial establishment, and although he was a favorite at court, he had a stormy relationship with the *Casa de Contratación*. Royal officials

Pedro Menéndez de Avilés. King Philip personally chose Menéndez to design the system for operating the treasure fleets. The king knew Menéndez well because the latter had commanded the fleet that had carried Philip to England for his wedding with Queen Mary. Menéndez's greed and ruthlessness were equal to that of any conquistador, *but, unlike the adventurers of the previous generation, he also had a grasp of how to plan and carry out a wide-ranging maritime strategy. (Photo courtesy of the Hispanic Society of America)*

arrested him on two occasions, in 1556 and 1563, and charged him with violating the *Casa's* elaborate rules. Philip, who respected Menendez's abilities, intervened to get the charges dismissed and made him a special adviser to the crown on maritime matters.[10]

From 1564 to 1566, the Council of the Indies issued a series of regulations for the treasure fleets that were based on over half a century of experience as well as Menéndez's personal views. These procedures were to be the basic guidelines for fleet operations for decades to come. Menéndez's more systematic methods for securely transferring precious metals provided a valuable complement to Toledo's efforts to increase production in the mines. The new plan adopted in the 1560s, which was cautious and defensive in nature but potentially extremely expensive, included three main elements:

- fortified bases at the fleets' main ports of call in the Indies.
- intensive naval patrols in the Caribbean and the Atlantic waters off Spain, at the vulnerable points where the treasure fleets began and ended their voyages.
- heavily guarded convoys operating on a regular schedule to shuttle ships between the strong points and protective squadrons.

Since the main threat was from the sea, the plan included few efforts to defend the chief political and economic centers of the New World, such as Mexico City, Lima, Potosí, and Zacatecas, which were safely located inland. The treasure fleets were to be almost entirely a maritime system, which eventually included ports and shipping lanes covering two thirds of the world.

Under the new procedures adopted in the 1560s, two great convoys, the *Tierra Firme* fleet and the New Spain fleet, were to depart Spain every year carrying supplies the colonists needed. The timing of their sailing was carefully calculated to take maximum advantage of winds and currents, to avoid the worst of the tropical heat in the summer, and to circumvent the violent storms of the Atlantic in the fall and winter. To reduce the risk of losing an entire year's production of gold and silver in a single storm, the fleets usually traveled separately. In time of war, however, when protection from enemy fleets was the main concern, all ships sailed together.

During the heyday of the treasure fleets, in the last half of the sixteenth century, 60 or more warships and merchant ships traveled in a convoy. There were also usually several smaller craft to patrol the surrounding waters and carry messages. Two warships usually accompanied the New Spain convoy, which the Spanish called the *flota* (fleet). An average of six or more warships traveled with the other convoy, the *Tierra Firme* fleet, which carried the bulk of the treasure because of the high productivity of Potosí. Because it was more heavily armed, the *Tierra Firme* convoy became known as the *galeones*, or galleons. Later, as production from the mines soared and frequent wars increased the threat to the flow of treasure, Spanish authorities often sent a third type of fleet, which was made up only of warships.

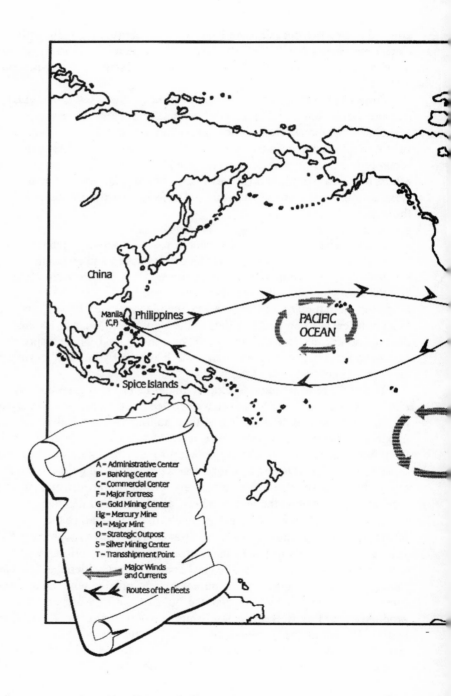

China

Manila Philippines
(C,F)

Spice Islands

PACIFIC
OCEAN

A = Administrative Center
B = Banking Center
C = Commercial Center
F = Major Fortress
G = Gold Mining Center
Hg = Mercury Mine
M = Major Mint
O = Strategic Outpost
S = Silver Mining Center
T = Transshipment Point

Major Winds
and Currents

Routes of the fleets

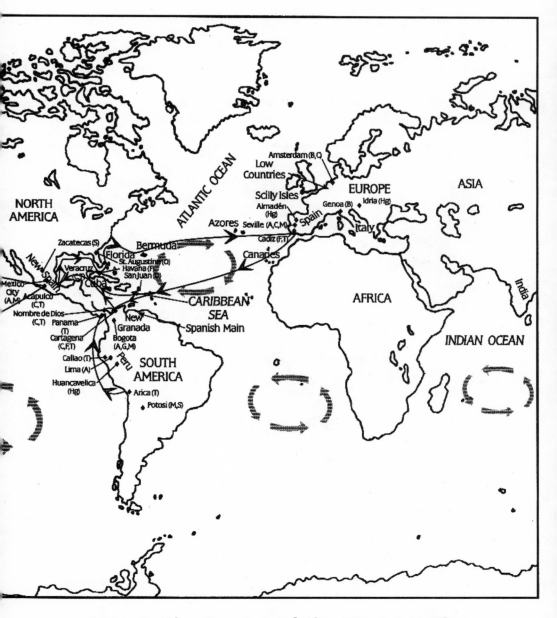

Map 2. The Routes of the Treasure Fleets

49

The merchant ships of the fleets usually operated on a two-year cycle and remained in the Caribbean over the winter months, while the warships carrying the treasure returned as quickly as possible to Spain. This schedule meant that there were long periods with few, if any, warships in the Caribbean, but Spanish authorities considered this an acceptable risk as long as foreign incursions were relatively rare.

Convoys were a traditional, but controversial, means of maritime defense. For centuries, Italian traders had organized their ships into great fleets that

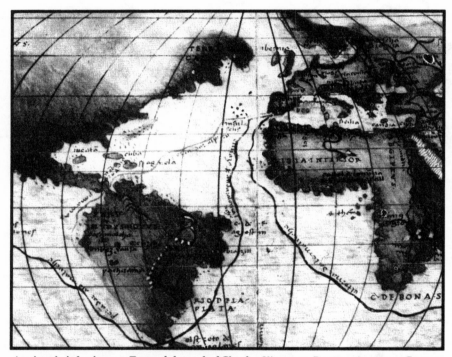

A prince's inheritance. Toward the end of Charles V's reign, Battista Agnese, a Genoese mapmaker, prepared an atlas of the world for Prince Philip. The lavishly produced book focused on the extensive Habsburg possessions around the globe. On this page, a dark blue line shows Magellan's route around the world. The map also shows the new conquests in the Western Hemisphere in considerable detail, with the route of the treasure fleets represented as a ribbon of gold running up the coast of Peru and then across the Caribbean and Atlantic to Spain. The path of the fleets shown on the map is inaccurate, reflecting the view of a landsman rather than a sailor. The route going northeast across the ocean is the shortest distance between the Caribbean and Spain. But because of winds and currents, the quickest way to make the voyage was actually to travel north at first, along the coast of North America, and then turn east. (Photo courtesy of the John Carter Brown Library at Brown University)

sailed to the Middle East, the Low Countries, and other destinations in European waters. Merchants often groused about sailing together because it meant all of the cargoes arrived at one time, which forced down prices. On the other hand, naval commanders, who were responsible for protecting the fleets, believed it was more efficient to protect one large group rather than dozens of individual ships. Maritime strategists in the sixteenth century, and for centuries afterward, also thought it made more sense to remain close to the likely target of an attack rather than to waste energy scouring the vast ocean looking for the enemy. As was usually the case with the treasure fleets, control and security were given top priority, and government officials overruled the merchants' objections to convoys. If they wanted to be defended, merchant ships would have to sail in convoys.

Both outbound fleets began their voyages by first sailing south to the Canary Islands, where the ships usually stopped for supplies. Then the convoys turned due west to take advantage of the trade winds. The two fleets left at different times, however.

Vessels bound for New Spain departed in the spring; and, traveling at a speed of about four knots, took nearly two months to reach Veracruz on an average voyage. When officials in Mexico City expected the fleet, they sent wagons or long mule trains to the port, carrying the silver that had been stored in the capital. After the fleet arrived, there was a great fair, at which the merchants from Seville exchanged their goods for silver. In the early years, the fair was held in Veracruz itself, but later the colonists moved it to a cooler and more healthy location slightly inland. Prices at the fair were high, but the merchants claimed they needed large profits to compensate them for the risks of the long voyage. Once the fair was over, the silver, which included the Spanish merchants' receipts, private funds of individuals living in New Spain, and the crown's share of the past year's silver production, was loaded onto ships for the voyage to Spain. During the first leg of the journey, winds and currents forced the fleet to travel along the coast bordering the Gulf of Mexico as it made its way to Havana.

In late summer, the *Tierra Firme*, or Mainland, fleet sailed from Seville bound for Cartagena, a voyage that took four to six weeks. The *Tierra Firme* fleet's mission was to pick up the gold and silver from the southern colonies. Once the fleet was safely in Cartagena, authorities sent word to Panama City, advising officials there to start shipment of the Peruvian silver that had been held on the far side of the isthmus to protect it from raiders in the Caribbean.

Silver came to Panama on the ships of the South Sea fleet, the link between the mines of Peru and the transit route over the isthmus. The South Sea fleet was smaller and less heavily armed than its Atlantic counterparts, because it was

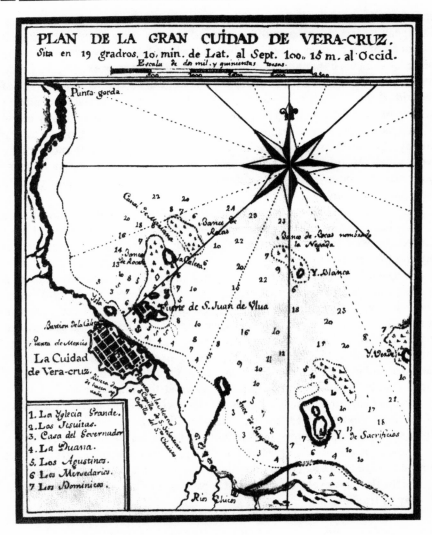

Map of Veracruz. Veracruz, the main Caribbean port of New Spain, was founded by Cortés. Protection from enemy attack was provided by the fort on San Juan de Ulua Island, just offshore. But Veracruz never become a major city in the colonial period. The area's heat and humidity made it too uncomfortable for full-time inhabitants, and it was a ghost town except when the fleet was in port. Moreover, ships had to anchor in an open roadstead, where they were exposed to storms. The one factor in its favor was that the distance between Mexico City and Veracruz was shorter than between the capital and any other port on the east coast. (Photo from the author's collection)

Map of Cartagena. This map shows the city, founded in 1533, at the lower left; the capacious harbor; and the narrow entrance, at the lower right, with its heavy fortifications. The map is inaccurate, however, in a number of details. For example, there is a second entrance to the harbor closer to the city, although this was too shallow for larger ships to use. Cartagena's advantages as a port and its proximity to the Magdalena River, which provided access to the goldfields of New Granada, made it the commercial center of the northern coast of mainland South America, the famous "Spanish Main." (Photo courtesy of North Wind Picture Archive)

believed to be almost impossible for foreign ships to make the long and dangerous passage through the Straits of Magellan, at the southern tip of South America, and into the Pacific. It took two months or more to move the silver to Panama from Arica and Callao, the main ports that served the Peruvian silver mines.

Panama City, founded in 1519, had a poor harbor and a terrible climate, but it was located at the narrowest part of the isthmus. From Panama City, mules and riverboats carried the silver overland to Nombre de Dios, where the fleet from Cartagena came to pick it up. Like Veracruz, Nombre de Dios was too unhealthy to be a permanent residence. It came to life only when the treasure ships were present and there was another great fair, similar to the one in Veracruz, to exchange silver for merchandise from Europe.

Both the New Spain and the *Tierra Firme* fleets made a stop at Havana before starting the return trip across the Atlantic, the longest part of the fleets' voyage. Colonial authorities set up a large shipyard in Havana because of the needs of the fleets and the abundant supplies of timber nearby. Unlike like so

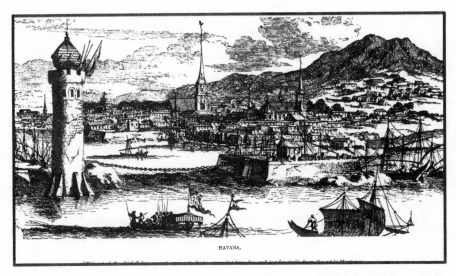

HAVANA.

View of Havana. Havana, founded in 1519, was probably the finest harbor in the Indies. Entire fleets could easily seek shelter there, and, like Cartagena, Havana had a narrow entrance that was easy to defend. For centuries it was one of the most important bases of Spanish power in the New World. (Photo courtesy of North Wind Picture Archives)

many ports in the Caribbean, Havana was a pleasant stop for Spanish mariners because it had a mild climate.

From Havana, the fleets traveled along the coast of Florida and rode the Gulf Stream, which had been discovered by Juan Ponce de León in 1513, as far as Cape Hatteras before turning east for the return to Spain. The trip along the coast of Florida was the most vulnerable part of the voyage. Winds and currents meant that virtually every ounce of gold and silver had to pass this way, but it was a region with dangerous shoals and hurricanes. Moreover, convoys starting out into the Atlantic were moving into a region not covered by the protective squadrons the Spanish planned to establish in Caribbean and Spanish home waters. Despite the dangerous shoals that surrounded Bermuda, the fleets usually passed close to that island in order to check their position before making the final run to Spain.

As the fleet entered dangerous European waters, where it was easier for Spain's enemies to operate, officials in Seville often sent a special escort squadron, the Armada of the Ocean Sea, to meet the treasure fleets in the Azores and escort them safely home. The final hurdle, a natural one, was the sandbar at the mouth of the Guadalquivir River. Once they were over that obstacle, the ships of the treasure fleets could be confident they would make it to Seville without further losses.[11]

Even after the routes of the treasure fleets had been established by regulations of the 1560s, there was still work to be done to strengthen the convoy system. Menéndez was especially concerned about Florida, where French Protestants had founded a colony in 1562. With his keen strategic sense, Menéndez realized that the Florida coast, which every treasure fleet had to pass, must be in Spanish hands. The fact that the intruders were Protestants made their destruction even more necessary in Spanish eyes. Menéndez asked Philip's permission to bring Florida under Spanish control, and in 1565 the king enthusiastically approved. In a ruthless campaign, Menendez captured the French settlements and slaughtered several hundred colonists after they had surrendered.

Menéndez became the first Spanish governor of Florida. He consolidated Spain's hold on the area by founding and fortifying St. Augustine. The new governor told King Philip that the purpose of the colony at St. Augustine was to "fix our frontier lines here, gain the waterway of the Bahamas, and work the mines of New Spain."

View of St. Augustine. This early view shows the settlement before the construction of Castillo de San Marcos, which was built in the late seventeenth century and is still standing. St. Augustine was the first permanent European settlement in what would later be the United States. The origins of the European influence that would have such a profound impact on the history of the United States arose from the need to protect the Spanish treasure fleets. (Photo courtesy of North Wind Picture Archives)

While serving as governor of Florida, Menéndez made tours of inspection throughout the region and tried to put into effect the defensive system for the Caribbean that he had helped to design. But his plans were too ambitious for the resources available, and the Spanish never fully implemented the plans for fortresses, escort squadrons, and convoys. Work started on extensive fortifications at Havana and Cartagena, but there was little progress at other locations. Although a protective fleet operated in Spanish waters, there was not enough money for the Caribbean-based escort squadron Menéndez had envisioned. Even the convoy system did not operate with 100 percent effectiveness, because Spanish officials allowed individual ships to go to isolated, smaller ports or to make speedy deliveries of the vital mercury.

Menéndez made one last voyage escorting a treasure fleet in 1571, and then Philip II put him in command of a new fleet of warships being prepared for use in the English Channel. When Menéndez died in 1574, he was working on a bold plan to establish a Spanish base in the Scilly Isles, off England's southwest coast. If his plan had been carried out, Spain would have been in a position to control the northern powers' main access to the Atlantic, because the long northern route around Scotland was impractical except in emergencies. But

Alvaro de Bazán, Marquis of Santa Cruz. The son of one of the main designers of the galleon, Bazán was the greatest Spanish naval commander of the time, and led successful squadrons at the Battle of Lepanto and the Spanish occupation of Portugal and the Azores. Bazán is wearing the insignia of the Order of Santiago, one of the crusading military orders founded during the reconquest of Spain from the Muslims. (Photo courtesy of Robert F. Marx)

such a distant base would have been difficult, if not impossible, for the Spanish to support, and Menéndez's plans were too advanced for their time.[12]

The long distances the treasure fleets traveled required ships that could remain at sea for extended periods and were well-equipped for defense. Fleet regulations specified a minimum size, armament, and crew for both merchantmen and warships to assure they could take care of themselves if attacked. The vessel that best satisfied these needs and served as the workhorse of the treasure fleets was the galleon. After years of experimenting, Alvaro de Bazán of Seville perfected the design of the galleon in the 1550s. In reward for his services, the king gave him the title of Marquis of Santa Cruz.

Santa Cruz had begun his work on designing the galleon by taking a hard look at the galley, the traditional warship of the Mediterranean. He concluded that the lightweight galley, with its limited cargo capacity, was unsuited for the rough weather and long voyages of the Atlantic. As an alternative, Santa Cruz built a larger and more heavily armed version of the sturdy caravels of the previous century. Galleons varied considerably in size and other characteristics, but an average one was about 100 feet long and 30 feet wide. They had three or four masts, a combination of square and lateen sails, and two or three internal

View of a Spanish galleon. (Photo courtesy of North Wind Picture Archives)

View of a Spanish galleon. (Photo courtesy of The Granger Collection, New York)

decks. A galleon sat high out of the water, a tactical advantage because it was easier to fire down into other ships and harder for enemies to scramble up its sides. To improve stability, tons of ballast stones were placed in the galleon's bottom to keep it on a even keel.

Besides being a formidable weapon, the galleon was also a superior way to move freight in an age when transport by sea was much more efficient than by land. Large and solidly built galleons could carry hefty cargoes in addition to the sizable amount of supplies that would be needed during long voyages to feed the crew of 200-300 men, including a company of about 100 soldiers. A sixteenth-century galleon had a carrying capacity of 500-600 tons, and the ships tended to get larger as time passed. This combination of size and strength meant that the galleon was the best possible way, given the technology of its time, to move vast amounts of valuable cargo such as gold and silver.

The galleon's size and solid construction also made it possible to carry considerable artillery, although the Spanish rarely used this weapon to its full potential. Galleons usually carried two or three dozen cannon. These guns came in a variety of sizes, but a typical large one was 12 feet or more in length, weighed 2-3 tons, and fired a ball of iron or stone weighing about 16 pounds.

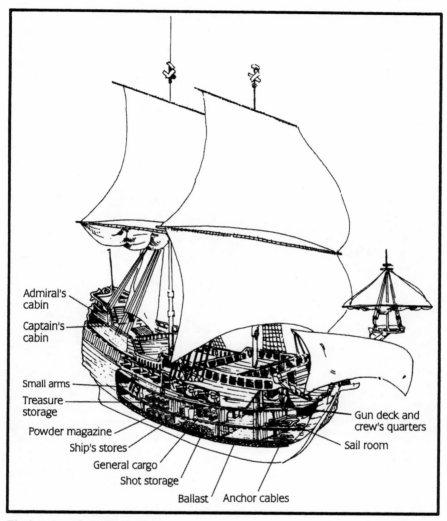

The interior of a typical galleon.

Cannon fire from such guns was slow and usually inaccurate at anything more than a couple of hundred yards. It took a long period of firing at close range to cause serious damage or to sink a stoutly constructed ship like a galleon. The most serious damage often came from splinters, which could decimate the crew.

In the eyes of sixteenth-century naval commanders, limited firepower was not necessarily a drawback. They saw victory at sea as a way to gain glory and profits rather than to destroy ships. Naval commanders believed it was preferable to capture an intact enemy ship that could be repaired and reused, or sold for a considerable sum. The Spanish also downplayed the use of shipboard artillery because most of their commanders came from a land-based military tradition and preferred to use hand-to-hand combat as their main tactic in battle. On board a galleon, the guns had the same long carriage, with two large wheels, that was used on land. Because it was difficult to pull these carriages back into the ship to reload, the Spanish often fired them only once as they closed with an enemy ship. After firing one broadside, the galleon would pull alongside an enemy vessel and send over a boarding party; the soldiers, with their pikes and

PVLVIS PYRIVS.
Manu quati tonitrua atq; fulmina ꞇDatum videtur inferis ab inuidis .

Cannon founding techniques in the sixteenth century. Sixteenth-century European cannon founders, the best of whom came from the Low Countries and northern Italy, produced cast bronze, muzzle-loading cannon that were much more effective than the guns used by earlier Europeans or by the contemporary Ottomans and the Chinese. To assure the quality of cannons and gunpowder, the Spanish government dropped its usual policy of working through contractors and operated the gun foundries and power mills itself, often with the help of foreign technicians. The Spanish usually preferred to use artillery made of bronze, which was expensive but more reliable; their English rivals made more use of the less costly iron cannon. (Photo courtesy of Robert F. Marx) swords, were expected to do the main work.

There were other drawbacks to a galleon as a weapon of war, besides its limited firepower. Many of the difficulties of the treasure fleets could be traced to the fact that Spain was basically a military power at sea rather than a true naval power. For example, officials at the *Casa de Contratación* usually entrusted command of fleets, and often of individual ships, to soldiers. This meant there was more emphasis on personal prowess and courage than on techniques of seamanship, such as ability to maneuver a ship or persistence in patrolling at sea for long periods. The government saw ship captains as technicians who followed the instructions of military men, and even senior mariners usually did not have the social rank or the battle experience that entitled them to command in the Spanish system. There were other problems, especially for the crew and passengers traveling on a galleon, including boring food, poor sanitation, disease, cramped quarters, and harsh discipline. Many of these hardships were exacerbated by the fact that the galleons had to operate in the heat of the tropics.[13]

The biggest single danger for the system of treasure fleets was destruction at sea by storm or faulty navigation. Losses from these causes were heavy because galleons were top-heavy and difficult to maneuver, techniques for coping with storms were primitive, and there were never enough experienced navigators. In 1554, for example, three ships from the New Spain fleet, the *Santa María de Yciar,* the *Espíritu Santo,* and the *San Esteban,* were lost in a storm off what would later become Padre Island, Texas. A few survivors managed to escape in a small boat. The rest tried to walk the hundreds of miles to the nearest Spanish outpost, but natives killed most of them. A salvage expedition was able to recover only about half of the 2 million pesos in treasure that had been lost. In 1567, six ships, carrying 3 million pesos, were wrecked in a storm off Dominica. The island's natives killed all the survivors. Salvage efforts were delayed by continuing bad weather, and a serious effort to recover the valuable cargo did not begin until the following year. When the salvage expedition finally arrived, the Spanish used every means at their disposal, including torturing the natives, to determine what happened to the treasure. They failed in their mission, however, and to this day the treasure has never been found. The year 1563 was the worst of the sixteenth century for losses, with seven ships going down in a storm at Nombre de Dios and another seven sinking off Cadiz.

There were other dangers that kept the fleets from operating more efficiently. One problem was the teredo, a warm-water mollusk that attached itself to ships and bored into the wooden hulls, creating leaks and eventually destroying the entire fabric of the ship. Shipbuilders sheathed the hulls with lead in an effort to halt the destruction from teredos, but the technique had only a limited success. Another difficulty was keeping experienced crews on the payroll. After surviving the dangerous voyage to the Indies, seamen often abandoned their ships to avoid the risks of crossing the ocean again and to try to make their fortune in the New World. At first Spanish authorities tolerated these casualties among the ships and men of the treasure fleets, because the cargoes of precious metals were less bulky than the outbound cargoes of supplies, and fewer vessels were needed for the return trip. As time passed, however, and the government was unable to come up with solutions to these difficulties, the mounting losses of ships and experienced sailors became a serious problem.

Another difficulty was the high expense of maintaining the galleons and forts that protected the treasure fleets. The *avería* tax, which had to be paid in addition to customs duties, was usually about 2 percent of the value of the cargo but could be three times as much in time of war. To raise the money, the prices of goods carried by the fleets had to be increased, and the colonists began to cast about for lower-cost sources of supplies.[14]

In the eyes of royal officials, however, the main threat to the treasure fleets was not enemy attack or hurricanes, but theft and tax evasion. A government inspector traveled on every ship as the personal representative of the crown, and he had the responsibility for seeing that the crew obeyed all the elaborate regulations. When a ship carried treasure, there was also a second watchdog aboard, the silver master, who received a fee of about 1 percent of the cargo if all the treasure arrived safely. To keep track of the gold and silver, officials and clerks prepared registers, in triplicate, listing every ingot and box of coins. The bureaucrats sent one copy of the register with the cargo, placed a second on another ship of the same fleet, and kept the third in the Indies, where it was kept for a year before sending it to Spain on another fleet.

When the treasure galleons reached Spain, no one was allowed to board or leave the ships until authorities from the *Casa de Contratación* arrived to verify the cargo and supervise its unloading. While a messenger rushed off to inform the king of the size of the treasure, officials transferred the ingots and chests of coins to the headquarters of the *Casa* in Seville for temporary storage. The royal share of the treasure usually went quickly to the bankers who had loaned money to the crown or to silver merchants who acted as brokers for the mint. Private individuals could claim their share once they verified their ownership and the fact that they had paid the appropriate taxes.[15]

Despite all the regulations, officials, and paper, the temptations involved in handling so much wealth were irresistible, and there were many attempts to cheat the system. The high value of the cargo and the extensive taxes on legal shipments made smuggling a profitable pursuit. One ship that ran aground in

The waterfront at Seville. *This modern view of Seville shows the area along the Guadalquivir River where the treasure fleets landed. The tower was built in the thirteenth century while the Muslims controlled the city, and they called it the Gold Tower because of the color of the tiles that had once decorated its sides. This name stuck after the Christians retook the city, and it became customary to unload treasure galleons at the base of the tower. The mint was only a block away, to the left across what was then an open plaza, and headquarters of the* Casa de Contratación *was a short distance beyond the mint. (Photo courtesy of The Image Works, Inc., Larry Mangino, Photographer)*

Spain in 1555 had a registered cargo of 150,000 pesos, but salvors found 350,000 in the wreck. On another occasion, the *Casa* accused Menéndez himself of taking bribes for permitting smuggling. He brazenly responded by claiming that any unregistered treasure had been only for his personal use and that, at any rate, whatever money he took from merchants had not affected his judgment as commander.[16]

Philip II was aware that there were problems with the maritime system that Menéndez and Santa Cruz had fashioned, and the king believed improvements could still be made. For example, traditionally the crown had leased merchant ships from private contractors, through *asientos*, and then converted these vessels to warships. The advantage of creating a fleet through *asientos* was that it was cheaper than maintaining a permanent government organization to build and equip galleons. Moreover, because there were few differences between merchant ships and warships in the sixteenth century, it was not difficult for civilian shipbuilders to do the work.

But Philip was not satisfied with this system. For one thing, the contractors, whose main concern was profit rather than quality work, sometimes cut costs by doing a shoddy job. In 1570, Philip II, in an effort to improve effectiveness and royal control in managing the naval squadrons, began a program of using tax money from New Spain and Peru to purchase specialized warships that would be directly owned by the government. He believed that the building and maintenance of warships, like the mercury trade, the cannon foundries, and the gunpowder mills, was too important to be left to private individuals. What the king envisioned was a professional navy, and this was the fleet that Menéndez was meant to command if he had lived. Philip found, however, that his income from the colonies was not rising quickly enough to finance the professional navy, and in the late 1570s he abandoned the plan.[17]

Despite its many drawbacks, the treasure fleet system of the sixteenth century was an impressive achievement. It depended on routine sailings and overwhelming power rather than flexibility and speed, but this proved to be a remarkably effective way to protect the growing volume of treasure. No major Atlantic shipment of precious metals was lost to enemy action during the period of over 40 years that Philip was on the throne. The treasure fleets were also quite dependable. Although there were delays, convoys sailed almost every year during Philip's reign.

In the sixteenth century, the galleon, and roughly similar ships from the other West European maritime powers, emerged as the main tool for establishing European control over the world's oceans. Even though its firepower was limited in comparison to the great ships of the line that sailed the seas in later centuries, the galleon's range and striking power made it an unrivaled seaborne weapon in its own age.

After a few futile attempts to resist, the native peoples in other regions gave up the effort to control the sealanes. Even a proud Chinese official acknowledged that Westerners were "extremely dangerous because of their artillery and their ships.... No weapon ever made since memorable antiquity is superior to their cannon." From the mid-sixteenth century onward, the struggle for mastery of the sea was conducted among European nations rather than between Europeans and indigenous powers.[18]

The Treasure Fleets of the Far East
Once production from the new mines in the Indies began in the mid-sixteenth century, it soon outstripped the traditional sources of gold and silver in Africa and central Europe. The gold and silver of the Indies amounted to about 3 million pesos' worth a year in the 1550s and increased to 5 million in the 1570s. Global trade patterns meant that much of this increasing flow of precious metals moved from west to east. After the shipments of gold and silver reached Spain, they were spread to the rest of Europe by the Habsburgs' commercial, banking,

and military activities. Large amounts then quickly moved further east because of Europe's negative trade balance with Asia. The largest share of the treasure that drained out of Europe, some 2 million pesos annually, belonged to the Portuguese, who had a virtual monopoly on the spice trade for most of the sixteenth century. Portuguese merchants raised gold and silver all over Europe, including the Habsburg lands, by selling spices and other Asian luxuries. Then they had to use much of the treasure for their newly developed direct trade with Asia, because Europe had so little else to offer the Asians in return for their products. Some of Europe's growing stock of precious metals also continued to travel along traditional pathways to the Ottoman Empire to pay for Asian products handled by Italian traders.[19]

These traditional trade patterns were challenged when Miguel López de Legazpi sailed west from New Spain in 1564. It was Legazpi who fulfilled Columbus' dream of traveling westward to establish direct contact between Spain and the Far East. Legazpi established a colony in the Philippines, and in 1571 moved its capital to Manila. The Spanish found that the Portuguese had consolidated their commanding position in the Asia trade by setting up a base in China, at Macao, in the 1550s. In the years after Legazpi arrived in the Philippines, there was a considerable rivalry between the Spanish and the Portuguese, and the latter were successful in keeping the Spanish out of the spice trade.

But Portugal did not contest Spain's right to deal in silk, and the silk trade became the foundation of Spain's trade with Asia. Despite the length of the voyage across the Pacific, a profitable exchange of silver for silk was soon taking place, because silk was cheap in China and much prized in the colonies and Spain. On the other hand, silver was easy to come by in America and much desired in China. The Spanish also used their silver to purchase Chinese porcelain and other luxury items. Because gold was relatively inexpensive in China, they sometimes exported it as well.

Initially, the Chinese did not use the silver imported from the West as currency. In the 1570s, only a limited amount of silver was coming into China, and the Chinese did not have a tradition of using precious metals for money. As a result, during the early years of the Western presence in the Far East, most of the silver that European traders paid to the Chinese usually ended up in hoards or was made into jewelry, and it did not have much economic, social, or political impact.[20]

The eastern terminus for Spain's Pacific trade was Acapulco. The sea voyage from Acapulco to Manila took eight to ten weeks on average. In the age of sail, the Pacific trade, like its Atlantic counterpart, operated on schedules that depended on weather patterns and currents. The westbound galleons usually

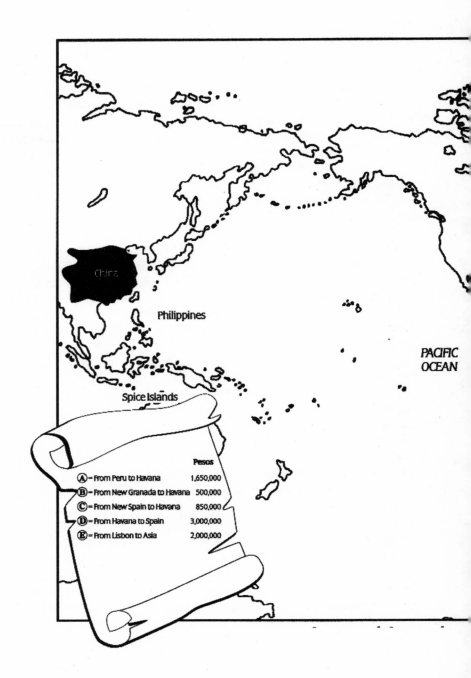

China

Philippines

PACIFIC
OCEAN

Spice Islands

	Pesos
Ⓐ = From Peru to Havana	1,650,000
Ⓑ = From New Granada to Havana	500,000
Ⓒ = From New Spain to Havana	850,000
Ⓓ = From Havana to Spain	3,000,000
Ⓔ = From Lisbon to Asia	2,000,000

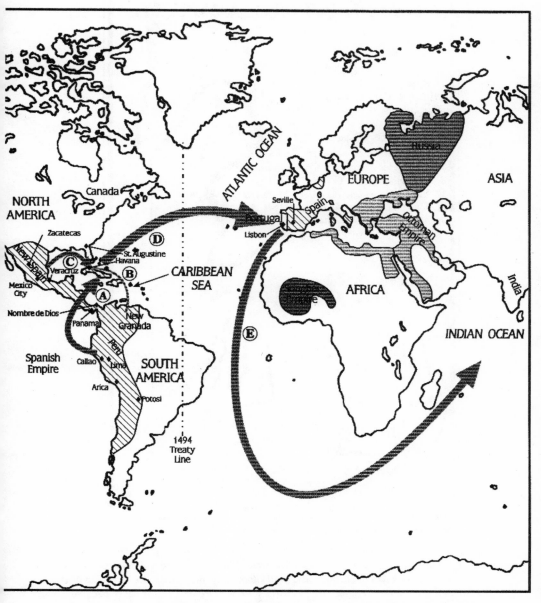

ATLANTIC OCEAN

NORTH
AMERICA

Canada

Zacatecas

New Spain

Veracruz

Mexico
City

Nombre de Dios

Panama

Spanish
Empire

Callao

Arica

Potosi

St. Augustine
Havana

New
Granada

Peru

Lima

SOUTH
AMERICA

1494
Treaty
Line

CARIBBEAN
SEA

Seville

Portugal

Lisbon

Spain

EUROPE

Ottoman
Empire

AFRICA

Russia

ASIA

India

INDIAN OCEAN

Ⓐ Ⓑ Ⓒ Ⓓ Ⓔ

Map 3. The Spanish Empire and Global Flows
of Precious Metals in 1550

Map of Acapulco. *Acapulco had an excellent harbor that was large, deep, and well-protected, and it was on a part of the western coast of New Spain that was relatively close to Mexico City, which was about 300 miles (480 kilometers) away. Acapulco was in an arid and isolated area, however, and, like Veracruz and Nombre de Dios, it never became a sizable city during the colonial era. It came to life only when the galleons were in port to take on silver or unload goods from Manila. (Photo from the author's collection)*

left Acapulco in the spring and traveled along a southerly route with the favorable winds. Their average cargo was 2 million to 3 million pieces of eight.

Manila, the western terminus of the Pacific galleon traffic, was probably the finest harbor in the Far East, and it became Spain's main strategic and commercial outpost in Asia. China's government discouraged foreigners from living in the Middle Kingdom, so a large Chinese colony grew up in Manila to handle the trade in silk and silver.

The return trip from Manila to Acapulco was the longest ocean navigation in the world and took from four to seven months. Galleons tried to leave Manila by June in order to avoid the typhoon season. Even if they left on schedule, the length of the voyage and the need to sail in the northern Pacific to find favorable winds made the voyage the most harrowing known to seamen. As early as 1568, one of the Manila galleons went down in a storm, the first of about 40 that would perish in the coming centuries, most of them on the long and dangerous eastbound route.[21]

Silver and State Power

In 1556, Philip II inherited Charles V's huge short-term debt of some 25 million pesos and another 70 million pesos worth of *juros*. Despite the increasing flow of silver from the Indies, he had no clear means to repay these obligations. The government had already pledged its revenues for the next five years to its creditors, and the bankers were becoming reluctant to make new loans. Philip used one of his father's techniques, and seized over 2 million in treasure meant for private individuals from the treasure fleet that arrived in 1556. Then, in desperation, early in 1557, Philip unilaterally suspended payments on the short-term *asiento* loans and offered long-term *juros* as compensation. Technically this was not a bankruptcy, because the debts were not totally repudiated, but it was a crushing blow to the crown's creditors. The hardest-hit were the German bankers, like the Fuggers, and as a result they sharply reduced their involvement in the financing of the Spanish government. After 1557, it was the Genoese who took over as the main royal bankers.[22]

In the lean years after the debt conversion of 1557, Philip II tried to control his expenditures by reducing the number of his enemies. His first step was to make peace with the French, who had been the main threat to Spain's empire in the New World. The Treaty of Câteau-Cambrésis, in 1559, finally brought a truce after more than 60 years of on-and-off warfare between Spain and France. It was a typical treaty of the time in that it combined territorial adjustments, religious issues, and royal marriages into a single package. The main result of the treaty was confirmation of Spain's mastery of Italy, completing the Habsburg ring around France. Exhausted by the decades of war, France slipped into religious strife and civil war in the decades that followed, and it ceased to be a serious challenge to Spain.

The Treaty of Câteau-Cambrésis was also interesting because the negotiations covered both European and colonial questions. Spanish negotiators tried to get the French to acknowledge Spain's monopoly in the Indies in the treaty, but the French refused. Such an agreement to disagree showed that although colonial problems were starting to become intertwined in European diplomacy, the connection was still very tenuous in the mid-sixteenth century. In its final form, the treaty acknowledged the reality that events outside Europe could not be closely controlled by European governments. As a result, the colonial struggle for control of the routes of the treasure fleets, including acts such as Menéndez's destruction of the French colony in Florida, would continue, even though the European powers were at peace in the Old World.[23]

Philip then decided to reduce the number of enemies further by dealing decisively with the threat from the Ottoman Empire. In 1571, Spain, the Papacy, and Venice formed an alliance, the Holy League, and gathered a fleet of over 200 galleys manned by 80,000 soldiers and sailors. Santa Cruz, son of one of the major designers of the galleon, commanded the Spanish squadron. Later that year, the allies defeated a Turkish fleet of roughly similar size at the Battle of Lepanto.

Lepanto was a great test of the tactics of galley warfare, the school in which the Spanish had learned how to fight at sea. Because galleys carried their guns in the bow and were most vulnerable along their sides, where there were no cannon and it was easy to destroy the long oars, the most advantageous arrangement was to place such ships side by side in line abreast. When two fleets of galleys met in battle, the individual captains tried to break through the line of opposing ships and thus expose the weak flanks of the enemy vessels to ramming and boarding. Gunnery played only a limited role in such fighting, and hand-to-hand combat was much more important. Lepanto turned out to be a great victory for the Christian forces, and this triumph convinced the Spanish that their tactics of coming alongside and boarding enemy ships was the key to victory at sea.

Soon after the battle, the jealousies of the members brought an end to the Holy League and there was no immediate follow-up to the great victory at Lepanto. Although the Turks would be a threat in the eastern Mediterranean for several more years, and on land in the Balkans for another century, the danger of a Turkish invasion of western Europe by sea was over. Lepanto was also the last great sea battle in the Mediterranean involving fleets comprised mostly of galleys, and unknowingly the Spanish had committed themselves to a form of warfare at sea that was becoming obsolete.[24]

With the Mediterranean secure, Philip could focus on the Atlantic. The greatest problem that remained there for him was unrest in the Low Countries. To understand why the revolt in the Low Countries became such an intractable struggle, and one that became closely interwoven with the operation of the treasure fleets, it is necessary to review its complex origins. The residents of the Low Countries had been fond of Charles V, who was born and lived among them, but they saw Philip as a distant and unsympathetic ruler. Moreover, the new king's mania for control and his efforts to assert royal authority in these wealthy and strategically important provinces clashed with the locals' traditional liberties. The main complaint was about increasing taxes to pay for the wars with France, but there was also resentment about having large Spanish armies based in the area. In addition, there were religious grievances because of the growing popularity of Protestantism and concern that Philip would bring in the Spanish Inquisition, the Catholic Church's tribunals for investigating and punishing heresy. Finally, there were economic problems because rising prices were causing discontent among the poor and the constant wars were disrupting trade.

In 1566, rioting broke out throughout the Low Countries. The following year Philip, emboldened by the arrival of an especially large treasure fleet, decided to take firm action and send the Duke of Alva and an army of 10,000 Spanish troops to reassert Spanish control. Alva was able to impose a tax increase by force, but his brutal methods led to an armed revolt on land and sea in 1572. The southern provinces, what is now Belgium, remained largely Catholic and loyal, while the north, the modern Netherlands, became a stronghold of Protestantism and independence.

Philip refused to accept the loss of the northern provinces, however, and the effort to suppress the revolt settled into a series of long and expensive sieges. By hiring mercenaries, the Spanish brought the total number of their troops in the area to about 60,000 men, and this massive Spanish army became a serious strategic threat to the neighboring countries of France and England, as well as to the minor princes of the Holy Roman Empire, who had long resented Habsburg power.[25]

The financial strain of the revolt in the Netherlands became enormous as time passed, but it was only part of Philip's financial problems. Although there was a vigorous growth of population, commerce, and industry in Spain during Philip's reign, increasing tax revenues did not keep up with spending. The king still had no state bank to help manage Spain's money supply, nor did he have an effective budgetary system to help match revenues with expenses. Only the great banking houses could provide the loans necessary to bridge the gap between income and expenditure. The bankers' international money market depended for its effectiveness on regular settlement of debts, but the crown's main sources of income—taxes and the treasure fleets—could be uncertain.

In 1567, for example, the treasure fleets were late in arriving, and the Genoese bankers told Philip there would be no more loans unless the ships arrived shortly. The king was so concerned that he became ill and retreated to his bed, ordering his aides to send the last few thousand pesos in the royal coffers to various churches and monasteries so there could prayers for the safe arrival of the treasure fleet. Shortly afterward, the galleons finally arrived, and there was general rejoicing among the courtiers, bankers, and priests.

Because of the king's many money problems, royal finance was a series of expedient short-term measures that involved juggling larger and larger sums. By the 1570s, Philip was collecting about 8 million pesos a year, including the royal share of over 1.5 million pesos from the treasure from the Indies, but this covered only half his expenditures. There was also constant pressure to increase spending, because inflation continued to undermine the purchasing power of the government's income. During the 1570s, the royal debt rose to nearly 70 million pesos, and one-third of the crown's income went to debt service. Royal officials did not, however, base their spending on budgetary calculations, but instead made decisions based on political and military necessity, as Philip tried to cope with the continuing Turkish threat in the Mediterranean and the revolt in the Netherlands.

Financial difficulties weighed heavily on the king, who made all important decisions himself. He readily admitted that he did not understand the complexities of international finance. In notes to his staff he acknowledged, "I have never been able to get this business of loans and interest into my head. I have never managed to understand it." Later, when dealing with other financial matters, he confessed, "To be frank, I do not understand a word of this. I do not know what I should do."

In 1575, Philip finally sought relief from his financial problems by reluctantly repudiating the short-term *asientos* with the bankers and merchants for the second time. Again he offered *juros* as compensation. The chief casualties of this second debt rescheduling were Spanish merchants, who had invested heavily in government loans. But the shock waves spread elsewhere as well, and the Genoese bankers, for example, stopped providing money for the Spanish forces fighting the rebellion in the Netherlands. The troops responded immediately with a mutiny and an unauthorized attack on Antwerp, which they pitilessly sacked in their search for money. Seven thousand people died in the onslaught, and this disaster virtually wiped out the city's ability to continue as the financial and commercial center of Europe.[26]

During the late sixteenth century, the increasing flow of silver from the Indies and the ever larger demands of royal finance were transforming the role of precious metals in Europe's economy. The massive imports of silver meant that gold was becoming relatively scarce and thus more valuable. This brought financial difficulties in areas such as Germany, where prosperity was linked to silver production, and for German bankers, like the Fuggers. While some scrambled to acquire as much as possible of the silver coming from America, the shrewder Genoese bought gold, correctly believing its value would rise.[27]

The increasing flow of precious metals was also arousing the interest of the English. Large-scale military operations in the Netherlands required vast amounts of money, because Philip's soldiers would work only for cash. Transferring funds by land to pay the soldiers became increasingly risky, and so large amounts of precious metals from the New World had to be shipped up the Channel, under the noses of the English. This was almost unbearable temptation. English merchants had already been siphoning off some of the wealth from the Spanish colonies through trade, but as political relations with Philip deteriorated, the English turned increasingly to officially sanctioned piracy against the vulnerable Spanish shipping lanes.

English Attacks on the Treasure Fleets

During the 1560s, France ceased to be the greatest outside threat to the treasure fleets, as the English, under Queen Elizabeth I, began flexing their muscles as a sea power. Under Elizabeth's father, King Henry VIII, England had had what was probably the largest fleet in Europe. Henry's warships had been used only in waters near England, however, and the English navy was greatly diminished in size by the time his daughter came to the throne. It would be the far-flung struggle with Spain's worldwide empire that would make the English a true global naval power for the first time.

England had been at peace with Spain for years, and traditionally the two had carried on a mutually profitable trade and shared a common interest in trying to contain France. Then, during the 1560s, tensions between Spain and England began to mount, and the rivalry spread to the maritime trade routes that now encircled the globe. One source of friction came when Spanish authorities restricted sales of English wool to the Low Countries, because they were concerned the commerce was also a channel for English aid to the Protestant rebels. Another issue was the large Spanish army in the Netherlands, which the English saw as a potential invasion force. Fear of Spanish power was also exacerbated by religious differences. Moreover, there were political suspicions because Philip knew about, and even encouraged, several plots against Elizabeth. Last, but far from least, there was a growing rivalry in the Indies. It was several incidents involving the treasure fleets that finally triggered the conflict between England and Spain.[28]

In 1568, a violent storm forced John Hawkins, an English merchant who had been illegally trading in the Caribbean, to take shelter in Veracruz. The next day, while he was still making repairs, the annual New Spain fleet arrived with a new viceroy on board. The Spanish and English agreed on a truce, but the viceroy, determined to uphold his authority and the Spanish monopoly, broke the truce and attacked. Like the French Protestants in Florida, Hawkins' presence in Veracruz was a challenge at a vital point that the Spanish could not ignore.

In the battle that followed, Hawkins sank a number of galleons, but the Spanish destroyed three of his five ships. The Spanish also captured a large number of English sailors, most of whom were executed or sent to work in the galleys. It was the first time the Spanish and English had come to blows in the Western Hemisphere. Hawkins made it back to England, along with the other ship, which was commanded by a relative of his, Francis Drake. Both men were now consumed with a desire for vengeance.

A few months after the battle at Veracruz, British ships seized four Spanish ships in the Channel carrying over 450,000 pesos for the Spanish soldiers in the Netherlands. The money was a loan from Genoese bankers. Elizabeth, who needed ready cash, took over the loan rather than return the money to Philip. Without the loan, Philip was forced to raise taxes in the Netherlands again, a move that further alienated the population there. The loss of the pay ships also demonstrated the vulnerability of the sea routes to the Netherlands. Philip was forced to begin the long and expensive task of organizing a safe land route to the Netherlands, known as the "Spanish Road," through the Habsburg lands of Milan, Franche-Comté, and allied countries in between. To retaliate against the English for the trouble they had caused him, Philip II seized English ships and goods in Spain and the Netherlands, a move which started a trade war between Spain and England.[29]

With relations between Spain and England deteriorating, Drake began planning to strike a blow at the source of Spanish power and to get his personal revenge. He believed that it was too risky to attack Spanish possessions in Europe but that the empire did have a vulnerable point at the Isthmus of Panama. Panama was the narrow funnel through which all the wealth of Potosí passed and also a point which English ships could reach. Elizabeth felt she could not offend Philip by openly sponsoring the attack on Panama. But as part of her campaign of diplomatic pressure on Spain, she did not object when Drake, with only two ships and 73 men, left for the Caribbean in 1572. The English queen apparently counted on the precedent from the negotiations at Câteau-Cambrésis, which showed that monarchs could remain at peace in Europe even though their subjects were fighting each other in the Indies.

At first, Drake was plagued by bad luck. When he arrived in Panama, he found that the treasure fleet had just left. Taking advantage of the fact that he had caught the Spanish by surprise, he briefly seized control of Nombre de Dios. Inside the town was a huge pile of silver ingots 70 feet long, 10 feet wide, and 12 feet high, but it was more than his small force could carry. After the failure to make off with the treasure at Nombre de Dios, Drake tried to cross the isthmus and capture Panama City, but that plan also failed.

Finally, he linked up with two extra sources of manpower: French privateers and escaped slaves who lived in the jungle with the natives and made a living from occasional raids on the Spanish. This additional strength gave him sufficient resources to make a third attempt against the Spanish, in 1573. During preparations for the third attack, the natives took Drake to a treetop vantage point from which he could see the Pacific Ocean, and the awed Englishman prayed for the opportunity to sail on the great sea. With his new allies, Drake waited until the 1573 *Tierra Firme* fleet arrived to pick up silver and then attacked one of the mule trains bringing treasure across the Isthmus. The Spanish put up a sharp fight, but Drake was able to capture a small fortune of over 100,000 pesos' worth of gold and silver and make his escape back to England.[30]

Three years later, John Oxenham, who had been on Drake's expedition, again tried to attack Panama. He managed to carry the parts for a small vessel across the isthmus and reassemble it on the Pacific side. Within a short time he captured a ship from the South Sea fleet, the first time the Spanish had lost a vessel in the Pacific. This time, however, local authorities were better prepared, and they managed to capture Oxenham. The Spanish sent him to Lima, for questioning by the Inquisition, and hanged him in 1580.[31]

In 1577, Elizabeth made the most ambitious probe yet of the Spanish Empire by allowing Drake to sail through the Straits of Magellan and become the first foreigner to break Spain's monopoly of the Pacific. Like his earlier voyage, this expedition was small, with only five ships and 164 men, and was financed by private individuals who hoped to gain a share of any treasure that Drake captured. After an arduous passage, Drake made it to the Pacific with only one ship. He immediately began raiding ports along the Peruvian coast, including Arica and Callao, and found the complacent Spanish too poorly prepared to resist effectively.

When he reached Callao, in 1579, he found that he had just missed the departure of a treasure-laden ship of the South Sea fleet, the *Nuestra Señora de la Concepción*, nicknamed the *Cacafuego*. He quickly pursued the vessel northward and caught it by surprise. After a brief fight, the vessel surrendered, and Drake and his crew began to count their booty. There were 1,300 bars of silver and 14 chests of coins in the registered cargo, valued at about 362,000 pesos. In addition, there was another 40,000 pesos' worth of illegal silver. When added to the treasure already captured, Drake had more than 25 tons of silver, worth about 750,000 pesos and equivalent to almost a year of Elizabeth's normal revenues.

With the whole coast of Peru up in arms behind him, there was no turning back, so Drake decided to return home by crossing the Pacific. During the first leg of his journey, he passed Acapulco but missed a galleon loading silver for the westbound transit. After stopping briefly in California, he visited the Spice Islands of southeast Asia and then headed home.

When Drake returned to England in 1580, he became a national hero. His was the second expedition to circumnavigate the globe, and he had convincingly demonstrated both the wealth and the weakness of the Spanish Empire. On a more mundane level, he was able to pay the wealthy men at court who had financed his voyage 47 times what they had invested. In fact, though, Drake's bravado had little long-term impact on the system of treasure fleets. Galleons continued to sail and silver continued to flow into the coffers of Philip II.[32]

During the 1560s and 1570s, forceful and creative Spanish commanders and administrators like Toledo, Legazpi, Santa Cruz, and Menéndez built a solid foundation for the Spanish Empire that would last for centuries. Many of the Spanish methods of managing production and shipment of the precious metals of the New World were brutal and exploitative. But it was a cruel and violent era; and the English and French, who denounced the Spanish in their political propaganda, wanted to profit from the Spanish system rather than dismantle it.

Menéndez, the key early figure in the design and operation of the treasure fleets, was unusual in Spain for his grasp of maritime strategy. He appreciated the importance of using the mobility and flexibility of sea power to concentrate resources at crucial points. The Spanish, along with the Portuguese, were the first to take advantage of the fact that the oceans of the world are open and interconnected, enabling ships of war and trade to bypass the political and physical barriers of the land. But the sea is also a hostile environment, and man's presence on the sea is impermanent by its very nature. In order to survive and prosper, Spain's empire would require a large-scale and continuous effort, along with wise choices in the use of maritime resources. This was the challenge Menéndez and the others left for their successors.

Powerful forces that would shape the world economy were set in motion during the consolidation of the Spanish Empire, especially by the founding of mints in the main silver-producing regions. As a result, a European-style monetary economy was firmly established in the Western Hemisphere, and silver coins became the main cargo of the treasure fleets. It was the treasure fleets that began the process of linking the continents together. The fleets rectified the global imbalance between regions in the New World with large but underutilized stocks of precious metals and areas, such as Europe and China, where gold and silver were in demand.

Whatever its problems, the Spanish system was a success in its early years because it served the needs of two powerful constituencies in Spain: the crown and the merchants of Seville. For the Council of the Indies, the fleets were a way to keep most of the treasure from getting into the hands of thieves or foreigners on its way to Spain, assure safe and more or less regular arrivals, and derive the maximum income from the shipments. For the *Consulado*, the fleets provided defense from pirates or countries at war with Spain, as well as protection within Spain for Seville's monopoly on the highly profitable Indies trade.

In the early years of his reign, Philip II grasped many of these realities and exhibited some of the key characteristics of successful political leadership by listening to wise counselors and realistically tailoring his goals to the means available to achieve them. When it became clear he did not have the money to defeat all his enemies, he made peace with the French and the Turks, a policy that enabled him to concentrate his resources against the rising power of the Dutch and the English. Philip also realized the importance of building institutions, such as a professional navy, to perpetuate his empire.

Although Philip and his officials were successful in diplomatic and strategic terms, they never solved the fundamental financial problems of their empire. This was their greatest failure. Temperamentally, the Castilians who dominated Spain's leadership were more concerned with glory and less worried about how to pay for it. Neither Philip nor his advisers, whatever their success in politics, had the education or experience to understand economic issues and thus how to retain control of the treasure of the Indies. Spain was sheltered from these realities by the growing flow of gold and silver from its colonies, which put off the time when the leadership would have to come to grips with Spain's economic deficiencies. Despite its problems, Spain, in the late sixteenth century, was still able to retain control over the wealth carried by the treasure fleets.

3. ascendancy, 1580–1620

he rewards of fortune and skill continued to come to the Spanish Empire in the 1580s. It was the age of Cervantes and El Greco, and Spain was at the peak of its glory. During this period, Portugal, with its vast and wealthy empire in Africa and Asia, came under Spain's control. In the Indies, production of precious metals was increasing year after year, and the treasure fleets were safely conveying this wealth around the world. King Philip II was at peace with all his enemies, except for the Dutch; and there was hope that even they might be reconciled, because the rebels in the northern half of the Low Countries had not officially left the empire. The question facing the Spanish government was: what was Philip going to do with all this wealth and power?

The Treasure Fleets at Their Zenith
The year 1580 brought a major turning point for the Spanish Empire, because the last legitimate claimant to the Portuguese throne died. Philip II, related to the royal family of the neighboring country through both his mother and his first wife, immediately asserted a claim to the crown and backed it up by sending to Portugal a fleet commanded by Santa Cruz and an army commanded by Alva. Dom Antonio, Prior of Crato, an illegitimate member of the Portuguese royal

family, tried to rally resistance to the Spanish from the Azores, the only bit of Portuguese territory that the Spanish did not immediately seize. With assistance from France, Antonio raised a mercenary fleet and army to defend his claim.

In 1582, Santa Cruz sailed to the Azores to enforce Philip's claim to the strategically located islands. There was a naval battle between the Spanish and the fleet financed by the French off Ponto Delgada; but it was a confused one, because it was the first clash between large fleets of galleons operating so far from the mainland. The captains on both sides, who were not familiar with handling galleons in formation, began the action by arranging themselves in a line abreast. This was the traditional tactic employed by the galley, which carried its few cannon in the bow. But such an alignment made it impossible for the rival fleets of galleons to bring to bear most of their larger number of guns, which were arrayed along the sides of the ships. Galleons lined up side by side were in a better position to fire at their friends than at their enemies. After the battle started, the ranks of ships were broken and there was a general melee. This enabled the galleons to use their superior firepower more effectively, and Santa Cruz defeated the mercenary fleet through a combination of gunfire and boarding.

Having gained command of the waters around the Azores, Santa Cruz returned the following year to take possession of the islands. This time, he had a surer sense of the appropriate tactics, and his assault was an impressive example of successful amphibious operations.

Adding Portugal to his realm meant that Philip II was now master of two of the world's great sources of wealth: the mines in America and the trade routes to Asia. The Portuguese accepted Philip as their king because he promised it would only be a personal union. He would be monarch of both countries, and Portugal and Spain would cooperate closely in naval and commercial matters, but Portugal would keep its own laws and institutions. One effect of the closer cooperation was to increase the circulation of silver in the world economy. Now it was easier for Portuguese merchants to sell African slaves to the Spanish colonists in the Western Hemisphere and then use the silver they earned to purchase silks and spices in the Far East.

The years after 1580 were the greatest days of Potosí. During this period, Spanish officials demonstrated the success of Toledo's more systematic methods of handling the mineral wealth of Peru. About 250 tons of silver, worth nearly 8 million pesos, came from the mines at Potosí every year. This was as much as all the other silver mines in the world were producing. Another 4 million pesos' worth of silver came from elsewhere in Peru. Potosí, the city at the foot of the silver mountain, had a population of about 160,000, or more people than Seville and all but a few of the other great cities of Europe.

Mural in the Escorial showing the Spanish attack on the Azores, 1583. *Soon after Santa Cruz's triumphant mission to the Azores, King Philip commissioned large frescoes for his palace outside Madrid, the Escorial, to commemorate the events. While the fleet of galleons, at right, remains at sea providing protection, galleys and smaller craft, at upper left above the door, take the soldiers ashore. This example of a successful seaborne invasion campaign gave the king much to contemplate as he pondered how to deal with his enemies, the English and the Dutch. (Photo courtesy of Robert F. Marx)*

Potosí had become a crossroads of the world's economy, and its market-place offered textiles from Europe, slaves from Africa, silk and porcelain from China, and carpets from Persia. It was a city of fabulous wealth but also an arena for violence, vice, and corruption. Because the city's fortune had been made so quickly, the prevailing mood was one of extravagance mixed with an acute sense that the power of chance could quickly take away wealth or even life itself. Potosí was a city fascinated with luck and money, supporting some 700 professional gamblers and 36 gaming houses. In 1585, a visiting judge claimed that the inhabitants were "the most perverse sort of people the world had created."[1]

Production of precious metals was also impressive elsewhere in the Indies. Although it was overshadowed by the spectacular production at Potosí, New Spain made an important contribution to the flow of silver by producing about 4 million pesos' worth a year, with about one-third of that coming from Zacatecas. By the early seventeenth century, the combined output of the silver

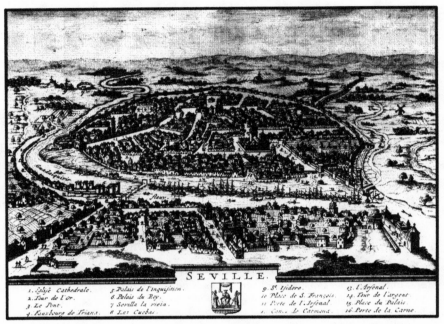

1. Eglise Cathedrale. 5. Palais de l'Inquisition. 9. St. Isidore. 13. l'Arsenal.
2. Tour de l'Or. 6. Palais du Roy. 10. Place de S. François. 14. Tour de l'argent
3. Le Pont. 7. Sevilla la vieja. 11. Porte de l'Arsenal. 15. Place du Palais.
4. Fauxbourg de Triana. 8. Las Cuebas. 12. Canal de Carmona. 16. Porte de la Carne.

View of Seville. *In the heart of the city were the great working monuments to the economic and political power of Spain: the Gold Tower, where the treasure ships were unloaded; the mint; and the new* Lonja *or Exchange building, which housed the headquarters of the* Casa de Contratación. *(Photo courtesy of the Hispanic Society of America)*

mines of New Spain and Peru was over seven times greater than European production. New Granada, for its part, produced about 800,000 pesos' worth of gold annually in the sixteenth century, or almost a fifth of the world's output. Of the total production of almost 17 million pesos that came from the mines of the Indies in the 1590s, over 11 million pesos a year was shipped directly to Spain.[2]

The wealth of the New World was carried to Europe and to Asia by the largest maritime system in the world at that time. The combined resources of Spain and Portugal gave Philip II a commercial fleet with more ships than the Dutch, three times as many as the French, and seven times as many as the English. This far-flung system was overwhelmingly preoccupied with handling bullion: some 80 percent of the value of the eastbound cargoes across the Atlantic was made up of precious metals, and 95 percent of that total, by weight, was silver. A Spanish official called the flow of treasure from the Indies "the

The headquarters of the **Casa de Contratación** *in Seville. To demonstrate their wealth and power, merchants of the* Casa *built a new headquarters during the last two decades of the sixteenth century. Juan de Herrera, who had designed Philip's palace, the Escorial, was the architect. The status of the* Casa *was also indicated by the building's prestigious location, just across the street from the cathedral. (Photo courtesy of Frerck/Odyssey Productions/ Chicago)*

lifeblood of the kingdom," and he thought that the sea routes were "the very veins that give life to this great and vast body." Another senior bureaucrat told the king, "everything is kept going by means of silver....Your Majesty's strength consists essentially of silver."[3]

The main threat to successful transfer of the gold and silver to Spain was the weather. Six ships sank in a storm at the mouth of the Guadalquivir in 1587 while on their way up the river to Seville. Large portions on the New Spain fleet were lost in the Caribbean in 1590, 1601, and 1614. The worst disaster of the period was in 1591, when a storm hit the combined fleets as they approached the Azores, sinking 20 ships that were carrying some 10 million pesos. The Spanish quickly launched a massive salvage operation and recovered about three-fourths of the loss. Another serious casualty was in 1605, when four ships of the *Tierra Firme* fleet, carrying more than 8 million pesos, went aground on the Serranilla Bank, southwest of Jamaica. In contrast to the situation in the Azores, where resources from Spain could be used more easily, the salvage effort on the Serranilla Bank was a failure and most of the treasure was lost.[4]

Seville, the main port of the Atlantic trade and the de facto capital of the empire in the Indies, was more prosperous and powerful than ever. It was the largest city in Spain, with a population of over 100,000, overshadowing Madrid, which had become the capital in 1560. The foundation of Seville's wealth, size, and power was the flow of precious metals through the city. In a burst of hyperbole, a history of Seville, published in 1587, claimed, "with the treasure imported into the city, every street could have been paved with gold and silver." Seville was the economic heart of a rich agricultural area that provided wine, cooking oil, and other valuable products. It was also an industrial center, where the ships, cannon, sails and other essentials for a maritime empire were made and repaired. Because Spain alone did not have the manpower to run its vast overseas empire, about 10 percent of the population of Seville were foreigners, and they provided many of the necessary commercial and industrial skills.[5]

Even at its height, however, the Spanish imperial system was showing signs of weakness, including, ironically, a shortage of money. There were basically two ways to make sure that Spain retained control of the treasure of the Indies: through taxes and through commerce. Although tax revenues continued to rise, the income from commerce was beginning to show some weakness. In the early sixteenth century, the countryside around Seville had been able to provide food that the settlers in the New World wanted. The colonists were willing and able to pay in gold and silver for these supplies, and the lively commerce in basic supplies brought considerable amounts of precious metals to Spain.

By the late sixteenth century, however, the colonies had become more mature and they craved manufactured products, such as textiles, weapons, glass, and paper. Spain produced only limited quantities of such goods, and then only at high prices. So the Seville merchants increasingly had to purchase foreign manufactured goods for re-export to the Spanish colonies, and this meant dividing the profits with outsiders and sending more silver abroad. The decline in profits from colonial trade was a serious blow to tax revenues. With less money in the hands of the merchants, the government could not raise as much from them through loans and confiscations. Even worse was when foreign merchants cut out the Seville middlemen and smuggled their goods directly to the Indies. In time, smuggling came to rival storms at sea as a cause of diversions from the flow of silver coming from the mines.

During the last decades of the sixteenth century, other factors also drained the riches of the Indies out of Spain. Philip II's ambitious foreign policy meant that vast sums had to be sent abroad to support fleets and armies. Moreover,

Spain, always short of arable land, had to import food to feed a growing population. The result was a continuing need to export precious metals. In 1590, the Spanish government finally had to go against mercantilist principles and authorize the legal export of bullion.

Another sign of weakness in the Spanish economy was massive inflation. This decline in the value of money took place elsewhere in Europe as well, but it seems to have been the worst in Spain. A number of factors contributed to the rise in prices in the sixteenth century, such as a rising population and the growing state debt, but the massive increase in the amount of silver coins in circulation also played an important role. The mining boom in central Europe in the last half of the fifteenth century had started the flood of precious metals into the European economy, and the torrent of silver from the Indies exacerbated the situation.

In the century that followed Columbus's discovery of the New World, about 170 tons of gold and over 8,200 tons of silver were legally imported into Spain from the Indies. Additional large amounts, by their nature impossible to quantify, reached Europe through smuggling. Because the amount of goods and services available expanded much more slowly than the money supply, there was inflation, and during the sixteenth century, prices in Spain quadrupled. This decline in the value of money was traumatic and mysterious, especially for people who believed that gold and silver had intrinsic value.

Since far more silver than gold came from the Indies, the imports of precious metals also changed the proportion of silver and gold in the European monetary system. In 1500, the ratio of silver to gold had been approximately 10 to 1, but by 1600 it was about 12 to 1, and by the mid-seventeenth century it was 15 to 1. One effect of lowering the relative value of silver was to increase the potential for profit in the trade with the Far East. In Asia, the ratio of value between silver and gold was as low as 5 to 1, meaning that silver could have as much as three times the purchasing power in the Orient as it did in Europe. On the other hand, the higher relative value of gold put considerable strain on the traditional bimetallic monetary system of Europe. It was difficult to maintain a monetary standard using two precious metals when their relative value was constantly changing.[6]

The Continuing Challenge from the Dutch and English

The stream of precious metals from the New World enabled King Philip of Spain to exert his will throughout western Europe and the Mediterranean, but his first priority was to defeat the Dutch rebels who had been defying him since 1567. Philip's generals had been able to restore control over the Spanish Netherlands, which remained largely Catholic. To the north, however, the

Protestant rebels renounced their allegiance to Philip in 1581, founded the independent country of the United Provinces, and continued the struggle against Spanish domination. The war against the Dutch required huge standing armies, expensive equipment like cannons, and long sieges, all a tremendous financial burden that drained Spain of much of the income brought by the treasure fleets. Spain's aristocratic generals complained that cash had become a more important tool of war than bravery or skill, and one complained that fighting had been reduced to "a sort of commerce in which he who has the most money wins."

Philip's extensive need for money to finance trade and war meant that most of the precious metals brought by the treasure fleets quickly left Spain. Because it was impossible to finance the massive effort against the Dutch rebels entirely from local sources in the rebellious provinces, large amounts of money had to be sent from Spain. By the late 1580s, Philip was shipping more than 4 million pesos a year from Spain to the Netherlands. The following decade, when the war was at its height, it was necessary to dispatch 5.5 million pesos annually. Another drain on the 11 million pesos a year that came from the Indies during the 1590s was the 4 million pesos sent abroad, mostly to France and Italy, to cover the trade deficit. Foreigners were eager to have the precious metals, especially the popular silver pieces of eight, to finance their trade with the Baltic region, the Ottoman Empire, and Asia.[7]

Transferring huge sums of cash to the Netherlands to support the war year after year was a daunting problem for the Spanish. Originally, most of the money had been sent in cash by sea; but French, Dutch, and English corsairs had made such transfers so dangerous that by the 1580s the Spanish preferred to send American silver to Italy, where Genoese bankers arranged for transfer to the Low Countries. The Genoese had two options, either of which earned them handsome profits. They could exchange the silver for gold, which was easier to ship and was also the method of payment preferred by the troops in the Netherlands, or they could convert the silver into bills of exchange payable in the Low Countries along the Spanish Road. Transferring specie could take four months, while sending a bill of exchange took about four weeks.[8]

As the Spanish became more deeply enmeshed in the war in the Netherlands, relations between Spain and England continued to deteriorate and the English began to prepare for war. During the 1580s, Hawkins, who still had scores to settle with Spain from the battle of Veracruz, become one of the leaders of the aggressive anti-Spanish camp in the government. As treasurer of the Navy Board during this period, he was determined to institute a more businesslike attitude toward running the navy and to ensure that the government got more value for the money it spent on its ships. Hawkins supervised

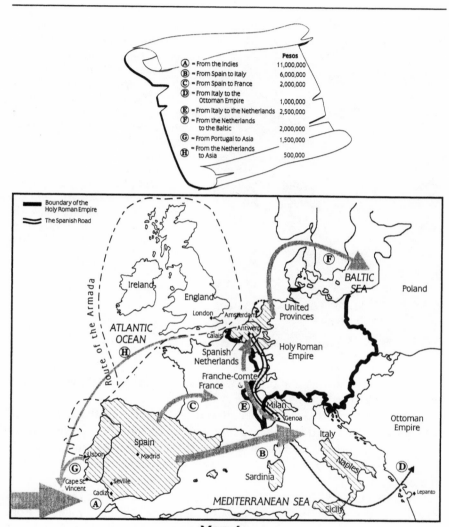

		Pesos
Ⓐ	= From the Indies	11,000,000
Ⓑ	= From Spain to Italy	6,000,000
Ⓒ	= From Spain to France	2,000,000
Ⓓ	= From Italy to the Ottoman Empire	1,000,000
Ⓔ	= From Italy to the Netherlands	2,500,000
Ⓕ	= From the Netherlands to the Baltic	2,000,000
Ⓖ	= From Portugal to Asia	1,500,000
Ⓗ	= From the Netherlands to Asia	500,000

Boundary of the Holy Roman Empire

The Spanish Road

Map 4.
European Possessions of Philip II and the
Flow of Precious Metals in 1590

Sir John Hawkins. For almost 30 years, Hawkins, shown in a portrait by Federigo Zuccaro that hangs in the City Art Gallery in Portsmouth, England, was the main nemesis of the Spanish maritime system. He violated Spain's claimed commercial monopoly, oversaw the design and construction of ships that bested the formidable galleons, commanded a squadron during the defense against Armada, and led raiding expeditions to the Caribbean. Hawkins was also one of the first and most vigorous proponents of a "blue water" English naval strategy, which emphasized operations at the far reaches of the deep, blue oceans of the world. (Photo courtesy of Robert F. Marx)

construction of a new generation of warships that were smaller, faster, and more maneuverable than Spain's galleons.

The English also made a greater effort to realize the potential of shipboard artillery. They designed a compact gun carriage, with four small wheels, which made it possible to pull the cannon back into the ships for reloading. This made it easier for English gun crews to fire their weapons repeatedly, a dramatic contrast to the single broadside often used by the Spanish.

Moreover, English ships tended to have more guns than their Spanish rivals. This was possible because English cannon were usually made of iron, which was heavier and less reliable than the bronze Spanish guns but which cost about a third less. Because the main striking power of the English fleet came from more effective shipboard artillery, English ships, unlike their Spanish counterparts, did not carry large numbers of soldiers. These smaller crews also helped keep costs down.[9]

The English were also developing a naval strategy in which control of the ocean's transport and communications routes, rather than possession of vast expanses of land, was the key to seizing a share of the precious metals of the Indies. As the English sea captains traveled further and further in search of plunder and trade, they came to believe that the most effective way to attack their country's enemies, and even to defend their own shores, was to send fleets to the far corners of the world. Later writers on maritime affairs labeled this the "blue water" strategy.

One of the chief proponents of a wide-ranging and hard-hitting fleet, Sir Francis Bacon, claimed, "He that commands the sea is at great liberty and may take as much or as little of the war as he will." Sir Walter Raleigh, another supporter of a blue-water navy, argued that the most effective way to reduce the threatening power of Philip of Spain was to cut off the flow of precious metals from the Indies because "it is his Indian gold that endangereth and disturbeth all the nations of Europe." Raleigh proposed that instead of raids, such as those that had been conducted by Drake, it would be more effective to establish permanent English bases in the Americas. In 1585, Raleigh sponsored the first attempt at an English colony, in what would later become North Carolina, with the goal of finding a location from which the English could monitor the movements of the treasure fleets. Hawkins, for his part, put forward an even bolder plan to seize and hold one of the main ports in the Spanish colonies.

The expeditions conceived by Raleigh and Hawkins were organized as joint stock companies, in which well-to-do merchants, landowners, and court-iers provided money, ships, and political support in return for a claim on a percentage of any treasure the adventurers captured. The English government often provided cannon and gunpowder from the royal arsenals for these joint stock ventures, and sometimes the queen even invested money. Usually, however, Elizabeth preferred to avoid provoking Spain by not openly partici-pating in such ostensibly private undertakings. In sum, Hawkins, Drake, Raleigh, and the other commanders of Elizabeth's navy were making great strides toward developing a distinctively maritime style of warfare rather than just adopting the tactics of battles on land for use at sea.[10]

As international tensions increased in the 1580s, Spanish leaders began to see the Dutch and the English challenges as interlinked and speculate whether the two problems could not be dealt with at the same time. In 1583, Santa Cruz sent Philip a plan for a seaborne invasion of England, which would be modeled on the successful conquest of the Azores that had been carried out that year. The plan would require building a huge fleet in Spain and then sending it across hundreds of miles of ocean to land on the English coast. He believed such a blow not only would knock out Philip's increasingly dangerous rival, Elizabeth, but also would undermine the Dutch revolt by removing English support.

The Duke of Parma, who commanded the army in the Netherlands, thought he and the army should take the lead in any great campaign against Philip's two main enemies, and he came up with a more conventional plan. Parma proposed that the first priority should be to pursue the campaign on land against the Dutch. Once the Netherlands were secure, he argued, the area could be used as a base for a surprise attack across the narrow Channel, thus obviating the need for a more risky campaign based in far-away Spain.

Philip believed that Santa Cruz's plan for a massive long-range strike by sea was too expensive and that Parma's ideas about subduing the Dutch first were impractical. So the king put off a decision on whether to go to war and decided to try other means of pressure first. Philip accepted the idea that the struggles against the English and the Dutch were linked, however. In 1585, he ordered Spain and its possessions to refuse to do business with both of them. Philip was emboldened to launch a trade war by a number of factors: the increase in strength provided by the addition of Portugal to his realms, the fact that France was weakened by sectarian civil war, the progress that Parma was making in capturing rebellious cities in the Netherlands, and last, but hardly least, the increasing flow of silver from the Indies.

This more confrontational attitude alarmed Elizabeth, who was concerned that she might lose her one continental ally, the Dutch, and who also felt that she had to stifle Spanish plots to overthrow her. Later in 1585, the queen responded to Philip's trade war by giving the Dutch a loan and sending troops to occupy several key cities in the Low Countries. The troops were to guarantee repayment of the loan and not to attack the Spanish, but Philip saw it as a provocation, nonetheless. Tensions rose even further that year after Drake, on another private expedition, raided the Spanish coast and then headed westward toward the Caribbean.

Sometime late in that eventful year of 1585, it appears that Philip finally determined what should be done with the massive wealth and power at his disposal. He decided to invade England. When he asked Santa Cruz what would be necessary to assure success, the old admiral replied that he would need a fleet of 50 galleons, 140 other large ships, more than 300 smaller support vessels, and 60,000 men. Santa Cruz himself took charge of a massive effort to organize such a fleet, which included building new ships and gathering existing ones from Castile, Portugal, Italy, and the Atlantic escort squadron for the treasure fleets.[11]

The First Worldwide War at Sea

Long before the Armada was ready to sail, the war between Spain and England had already started. In 1585, Drake sailed for the Caribbean to carry out another of his raids on the bases from which the treasure fleets operated. This was a much more ambitious undertaking than his earlier expeditions, and Drake had more than 25 ships and about 2,000 men under his command. As part of her campaign to signal her resolve without going to war, Elizabeth herself participated more openly in outfitting the fleet by providing two royal warships. It was the first great foreign fleet to make the long trip to the Caribbean.

Once there, Drake captured Santo Domingo, an important administrative center but not a major stop for the treasure fleets. Then he went on to take Cartagena and St. Augustine, much more important bases in the Spanish convoy system. In Santo Domingo and Cartagena, he was able to extract modest cash ransoms, but the main prizes, the treasure fleets, managed to escape. Moreover, the Spanish were able to save much of the other treasure in the Caribbean cities by sending it inland for safekeeping.

After more than a year in the Caribbean, Drake's forces were too weakened by disease to attack other strong points like Nombre de Dios or Havana or to hold any ports as a permanent base, so he decided to withdraw. Countermeasures against sickness were still primitive in the sixteenth century, and, like many other commanders that would follow, Drake found that dietary and other illnesses usually killed more soldiers and sailors than combat, especially in the distant tropics.

On the way home in 1586, Drake evacuated Raleigh's disheartened colonists from North Carolina, thus bringing to a close the first English attempt to found a permanent colony in the Western Hemisphere. When they finally returned to England, Drake and the other participants viewed the expedition as only a limited success, since they captured no permanent bases and the money raised from ransoms was not even enough to cover expenses.[12]

Drake's attack was a sobering experience for the Spanish, however, and Philip II ordered immediate countermeasures. In line with Menéndez's strategic outline of 20 years before, the king dispatched extra warships to the Caribbean and began a massive program of strengthening fortifications at the main ports. The most extensive construction was at Havana, Cartagena, Veracruz, Santo Domingo, and San Juan on Puerto Rico. Smaller installations were also begun at St. Augustine and Nombre de Dios.

The colonial government spent huge sums on these fortifications, which meant that there was less silver available to send to Spain. The Duke of Medina Sidonia, the largest landowner in southern Spain and the man who oversaw the preparation of the fleets at Seville in the name of the king, worried about the expense of the fortifications and proposed another approach. Medina Sidonia argued that it was cheaper to protect the mines and treasure fleets by invading England and destroying Drake and the other marauders at the source, rather than attempting to fortify all the many key points in the distant colonies. Medina Sidonia's plan, with its emphasis on an seaborne invasion launched from Spain, was similar to Santa Cruz's strategy and showed that it was not only the English who could think in blue-water terms. Philip was impressed by Medina Sidonia's

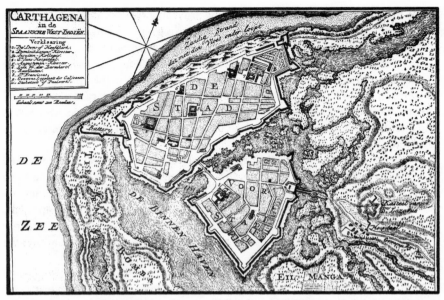

Map of part of the fortifications at Cartagena. Massive fortifications were an important component of the defensive strategy the Spanish followed in protecting the treasure fleets. Although thick walls provided some assurance that crucial ports would not be quickly overrun by enemy forces, they were expensive and gave pause even to Philip II, who lavished millions of pesos on his armies and fleets. According to a perhaps apocryphal story, a courtier once asked the king why he was staring out a window that faced west. Philip replied, "I am looking for the walls of Cartagena. They cost so much, they must be visible from here. " (Photo courtesy of North Wind Picture Archives)

recommendations and urged renewed vigor in the preparations for an invasion of England.[13]

With the war underway, the English also decided to expand their scope and strike at the treasure fleets in the Pacific. Following Drake's path of almost a decade earlier, Thomas Cavendish left England in 1586 with two ships to sail around South America. He raided cities along the Peruvian coast and finally intercepted an eastbound Manila galleon, the *Santa Ana*, off California in 1587. Like most Spanish ships that sailed the Pacific, the galleon was only lightly armed because intruders were so rare, and after a short fight it surrendered. The vessel's cargo of gold and silk from the Far East was worth about 2 million pesos. This was the first time foreigners had seized one of the Manila galleons. Cavendish returned home by continuing westward, and was the third captain to circumnavigate the globe.[14]

Meanwhile, back in the Atlantic, Elizabeth and her naval commanders were well aware that the Spanish were planning to invade England. In 1587, the queen sent Drake and a fleet of more than 20 ships to disrupt Spanish preparations. First, Drake boldly sailed into Cadiz harbor and sank dozens of ships being prepared for use in the treasure fleets and the invasion Armada. A few galleys stationed at Cadiz tried to block his attack, but they were quickly swept aside by the power of the English gunfire.

Drake then proceeded to Cape St. Vincent, which he used as a base for a partial blockade of the Spanish coast. This phase of the operation was a disappointment for Drake and his crews because, instead of valuable booty, all they were able to capture or destroy were a number of small supply ships carrying prosaic cargoes, such as food for the Spanish fleet and seasoned wooden staves for making barrels. Although barrel staves seemed unimportant at the time, wooden barrels were one of the main storage containers for supplies being gathered for the Armada. As a result of Drake's attack, the Spanish fleet would have to make do with inferior barrels for carrying food and water. This would not be important if the Spanish gained a quick victory, but if the campaign was a long one, their supplies would quickly spoil.

During the final phase of his cruise in Spanish waters, Drake blockaded Lisbon, Santa Cruz's headquarters for the preparation of the Armada, and also tried to cut off the 1587 treasure fleets by cruising off the Azores. He got to the Azores before the fleets, though, and had to content himself with the rich cargo of a Portuguese ship returning from the Far East. Philip's response to Drake's marauding was to dispatch Santa Cruz and a fleet to the Azores, where they met up with the treasure fleet and safely escorted it home. The success of Drake's cruise inspired Hawkins to propose setting up a permanent blockade of the Spanish coast, but there were not enough ships for such an ambitious project, and Elizabeth rejected the plan.[15]

In 1588, the Spanish did not send the regular fleets to the Indies to bring back the treasure, because of the heightened insecurity after Drake's raid and the need to conserve shipping in Europe for use in the Armada. Instead, a new strategy was tried, and small ships, called *zabras*, fast and well-armed, went out alone or in small groups. Their job was to take out the mercury essential for refining silver and then return with precious metals from the mines of Peru, New Spain, and New Granada.[16]

In Spain, preparations for the launching of the Armada continued. Despite English attacks, Santa Cruz had managed to gather a fleet of 130 ships, including 20 Spanish and Portuguese galleons and four galleasses, hybrid ships that combined the firepower of galleons with the maneuverability of galleys. Most of the rest of the vessels were heavily armed ships normally used in commerce. But even this large number was still far short of what the admiral believed necessary for success. As a result of old age and the strain of the extensive work needed to prepare the Armada, Santa Cruz died early in 1588, without seeing his plans come to fruition.

Philip II ordered Medina Sidonia to take command of the fleet and press ahead with the much-delayed preparations. The final campaign plan was a combination of Santa Cruz's and Parma's earlier proposals. A large fleet would sail from Spain with 18,000 fighting men and establish control over the Channel at its narrowest point, the Straits of Dover. Then the fleet would cover the landing of both the troops it had brought with it and another 16,000 soldiers from Parma's forces in the Netherlands.

Although it was scaled back from Santa Cruz's original project, in terms of size and distance this was the most ambitious undertaking in naval history to that date. Naturally, the plan to invade England required vast amounts of money, and Parma wrote to Philip that, "I will only remind you now of the importance of the question of money, and of its timely supply." The king, still groping for solutions to his money problems, jotted in the margin of Parma's report, "This is the matter which gives me the most anxiety."

The goals of the Armada were as extensive as the preparations. Philip hoped to restore Catholicism in England, knock out an important source of foreign support for the Dutch rebels, and end the attacks on the treasure fleets. The need to accomplish this last goal was reinforced by Drake's recent exploits in the Caribbean and the waters off Spain. Medina Sidonia acknowledged the importance of protecting the treasure fleets traveling between the Indies and Spain when he told Philip, "The link between the two continents is the foundation of the wealth and power we have here."[17]

In the summer of 1588, the great Spanish Armada finally sailed up the English Channel bound for its rendezvous with Parma's army in the Netherlands. Many of the captains and planners who had prepared the Armada were veterans of the treasure fleets, and this experience shaped their approach to the invasion of England. The Armada used the same strategy as the treasure fleets, stressing massive strength focused on vital points. Moreover, the Armada's formation, with the warships providing a protective shell around the supply vessels, was similar to that used for the Atlantic convoys.

When the Spanish and English fleets first clashed, during a week-long transit of the English Channel, the Spanish tried to use their traditional tactics of grappling and boarding. On the other hand, the English, under Charles Lord Howard of Effingham, the Lord High Admiral of England, used the tactics they had been developing for the last 20 years, which stressed maneuverability and cannon fire. The English knew and respected the prowess of the infantry on

Spanish ships, and Howard and his commanders sought to avoid coming too close to the Spanish fleet. Individual English ships, commanded by captains such as Drake and Hawkins, again and again demonstrated superior seamanship by darting in, firing, and then withdrawing before the Spanish could catch them.

The English had less success, however, in the management of the dozens of ships at their disposal, and the disciplined Spanish formation proved to be a difficult target and a better way to handle a large fleet. To strike more effectively at the Spanish, the English tried a variety of techniques, including dividing up into squadrons and firing in organized sequence, but they were unable to break the Spanish formation or to cause serious damage to the ships. Although both sides expended a tremendous volume of powder and shot during the running battle up the Channel, neither contender was able to sink any of the other's ships and the only losses were through accidents.

When the Armada reached Calais, a neutral French port, it had to wait because the Dutch fleet was keeping Parma from leaving his bases in the Netherlands. This situation left the Armada stymied, because it could not carry out its plan of linking up with Parma's troops and it had no safe port. Before Medina Sidonia could come up with an alternate plan, the English, who by now had gathered roughly the same number of ships as the Spanish, used fire ships to scatter the enemy formation and then attacked with renewed vigor.

Even after its arduous trip and the sharp fight off Calais, the Armada was still intact and prepared to fight. Its total losses, from both accidents and English fire, were only six ships. At this point, the weather turned against the Spanish, and strong contrary winds forced the Armada to return home by sailing north around Scotland. During the long trip back to Spain, the loss of the seasoned wood for barrels, which had taken place the year before as a result of Drake's raid, took on great importance, and the Armada ran short of fresh supplies. In addition, the weather continued to be bad week after week, and about 20 ships were lost along the coast of Ireland.

In the end, only about half of the ships returned to Spain. Philip claimed that the Armada had cost him nearly 14 million pesos. It was a serious, but not fatal, blow to the Spanish navy, because Philip still had the resources to rebuild his fleet. As long as the treasure from the Indies kept flowing, Spain could recover, even from a defeat as great as that of 1588.[18]

In English eyes, enough of the Spanish ships had survived to present a threat, and the English captains urged Elizabeth to finish the job of defeating the Armada by striking back at the weakened Spanish before they could rebuild their fleet. The queen's advisers, still groping for an effective strategy to use against Spain, disagreed over how to proceed. Drake called for a large-scale attack to destroy the remains of the Spanish fleet in its home waters. If they were

The Spanish Armada in the English Channel, 1588. *This sixteenth-century print conveys the discipline of the Spanish formation and the rather haphazard English countermeasures. In the left foreground, Drake, in the* Revenge, *is capturing a galleon that suffered an accident and had to drop out of formation. As long as the Spanish ships stayed together and supported*

spanish treasure fleets

each other, they were invulnerable. The print is somewhat inaccurate, however, in portray-
ing the details of the Spanish formation. In fact, most of the ships in the Armada probably
sailed in a long, thin line abreast. If the ships had sailed bunched up, as shown, those in the
rear would have taken the wind from the sails of those ahead and caused great confusion.
(Photo courtesy of North Wind Picture Archives)

successful, he argued, the English would be able to collect the riches of the Indies at their leisure. Hawkins, for his part, again recommended a long-term blockade of the Spanish coast, using the Azores as a base. As a compromise, they agreed to recommend an attack on both the Spanish ports and the Azores in a single expedition. Elizabeth was less certain than her captains that the best way to defend her realm was to send her main strategic asset, her fleet, away from home waters, but she reluctantly authorized the expedition.

The fact that so many of the English naval commanders came from a privateering tradition gave rise to distractions from the worthwhile and practical, if difficult, goals of attacking the Spanish fleet in its home ports and lying in wait for the treasure fleets in the Azores. An attack on Lisbon, with the opportunity to loot that wealthy city, was also added to the plan, which was now hopelessly overburdened and ambitious.

In the spring of 1589, Drake, with nearly 200 ships of various sizes and 13,000 troops, sailed for Spain and Portugal. Bad weather disrupted the planned assault on the remains of the Armada; and because there was much danger and little chance of plunder, the English fleet did not persist in the attack on the northern Spanish ports. Then the English fleet sailed on to Lisbon, but had no success there because the Portuguese refused to rise up against the Spanish. The discouraged English forces were now suffering from hunger and disease, and Drake decided to withdraw without making an attempt to seize the Azores. Soon after the English left Spanish waters, the 1589 treasure fleet arrived safely. The great English fleet, one of the largest they ever mustered, had failed to achieve any of its goals.[19]

In the meantime, the situation in France was deteriorating, from the Spanish point of view, because it looked like a Protestant, Henry of Navarre, might inherit the throne. In 1584, Philip had promised the French Catholics a subsidy of nearly 70,000 pesos a year. He hoped that money alone would be enough to keep France Catholic, but he also agreed to provide troops, if it became necessary. Five years later, Henry became king of France, and Philip decided the time had come to increase his commitment by sending Spanish soldiers, even though the war with the English and the Dutch was still underway.

It was a classic case of providing too little too late. Spanish forces were not powerful enough to prevent Henry from successfully asserting his claim to the throne, and Philip had gained an additional enemy. Although the fighting was confined to land, it became another costly and lengthy commitment. There was a Spanish garrison in Paris from 1590 to 1594, and even after the Spanish withdrew from the capital, the French kept up the fight.[20]

Philip was now at war with all three of the other major states of western

Europe: the United Provinces, England, and France. In the 1590s, his response to the crisis was to redouble his efforts to achieve victory. The defeat of the Armada was not the end of the effort to make Spain a great sea power but only a spur to further effort. Treasure from the Indies was still flowing across the Atlantic in record amounts, and communications were improved by having more small, fast vessels carrying information and orders across the Atlantic. Philip's armies and navies held strategic positions all over western Europe, and he remained on the lookout for an opportunity to seize a port in France that could provide a base for another attack on England.

Naturally, one of the king's chief goals, if he were to continue the war, was to rebuild the Spanish fleet after the disaster of the Armada. To pay for a new fleet, Philip raised taxes. To improve efficiency, he revitalized his plans of the 1570s and made renewed efforts to construct a professional navy. As before, the goal was to have a fleet of specialized warships owned and operated by the government without having to depend on contractors. The fleet built in the 1590s was Spain's first permanent royal navy, and by 1598 there were nearly 30 ships available, although this was still less than half the Spanish battle fleet.[21]

As the war dragged on, Spain's enemies turned more and more to plans to strike at the treasure fleets as a way to undermine the sources of Spanish power. There were basically two strategies for attacking the convoys: catching them at sea or capturing the bases from which they operated. The English and Dutch tried both strategies, and they found both equally difficult. After the failure of the attacks on Spain and Portugal in 1589, the British turned to pure deep-water operations, and started by stationing a squadron off the Azores later that same year. When the treasure fleet arrived, the English found themselves outnumbered more than two to one, and they let the Spanish ships pass without engaging them. It was a close call, though, and Philip was unwilling to run the risk of keeping to the regular fleet schedule. Instead, the king ordered the 1590 fleet of galleons to remain in the Caribbean and used *zabras* to ferry the treasure.

In 1591, the Spanish divided the treasure between the *zabras* and a regular fleet, and the English again went to the Azores and tried to maintain a blockade there with about 20 ships. The *zabras* slipped past the English, but Elizabeth's captains doggedly tried to maintain a blockade to intercept the main fleet. With their ships and crews suffering from the extended time at sea, they went ashore in an isolated area to make repairs and to look for water and fresh food.

In the meantime, a Spanish escort fleet of over 50 ships, under the command of Alonso de Bazán, the brother of the Marquis de Santa Cruz, headed for the Azores to meet the treasure fleet. When they realized they would be vastly outnumbered by the converging Spanish fleets, the English quickly interrupted their repairs and tried to escape. Many of Bazán's captains were veterans of the

The last battle of the **Revenge,** *1591. The only captain unable to withdraw in time when the more powerful Spanish fleet arrived was Sir Richard Grenville, commanding the* **Revenge,** *Drake's flagship during the fight against the Armada. In a gallant but hopeless struggle,*

Grenville and his crew engaged 15 Spanish ships for over 12 hours, sinking two and badly damaging two others. They surrendered only after they had exhausted their ammunition. Grenville, who was seriously wounded, died shortly after the battle. (Photo courtesy of Robert F. Marx)

Armada, eager to settle scores, and they attacked as soon as they sighted the English. All of the English ships managed to get away, except for the *Revenge*. Soon after the capture of the *Revenge*, the main fleet from the Indies arrived. While the combined Spanish fleet was still in the Azores, a violent storm destroyed many of the Spanish ships, along with the shattered hulk of Grenville's ship. As noted earlier, about 10 million pesos' worth of treasure was also lost in this storm. Even though much of the treasure that went down with the ships was later salvaged, it was one of the worst disasters of the period. King Philip was so unnerved by the attacks on Spanish and Portuguese ports and the efforts to establish a blockade that he ordered that no treasure ships, either galleons or *zabras*, should sail in 1594, despite the fact that he desperately needed the money. This was the first year in which no treasure had arrived since the reorganization of the fleet system in the mid-1560s.[22]

By 1595, the English were almost exhausted, but they decided to make one last attempt to cut off the silver fleets at their point of origin. Drake and Hawkins began preparing another expedition for the Caribbean, but because of a Spanish attack on Cornwall, the only time during the war that Spanish forces actually landed in England, Elizabeth refused to allow their departure. Once it was clear that the Spanish strike in Cornwall was only a raid, not a prelude to an invasion, the queen was more willing to release her most famous captains.

Final orders for departure were prompted by a report about the vulnerability of a galleon with more than 3 million pesos on board. The Spanish ship had been caught in a storm off Florida, and it was so badly damaged that it could not continue and had to take shelter in San Juan, Puerto Rico. Drake and Hawkins set out with nearly 30 ships for what was to be their last great strike at the treasure fleets. This tragic and futile expedition made it clear, however, that both men were well past their prime. They failed to locate the treasure fleets during their transit of the Atlantic, and had little more success in attacking the ports of the Caribbean. As a result of Philip's massive construction projects, the English found that the defenses in the Caribbean were much improved. Drake and Hawkins were unable to capture the fortress at Puerto Rico or the battered galleon that had sought refuge there. The English then went on to Nombre de Dios. Although they seized the port, they found that there was little treasure present. Weakened by disease, the English forces were unable to press on to Panama City, where, unknown to them, 5 million pesos were waiting to be picked up by the treasure fleet.

Both Drake and Hawkins died during the 1595 expedition to the Caribbean. With their legendary leaders gone and no major success to their credit, the demoralized English decided to withdraw. While the much-reduced English force was leaving the Caribbean, it encountered a Spanish squadron off Cuba and had to fight its way out. Although the English had little to show for their troubles, their sack of Nombre de Dios was so thorough that the Spanish stopped using the town as a port for the treasure fleets. After 1595, the Spanish preferred to use Porto Bello as the terminus on the Caribbean shore for the path across the Isthmus of Panama. Although Porto Bello, like most ports in the West Indies, was usually hot and a source of tropical fevers, it had a better harbor than Nombre de Dios and soon became an important port of call for the treasure fleets.[23]

For the rest of the war, the English were unable to risk sending another large fleet so far from home, but they did manage to muster several smaller expeditions. In 1595, Raleigh revived his efforts to found a permanent base in the Western Hemisphere and set off with a small force of five ships and 150 men. This time his destination was Guiana, a region at the mouth of the Orinoco River that was thinly populated but near the heart of the Spanish Empire. The English had heard the stories about *El Dorado* and hoped they might be the ones to uncover the secrets of the lost kingdom.

Raleigh's strategy was to befriend the natives and use them as allies in capturing a base for carving out an English empire in South America and attacking the treasure fleets. Although Raleigh did treat the natives kindly and was able to strike up a friendly relationship with them, the expedition was a failure. Ore samples, allegedly containing gold, turned out to be of little value, and Raleigh's force was too weak for direct attacks on Spanish fleets or ports. After several months of effort, Raleigh gave up and returned to England.

In 1598, an English expedition under the Earl of Cumberland made one last attempt to establish a toehold in the Caribbean by attacking Puerto Rico. Cumberland was able to capture San Juan, but was too weak to hold the fortress and had to evacuate his forces.[24]

Back in European waters, the war continued. Energy and resources were flagging on both sides, but the Spanish capture of Calais had added new urgency to the aging Elizabeth's desire for a decisive victory that would assure the security of her island realm. In 1596, the English and Dutch sent another large fleet of about 100 ships to Cadiz under Howard, Raleigh, and the Earl of Essex. The Spanish Atlantic squadron was distracted by efforts to catch Drake and Hawkins in the Caribbean, and the English correctly calculated that Cadiz would be dangerously exposed. Raleigh led a daring charge of the fleet into the harbor of Cadiz, and the allies destroyed or seized more than 20 ships and millions of pesos' worth of merchandise. Essex proposed that the allies build on their success by establishing a blockade of Spain, but he could not convince the other captains to remain so far from home for an indefinite period. Yet again, the English captains and sailors preferred loot to strategic advantage, and they withdrew from Spanish waters for the last time during the war.

A short while after the English left, the treasure fleet arrived safely. Essex and Raleigh tried to catch the treasure fleet in the Azores in 1597, but a storm scattered their forces. The combined New Spain and *Tierra Firme* fleets, with over 10 million pesos on board, slipped through. In a report summing up two years of efforts to seize the treasure fleets, Essex recommended that the English try to capture a port in Spain that would provide a permanent base for striking at Spanish shipping, but in the 1590s, England did not have the resources for such a bold operation.[25]

The Spanish responded to these attacks by reviving plans for an invasion of England, but their efforts were hampered by bad luck and the strains of the long war. By 1596, their ship-building program was progressing well enough that they could assemble another Armada. Philip's plan was to send more than 100 ships to assist a rebellion by the Irish Catholics, but storms that year damaged many ships and kept the fleet from sailing to England.

In 1597, the Spanish tried yet again to launch an invasion, and this time they were able to achieve complete surprise and arrive undetected almost within sight of the English coast. As before, however, the notoriously bad weather in the Channel disrupted their effort. Just at that moment, Raleigh and Essex returned from their expedition to the Azores, and the Spanish decided to withdraw.

The Spanish made one last attempt to strike directly at the British Isles by landing 4,500 troops in Ireland in 1601. An alliance with the Irish Catholics made a great deal of sense, but the Spanish and Irish did not coordinate their efforts, and the Spanish committed too few forces to be effective. The small Spanish fleet had to abandon the army in Ireland, and the English were then able to defeat the combined Irish and Spanish land force.

These expensive but unsuccessful attacks, combined with the heavy burden of keeping up a worldwide fight against his many enemies, meant that Philip was again forced to abandon his plans for a professional navy. Like their equally exhausted English enemies, the Spanish were unable to muster the resources for ambitious projects, even if the ideas had merit. These compromises with reality affected things such as the production of cannon and gunpowder, sectors of the economy that the authorities, in the past, had believed were too vital to leave to private entrepreneurs. In the 1590s, the Spanish government reluctantly had to opt for the less expensive alternative and turn some work over to contractors.[26]

All during the worldwide war at sea of the 1580s and 1590s, the Dutch, Spain's most tenacious enemies, were making strategic and commercial gains. Philip II's economic and military pressure on the Netherlands in Europe had forced the Dutch to go farther afield to raise money and continue the fight against Spain. The Dutch also took advantage of the fact that the Spanish were preoccupied by the fighting in Europe and the Caribbean.

At first, the Dutch had mostly bad luck against the Spanish. In 1597, the Dutch made their first foray into the Pacific via Cape Horn, but local Spanish forces sank or captured all the ships. A Dutch expedition of 1598-1601 was more successful, and became the fourth European expedition to circumnavigate the globe. Dutch fleets returned to the Pacific in 1615, but had little luck in seizing any Spanish treasure from ports or ships, and the Manila galleons continued to sail unimpeded. During this period, Dutch forces also traveled eastward across the Indian Ocean and attacked Manila on several occasions, but they were always beaten off. The first real Dutch successes were in the Spice Islands, a traditional Portuguese preserve, and Dutch fleets captured several important islands there. In 1619, they seized Jakarta from the local ruler, renamed it Batavia, and made the city their headquarters in Asia.

While naval attacks brought only limited gains, the Dutch had more success with commercial ventures. They were finding they could tap into the wealth of the Spanish Empire by smuggling merchandise. Even though it was illegal, Spanish colonists in the Western Hemisphere were eager to trade their silver for the high-quality and low-priced goods brought in by the Dutch. In time, Dutch smugglers built their illicit trade into such a large operation that Spanish merchants found it difficult to compete. The contraband trade not only generated private profit but also served the purposes of the rebel government of the United Provinces by reducing the Spanish government's income from customs duties.[27]

As the war dragged on and expenses mounted, the Spanish finally became reconciled to the need to use diplomacy to reduce the number of their enemies. Philip II made peace with France in 1598, a few months before he died. His son and successor, Philip III, was also disposed to peace and retrenchment, and he arranged a peace treaty with England in 1604. The English were so discouraged by the costly and indecisive struggle that they granted the Spanish much of what Philip II had sought when he sent the Armada: an end to English support for the Dutch rebels, freedom of transit in the Channel for Spanish ships, and tolerance of Catholics in England. About the only thing the English gained was an easing of restrictions on their trade with Spain.

Even after the others had dropped out of the war, the rebels in the Netherlands kept up their struggle, and remained Spain's most persistent enemy. In 1607, the Dutch defeated a Spanish fleet off Gibraltar, and the Spanish government had to suspend payments on its debts again. Even the proud officials in Madrid were forced to recognize that they could not continue the fight against the Dutch. Spain and the United Provinces finally signed a truce in 1609, and the Spanish were at peace for the first time in more than 35 years.

Spain made very few concessions in these peace treaties and stubbornly tried to maintain control of its empire in the Americas. The government's diplomatic and military success in holding on to its colonies, which were the world's greatest source of precious metals, demonstrated that Spain was still the greatest power in Europe. The Treaty of London in 1604 with the English and the Truce of Antwerp in 1609 with the Dutch both included clauses which recognized the Spanish claim to a colonial monopoly in the areas they already occupied, but the English and Dutch refused to accept Spanish claims in areas they did not occupy. In time, this principle of effective occupation became an important part of international law.

In the early seventeenth century, such discussions were a sign that other powers were moving closer to encroaching on Spanish possessions by founding permanent settlements in the Western Hemisphere. In contrast to the Treaty of Câteau-Cambrésis, half a century before, colonial matters were now closely interwoven with European diplomatic settlements, and the affairs of distant continents were proving to be more susceptible to control from Europe. The world system begun as an economic enterprise a century before was taking on political importance.

During the reign of Philip III, other powers made the first tentative steps toward permanent settlements in the Western Hemisphere. These early colonies by outsiders were in areas far from the sources of colonial wealth in New Spain and Peru. Given the financial difficulties and military exhaustion of the time, the Spanish did not respond. The English founded Jamestown in 1607, the French established Quebec in 1608, and the Dutch set up a trading post on Manhattan Island in 1613.

The one probe by foreigners that did elicit a violent response from the Spanish was Raleigh's last voyage in 1617. Raleigh had outlived all the other Elizabethan sea dogs, but his vision, daring, and anti-Spanish attitudes were seriously out of date in an era of peace. Nonetheless, King James I, who had succeeded Elizabeth in 1603, needed money and was seduced by Raleigh's tales of the gold available in South America. Although Raleigh no longer believed in *El Dorado*, the rich kingdom rumored to be somewhere deep in the jungle, he was confident that there were gold mines yet to be found in Guiana.

James authorized Raleigh to go in search of the mines, but he issued strict orders not to seize gold by force. To lessen any possible objections from Madrid, James informed the Spanish about Raleigh's plans. Despite instructions to conduct peaceful exploration, there were violent encounters with the Spanish in Guiana, and Raleigh's own son was killed in the fighting. Raleigh found only a little gold, and, heartbroken, he returned to England, where James dredged up old charges of treason and executed the last of the sea dogs.[28]

Increasing Financial Pressure on Spain

Paying for all of Philip II's wars was a staggering burden for Spain, and the government was desperate to lay its hands on the wealth of the Indies in any way it could. By the 1590s, Philip had managed to increase his income to almost 14 million pesos a year, which included about 3 million annually from the *quinto*, the royal share of the gold and silver from the mines in the Indies. Philip also could collect more of the wealth of the Indies that went into private hands by increasing taxes. For example, the *averia* tax, the main source of money for defending the treasure fleets, rose from less than 2 percent to 8 percent of the value of the cargoes. Between 1575 and 1598, the government also raised money by selling about 55 million pesos' worth of long-term *juros*.

But expenditures were rising even faster than income and eventually reached over 27 million pesos a year, or about 10 percent of Spain's gross national product at the time. The only way to make up the difference was through loans, and Philip borrowed more and more from the merchants and bankers who had profited from the Indies trade. By the 1590s, over half the royal income was committed to repaying debts. Making payments on these loans was becoming increasingly difficult because precious metals continued to drain out of Spain to pay soldiers, repay foreign creditors, and finance a growing trade deficit.[29]

In 1596, the desperate situation forced Philip to suspend payment on his short-term debts for the third time, in part because no treasure had been received in 1594. The government's failure to pay its obligations further undermined the finances of the wealthy businessmen who provided most of the loans. The 1596 suspension of payments was the final blow for the Spanish commercial money market that had operated at the fairs of Medina del Campo. Government borrowing had absorbed most of the resources of Spain's domestic money market, and yet another suspension of payment virtually destroyed that market. As a result, after 1596 there was no large and reliable source of loans for private commerce and industry, and Spain's economy was seriously weakened.

For the next century, most of the borrowing in Spain was done on behalf of the government, and much of the money the crown raised was used for unproductive foreign wars. When Philip II died in 1598, he had more than 100 million pesos in debts outstanding, and more than half the budget was required for debt service.[30]

After Philip III came to the throne, he also cast about for expedients that would increase his income. Charles V had seized private funds from the treasure fleets, and Philip II had repudiated debts. Philip III went even further. For the first time in more than a century, the king of Spain, who ironically was the master of the treasure house of the Indies, debased the Spanish currency. In 1599, the government recalled the *vellón* coins, small denomination pieces that were a mixture of copper and silver, and melted them down to extract the silver. Royal officials then defrauded the public by reissuing the coins in only copper at their old value. Four years later, the copper coins were recalled again, stamped at twice their value, and then put back into circulation. The government was returning to the devaluations of the medieval period and attempting to create a fiat currency, with little intrinsic worth and a value in trade that was only what the government said it was.

Since this manipulation involved the currency used in small, day-to-day transactions, it had an impact on most of the population and especially on the poor. The royal treasury made large short-term profits as a result of these operations, but such measures also undermined faith in the currency and the government. As a result of public protests, in 1608 the government promised to stop minting the debased *vellón* coins. But the hard-pressed authorities, who still could not balance the budget, reneged on this commitment in 1617, a move which further undermined the Spanish economy. Although Spaniards had no choice but to take the debased currency, foreigners were not so accommodating. Because Spain's imperial policy still demanded large amounts of hard currency that would be acceptable abroad, the silver pesos of New Spain and Peru were kept at their full weight and purity.[31]

Maintaining the silver content of the colonial pesos made only a minor contribution to ameliorating the Spanish government's financial problems. One of the chief remaining difficulties was the inability to predict accurately the size or date of the arrival of the cargoes of the treasure fleets. In 1606, the treasure fleets were delayed, and the troops in the Netherlands mutinied because they had not received their pay. The following year, due in part to uncertainty about the security of the overseas lifelines, there was yet another suspension of payments on the government's short-term debt. One footnote to the 1607 suspension was that it finally drove the Fuggers out of the business of royal finance.

Spanish Silver Throughout the World

By the late sixteenth century, Spanish coins, especially the silver pieces of 8 *reales*, were the most widely circulated currency in Europe. International financial transactions, such as trade contracts or ransoms for prisoners seized by the Turks, often specified that payment should be in pieces of eight. Much of this Spanish money, however, was falling under the control of foreigners. The English and the Dutch were pioneering new techniques that would enable them to divert more and more of the Spanish silver without territorial conquests in either the Indies or Europe.

In 1600, a group of English merchants founded the English East India Company, and two years later the United Provinces set up the Dutch East India Company. Because of the vast distances involved and the governments' shortage of resources, these companies assumed many of the powers in Asia that national governments held in Europe. The trading companies made laws, negotiated treaties, operated fleets and armies, and declared war without referring to the home governments. In Asia, the Dutch company soon outdistanced both the old Portuguese state-run trading system and the new British private company. Silver was still the key to success in the Asian trade, and the Dutch raised what they needed by legally selling colonial products in Europe and by smuggling goods into the Spanish colonies in the Indies. As the seventeenth century went on, it was increasingly the Dutch rather than the Portuguese who controlled the flow of silver eastward to Asia.[32]

In Europe, Amsterdam had taken over from Antwerp as the commercial and financial center of the continent, with the difference that the focal point was now in a virtually independent country rather than a province loyal to the Habsburgs. The Dutch even made a good profit by providing supplies and financial services for the Spanish government they were rebelling against. Because of Dutch skill, the net result of doing business with the enemy was to undermine Spanish power rather than increase it. Dutch financial power was symbolized by the founding in 1609 of another important private corporation, the Bank of Amsterdam. The bank operated full time and took over many functions of the periodic fairs, which had provided a forum for the commercial money market in the previous century. The Bank of Amsterdam safely and efficiently accepted bills of exchange, took deposits of coins and bullion, and made transfers among its account holders. This bank was still not a national central bank in the modern sense, however, because it did not make loans or issue bank notes.

Through the mechanisms of the Bank of Amsterdam and their vast trade connections, the Dutch managed the flow of silver to areas where western Europe had large trade deficit, such as the Baltic, the Ottoman Empire, and the Far East. With its huge reserves of precious metals, the bank was able to improve on the crude Spanish financial system by creating a mechanism that could support large-scale commercial operations and smooth out the differences between the irregular arrivals of the treasure fleets from the Indies.[33]

In the Far East, silver continued to be the one thing Asians would readily accept in return for silks and spices. According to an Italian merchant of the time, "The Chinese, among all the peoples of Asia, are wild about silver as everywhere else men are about gold." Although high demand stimulated domestic production, China's mines still did not produce enough of the silver needed to support its large and vibrant economy. Therefore, resistance diminished to the idea of earning silver through trade with foreigners. These developments meant that by the early seventeenth century there was enough silver that it began to come out of hoards and circulate as currency. The mandarins who ran the Chinese government noticed this and began to levy taxes in silver rather than in kind or in labor. These real benefits to the economy meant that the Chinese developed an ambivalent attitude toward trade and its profits.

China's mandarins traditionally saw trade with the West in terms of tribute, a privilege granted to less civilized outsiders so they would have a means to pay homage to the superior culture of the Middle Kingdom, and they assigned a low value to the work of merchants, both Chinese and foreign. Official disdain for the needs of commerce was shown by the fact that the government still made no effort to mint coins from the rising tide of silver. But at the same time, the government welcomed the increased revenues in silver that were made possible by expanded intercontinental trade. The Chinese emperors shared this equivocal attitude. While they criticized the low level of culture of the Western barbarians, they also enviously referred to their counterpart, the Spanish monarch, as "the King of Silver." Chinese merchants, on the other hand, were more open and sincere in their appreciation of the rising flow of silver, which increased their wealth and made their work easier.[34]

Around 1600, a world commercial system, financed largely by silver, was

Chopmarked sixteenth-century peso. With no silver coins of their own, Chinese traders were particularly fond of Spanish coins, a more useful and reliable form of money than their country's discredited paper currency, awkward bronze cash coins, or silver sycee ingots. However, Chinese who dealt in silver were aware of the possibility that the oddly shaped silver cobs from Spanish colonial mints could easily have had some of the silver clipped off before they reached Asia. So businessmen in China began to stamp the pesos with chopmarks to record that the coins had been tested for weight and purity, as was done on this example from the Mexico City mint. Many Chinese merchants would only accept a coin that had been stamped with their personal mark. (Photo from the author's collection)

firmly in place. The Spanish, in conjunction with the Portuguese, controlled most of the seaborne channels through which precious metals were spread around the world; but the Dutch were encroaching on the networks of the Iberian powers. At this time, about 16 million pesos' worth of precious metals came from the mines in the Indies every year. The silver then went in two great streams: one to the east and one to the west.

The largest flow of silver was the 11 million pesos shipped across the Atlantic. Much of this immediately left Spain to go to Italy and the Netherlands to pay for imports, loans, and wars. The Dutch, in turn, sent some 2 million pesos' worth of silver a year to the Baltic for grain and naval supplies. Of the 11 million pesos coming across the Atlantic each year, the Portuguese re-exported about 1.5 million to the Far East and the Dutch sent another 500,000 or so. As the Dutch expanded their direct trade with Asia in the early seventeenth century, they found it practical to ship silver in the form of pieces of eight, which were accepted throughout Asia. Although the Dutch minted some of their silver into trade coins for their growing commerce, they transported pieces of eight intact, because of the coin's high silver content and widespread acceptance.[35]

The other great stream of silver was the approximately 5 million pesos a year that the Spanish sent westward directly to China via the Manila galleons. This abundant and steady supply of silver meant that Manila, Spain's foothold in Asia, became the center of a thriving trade. This transpacific commerce was lucrative but also had its risks and problems. As in the other seas of the world, severe weather took its toll on Spanish shipping in the Pacific. For example, in both 1600 and 1603, Manila galleons, each with about 1.5 million pesos on board, were lost in storms.

Moreover, the textile merchants in the Seville *Consulado* became so worried about the competition from Chinese silk that they petitioned the government to restrict the trade. The government, which had concerns based on mercantilist doctrines about the outflow of silver, was responsive to the merchants' complaints. In 1593, Spanish authorities issued new regulations limiting the number of annual galleons to two and permitting only 500,000 pesos in silver to be exported from America. Strict limitations on the flow of silver was counterproductive in the long run, however. As in the Atlantic, the regulations were often thwarted through smuggling. In addition, one consequence of limiting the amount of silver sent to the Far East was that the Spaniards effectively relinquished leadership of the trade with China to the Dutch, who were willing to ship unlimited amounts of silver to Asia.[36]

By the beginning of the seventeenth century, only a century after Colum-

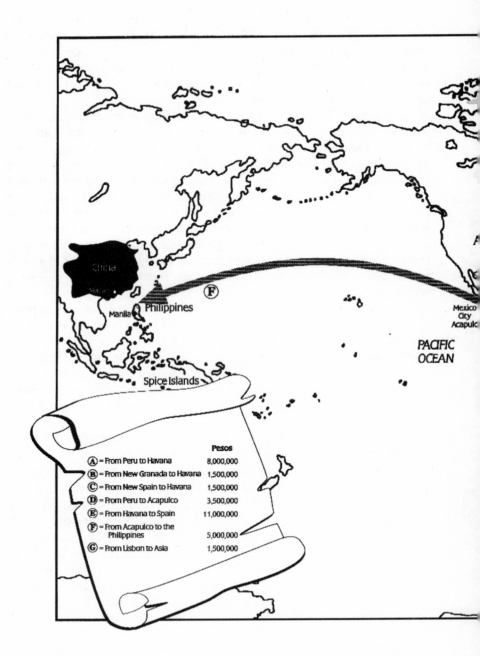

China

Macao

Ⓕ

Manila Philippines

Mexico
City
Acapulco

PACIFIC
OCEAN

Spice Islands

		Pesos
Ⓐ	= From Peru to Havana	8,000,000
Ⓑ	= From New Granada to Havana	1,500,000
Ⓒ	= From New Spain to Havana	1,500,000
Ⓓ	= From Peru to Acapulco	3,500,000
Ⓔ	= From Havana to Spain	11,000,000
Ⓕ	= From Acapulco to the Philippines	5,000,000
Ⓖ	= From Lisbon to Asia	1,500,000

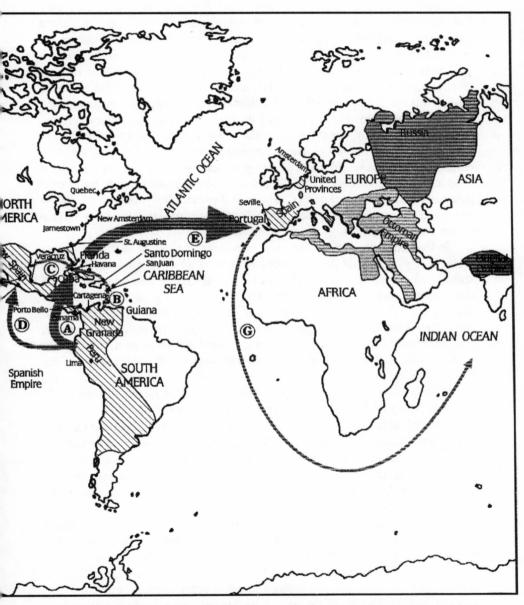

Map 5. The Spanish Empire and Global Flows
of Precious Metals in 1600

bus, a global economic and political system was in operation. Areas of the world that had been isolated from each other found that their histories had become interconnected. For instance, a Spanish embargo of Dutch shipping in Europe led to the Dutch becoming the leading commercial power in Asia; or the interruption of the flow of silver from the mines of Peru forced the Spanish government to reschedule its debts, which in turn caused economic distress throughout Europe. The rising output from colonial mints and the fact that more money was remaining in the Spanish colonies to pay for defense meant that the entire Western Hemisphere was being drawn into a global monetary system.

During the late sixteenth century, the treasure fleets also spread to the Far East the European custom of using currency made from precious metals. As a result, most of the world was caught up in economic rhythms based on the production and distribution of gold and silver, in addition to more traditional patterns based on factors such as weather and agricultural productivity. Silver pesos and galleons became potent symbols of how Europe was fastening its grip on the rest of the world.

In the sixteenth century, the most important participant in this emerging worldwide system was the combined empire of Spain and Portugal, which spread across five continents. This vast colonial system was financed by the cumbersome method of transporting huge amounts of gold and silver from place to place. Because much of the silver was shipped in the form of pieces of eight, these coins became a world currency. Although such financing was risky, and there were losses, it worked. Even the Spanish government, notoriously irresponsible in financial matters, dared not tamper with the integrity of the pieces of eight.

Spain's power made its monarch, Philip II, overconfident. Instead of his previous policy of dealing with his enemies one or two at a time, in the 1590s Philip ended up at war with all the major maritime powers of Western Europe. Spain soon found, however, that it could not be strong everywhere. The Spanish also learned that the sea could be a highway to its empire as well as a moat; it could bring intruders as well as security. By the early seventeenth century incursions by foreigners, rare during the first century of Spanish rule in the Americas, had become commonplace.

Even after incurring heavy losses responding to these threats from rivals abroad, such as the destruction of much of the Armada of 1588, Philip kept trying to maintain his empire by fighting rather than negotiating and making concessions. This policy ran the risk of bringing even more damage to Spain's international position and also created a host of bitter enemies, especially the English and the Dutch. In the end, a negotiated peace became imperative. Spain's empire emerged intact from the wars of the late sixteenth century, but it was not clear that the Spanish system could continue to stand the strain.

The key to Spain's continued success would be retaining access to its far-flung colonies. Spain remained a mighty empire despite the attacks of the English and Dutch, and still had considerable sources of strength. For example, the great oceanic war at the end of the seventeenth century demonstrated how difficult it was to locate the treasure fleets once they were at sea. But there were danger signs. Spain was losing control of the trade of its empire, in large part because other countries were pioneering new techniques of commercial success, such as large trading companies and banks. Spain was slipping behind; if it became involved in war again, the challenge would be even greater while the resources available would be fewer.

4. Decline, 1621–1715

uring the seventeenth century, Spain's enemies exerted pressure on the empire on all fronts. If Spain was to retain its position of international hegemony against this onslaught, the country would have to maintain control of the flow of precious metals from the Indies. Command of the main sources of gold and silver was one of the key assets that made an intrinsically poor and increasingly backward country like Spain a major power. Control required managing production at the mines efficiently, assuring that the sea lanes remained open and safe for the treasure fleets, and adopting commercial and diplomatic policies that kept foreign expenditures to a minimum.

The Decision to Go to War

When a dispute between Protestants and Catholics in the Holy Roman Empire unleashed the Thirty Years' War in 1618, the peacefully inclined Philip III was still on the throne of Spain. Although his Austrian relations were heavily engaged in the fighting, Philip initially remained on the sidelines. As the war widened, however, it began to encroach on Spanish interests, especially in strategically important Italy.

In 1621, Philip III died and his son, Philip IV, became king. Philip IV was young and eager to seek glorious victories for himself, his relatives in central Europe, and his religion. A few weeks after he came to power, the truce with the Dutch rebels expired, and this was the event that triggered the Spanish decision to join the Thirty Years' War. Philip and his chief minister, the Duke of Olivares, decided to resume the effort to regain control of the United Provinces not only because the Dutch were Protestants who continued to flout Spanish authority in Europe, but also because the Dutch were encroaching on Spanish and Portuguese trade in the Indies and in Asia. Philip's advisers apparently assumed that the risk of going to war would be minimal because their main potential enemy, France, was still weakened by internal problems. Spanish officials realized they would need reliable financial resources to conduct the war successfully, for as Olivares admitted, "Kings cannot achieve heroic actions without money." Spain's leaders were confident, however, that the torrent of precious metals still coming from the Indies would provide the funds they needed.

Because of the nature of Spain's far-flung empire and the enemies to be fought, it was clear that much of the war would be fought at sea, and the Spanish believed they were ready for this, as well. An important factor behind the fateful decision to go to war was the confidence generated by the fact that the government had been rebuilding the fleet since 1617, in response to rising international tensions. Once Spain joined the conflict, work on the fleet was pursued with renewed vigor and expenditures on the army and navy more than doubled. Philip IV was sure he would have the money, but to get large numbers of warships quickly, he rejected the option of expending the time and effort necessary for a professional navy. Instead, the government again negotiated *asientos* for building and outfitting ships. The demands of war soon made it impossible to follow any policy other than to depend on the contractors. This meant that for the remainder of the century, Spain would have a parsimoniously managed fleet, with old-fashioned ships and poorly trained officers.[1]

Initially, the war went well for Spain. Her armies were victorious in Italy, the Holy Roman Empire, and the Netherlands, and her fleets defeated the Dutch in the Caribbean and in the waters off Spain. To his credit, Olivares realized that traditional methods would not be sufficient to maintain Spain's position. In 1624, he proposed that the burdens of empire, which for over a century had fallen most heavily on Castile, should be spread more evenly among the various provinces. Olivares suggested that all the provinces contribute to a common pool of troops and money, which would be drawn upon to defend any portion of the empire that came under attack. He hoped that this plan, known as the Union of Arms, would alleviate the century-old problem of the empire being so scattered and diverse that there was little or no sense of common interest. Some provinces grudgingly contributed money to the Union of Arms, but they were extremely reluctant to send their troops very far from home. Olivares kept pushing for contributions, however, and his exactions caused increasing resentment.[2]

In the 1630s, the war began to go against Spain. France, traditionally the Habsburgs' greatest enemy, was coming out of a period of decline and rebuilding the power of the central government under the leadership of Cardinal Richelieu. Once France threw its weight into the war in 1635, it was impossible for Spain to maintain its hegemony in Europe. France began to assault the territorial foundations of Spanish power on land, while the Dutch and the English struck at the sea routes. Spain again found itself overcommitted and unable to isolate problems to deal with them one at a time. For most of the seventeenth century, Spain would be at war against increasingly more powerful enemies. One of the main targets in these conflicts would be the treasure fleets.

Attacks on the Treasure Fleets during Spain's Decline

Probably the most obvious sign of Spain's weakness in the early seventeenth century was that other European powers were able to take advantage of the fact that the government in Madrid was distracted by war in Europe. For the first time, outsiders were able to establish permanent colonies along the routes of the treasure fleets. The initial targets were the small islands of the Caribbean, largely ignored by the Spanish because there were no precious metals and no open country for ranching. In 1624, the first permanent settlement in the Caribbean by foreigners was established when a small group of English founded a colony on St. Kitts. A few months later, a shipload of French privateers turned up, and the British and French decided to develop the island jointly. The Spanish soon responded, and in 1629, a fleet on its way to pick up treasure in the Caribbean stopped at St. Kitts, attacked the English and French settlements, and killed or captured most of the colonists. The colony was not completely eliminated, however, because a few colonists survived on the island and the Spanish did not have the resources to station a permanent garrison there. The English founded a second colony on Barbados in 1627 and the French expanded to Guadeloupe and Martinique in 1635.

These first colonies were only tentative signs of rival nations' interest in the Caribbean. Moreover, they were not very threatening because the settlements were small agricultural enterprises founded by private groups rather than naval bases or trading stations under the control of the government or the great trading companies. A much more serious threat came from the Dutch, who founded the Dutch West India Company in 1621. Like its counterpart in the East Indies, the company was designed for both war and profit. An expedition sent out by the

Piet Heyn. The Dutch admiral was the quintessential seventeenth-century man on the make. He came from a humble background but shrewdly and aggressively worked his way to the senior ranks of what was the world's greatest navy at the time. Heyn had once been a privateer and had spent four years as a Spanish galley slave. Based on his years of experience at sea, Heyn had a good idea of the Spanish fleets' schedules and routes and turned this knowledge to his advantage. He was the only naval commander to capture the entire cargo of a Spanish treasure fleet. (Photo courtesy of Robert F. Marx)

25 Piet Hein.

Dutch West India Company seized Curacao in 1634 and used it as a major base for smuggling operations.[3]

The most striking sign of the decay of the Spanish maritime system in the early seventeenth century was a crippling series of Dutch naval victories in the Caribbean and in Europe. In 1628, the West India Company sent a fleet of more than 30 ships to the Caribbean under the command of Admiral Piet Heyn. Heyn's goal was to capture one of the treasure fleets, and once he reached the Caribbean he sent out patrols to find the treasure galleons. Spain's own patrols detected Heyn's movements and warned the treasure ships to remain in Cartagena and Veracruz. When part of Heyn's fleet returned to Europe, Spanish authorities mistook it for his entire force and allowed the New Spain fleet, made up of 11 merchantmen and 4 galleons, to sail. Meanwhile, Heyn, with the main body of his fleet, cruised off Havana, knowing that sooner or later the Spanish ships would have to pass that way. Spanish patrols spotted Heyn's fleet, but their warning to the treasure fleet did not arrive in time. As the Spanish fleet, ignorant of the danger, approached Havana, they sailed right into Heyn's net of patrols.[4]

Coincidentally, the commander of the fleet, Juan de Benavides y Bazán, had been captain of one of the galleys on which Heyn had served as a prisoner. Benavides was not one of Spain's greatest commanders, and the fact that he held such an important post showed how corrupt the system of managing the treasure fleets had become. He had little knowledge of seamanship, and he had made an illegal fortune carrying contraband on his ships. Benavides' career had prospered mainly because of the protection provided by his sister, one of Philip IV's mistresses.

In 1628, his laxity and lack of judgment were his undoing. The Spanish ships were so overloaded with cargo and passengers that the crews could not clear enough room to operate their guns. After sighting the Dutch, Benavides decided to sail to Matanzas Bay, 50 miles (80 kilometers) east of Havana, to unload the treasure and take it inland to safety. Inside the bay, Heyn's fleet caught up to the Spanish before they could carry out their plan.

This was the first time all the treasure galleons of a fleet were captured or destroyed, and the only instance in the history of the treasure fleets when an entire shipment of precious metals was lost. The Dutch booty from this action was 90 tons of gold and silver worth about 3 million pesos. On the way back to Spain, the Dutch lost some of their loot when two captured Spanish ships, with some of the treasure on board, sank in a storm in the Bahamas.[5]

The unprecedented capture of all the treasure in one of the annual fleets sent the West India Company into ecstasy and the Spanish into despair. For its part, the company was able to pay a 50 percent dividend. Although Heyn became a national hero, his share of the profits amounted to only 2,500 pesos; in disgust, he soon resigned his post with the company. For the Spanish, the encounter at Matanzas Bay meant a loss of about one-third of the ships then involved in the Atlantic trade. Philip IV suffered a nervous collapse when he received the news and did not appear in public for five days. Later, the king, exceedingly sensitive to questions of prestige, lamented that, "Whenever I speak of the disaster the blood runs cold in my veins, not for the loss of treasure but because we lost our reputation in that infamous defeat, caused as it was by fear and cowardice." Benavides' sister was able to protect him from the worst, and initially the courts only convicted him of dereliction of duty. After she died, however, he was executed in 1634.[6]

Such a loss was a disaster, but Spain still had the resources to respond vigorously, and a stream of countermeasures soon flowed from the government. The authorities in Madrid and Seville ordered the treasure fleets to sail together so they would be easier to protect. In addition, the government made an effort to keep warships in the Caribbean on a permanent basis, as Menéndez had originally proposed. From 1629 to 1632, the fleets were comprised almost entirely of warships, which took out the vital mercury and returned with

The Battle of Matanzas Bay, 1628. The awkward Spanish galleons towered over the smaller, but more nimble, Dutch ships during the battle. The treasure ships accomplished the first phase of their plan by making it into the bay, but Heyn pursued the Spanish so relentlessly that Benavides panicked and issued orders to destroy the ships. In the confusion that

Havana

followed, the Dutch were able to capture all the treasure galleons and all but three of the merchant ships without a serious fight. But the victory was not a result of superior firepower or skill at hand-to-hand combat; Spanish panic and confusion made them easy victims. (Photo courtesy of Robert F. Marx) treasure, and only a few commercial ships sailed. The 1629 fleet, for example, was made up of more than 20 galleons and carried nearly 4,000 troops, all under Fadrique de Toledo y Osorio and Antonio de Oquendo, two of Spain's best commanders. As already noted, this large force took the opportunity to attack English and French colonists on St. Kitts before bringing back more than 5 million pesos in treasure the following year. By 1638, enough improvements in defenses had been made that, when the Dutch tried again to capture the *Tierra Firme* fleet in the Caribbean, they were driven off after a week-long battle.

Sending fleets to the West Indies made up almost entirely of warships intimidated Spain's enemies, but it was an expensive policy for the government. With little or no trade to tax, the royal treasury had to pay all the costs of the fleets. Moreover, sending so many galleons to one region meant that the fleet was weak elsewhere. After a few years, Spanish authorities gave up trying to defend the Caribbean with such a large and expensive force, and the king ordered the warships back to Europe.[7]

Spain needed every ship she could muster to keep open maritime lines of communication in Europe. Among other projects, the Spanish government was determined to regain control of the English Channel, an essential goal in light of the pressure the French expansionist policy was putting on the Spanish Road, the Spanish-controlled route from Genoa to Antwerp that enabled them to shift resources across Europe. When the 1639 treasure fleet arrived in Spain, it was carrying more than 6 million pesos, which was badly needed to pay the troops in the Netherlands. Spanish authorities loaded 20,000 men and 4 million pesos onto more than 80 ships and sent them up the Channel under the command of Admiral Oquendo. There they were met by a force of about 30 Dutch ships, commanded by Admiral Martin Van Tromp.

A sharp fight ensued, and the smaller Dutch fleet caused considerable damage to the Spanish because of two innovations. First, the Dutch were using a new type of ship, the frigate, half the size of a galleon but faster and able to carry as many guns as the larger ships. Second, the Dutch, who agreed with the English in preferring cannon fire to boarding, were better organized. Instead of the usual chaotic melee of war at sea, they lined their ships up in single file to provide the maximum field of fire from the sides of the ships, where most of the guns were located. This formation also reduced exposure of the vulnerable bows and sterns of their vessels. Although arranging ships in line ahead had been used from time to time before, after this battle it became the standard naval tactical formation for the next 200 years.

The Spanish were badly shaken but not defeated during the fight in the Channel. Oquendo decided that, before proceeding to the Netherlands, it would be prudent to withdraw to neutral English waters at the Downs, off England's

The Battle of the Downs, 1639. *Van Tromp's attack on Oquendo's fleet off the southeast coast of England was one of the worst Spanish defeats of the seventeenth century. The Spanish lost 6,000 men and over 30 ships. It would be more than a century before large Spanish fleets operated in the Channel again. (Photo courtesy of the National Maritime Museum, London)*

southeast coast, to replenish his supplies. The Dutch blockaded the Spanish fleet there and summoned other warships until their fleet numbered more than 100. While the stalemate at the Downs continued, the Spanish were able to get most of the treasure and many of the troops through the blockade on small ships. After a few weeks of waiting, the Dutch were concerned that their prey was slipping away. Van Tromp ignored protests from London and violated England's neutrality by attacking the Spanish ships in English waters. The Spanish fleet was virtually destroyed, and the losses at the Downs were compounded when the Dutch defeated another Spanish fleet off Brazil a few months later.[8]

With much of Spain's navy destroyed, its options for protecting the treasure fleets were severely limited. The government apparently lacked the energy and creativity to come up with any alternative to the defensive strategy in use since Menéndez's time. But, at the same time, it was impossible to implement properly the Menéndez strategy, which called for heavy fortifications and large protective squadrons, because such an approach was so expensive. Instead, the Spanish authorities resorted to measures such as holding the fleets in port when there were known dangers or sending them to sea and hoping the vastness of the ocean would provide a degree of protection.

Now that Spain was so seriously weakened, disaster followed disaster. In 1640, both Catalonia and Portugal revolted. It would take nearly 20 years of fighting before the Spanish recovered Catalonia. Another long and expensive struggle took place in Portugal, but here the Spanish failed to re-establish control and had to recognize Portuguese independence in 1668. There were also a series of short-lived revolts in Spain's Italian provinces in 1647. Moreover, there were defeats for the Spanish army, once considered the best in Europe. In 1643, the French crippled a Spanish force at Rocroi, along the border between the Spanish Netherlands and France, when they inflicted 14,000 casualties on a Spanish army of 20,000 men. Although there were no immediate strategic effects from the defeat, and the Spanish retained their hold on the southern Netherlands, the Battle of Rocroi shattered the Spanish infantry's reputation for invincibility. That same year Philip IV dismissed Olivares, who became a scapegoat for Spanish failures, and decided to continue the war with France.

Meanwhile, developments in England, where a revolutionary government had overthrown and executed the king, were bringing a dramatic change in the English role in the world. During the first half of the seventeenth century, under the first two Stuart kings, James I and Charles I, England had been preoccupied with internal politics, and it was weak and ineffective on the few occasions when it did act overseas. In contrast, the new revolutionary government of the Commonwealth was more sympathetic to commercial interests and eager to demonstrate that it could expand and protect England's interests abroad. Two

King Philip IV of Spain by Velázquez. For over 30 years, Velázquez chronicled the King's transformation from a naive and somewhat arrogant youth to an old man weighed down with having to preside over the decline of an empire. This portrait, now in New York's Frick collection, shows Philip in the 1640s. Although he is splendidly attired in a coat and sash embroidered with silver, the symbols of glory that were often in earlier portraits have vanished and the monarch's face reflects the burdens of his position. (Photo courtesy of the Bettmann Archive)

other countries stood in the English Commonwealth's way as it sought to expand its power overseas: the United Provinces, in the full bloom of their wealth and power, and Spain, with great resources but a waning ability to defend them.

Oliver Cromwell, who became Lord Protector of the Commonwealth in 1653, gave a high priority to strengthening the navy as a means to exert English influence. Under James I and Charles I, the English navy had been allowed to deteriorate in size and effectiveness. During the Civil War, this attitude changed as the parliamentary forces came to see the navy as an essential tool for preventing outside help from reaching the royalists and making sure that a steady income from customs duties flowed into government coffers.

Once he had come to power, Cromwell reinvigorated the navy and made it an important part of a mercantilist policy that stressed building up England's trade, colonies, and merchant marine. It was Cromwell who began the task of making the English navy a professional force that would dominate the world's oceans for over two centuries. His goals were to make administration ashore more efficient and less subject to corruption, impose stricter discipline at sea, and more carefully recruit and train officers. Cromwell also wanted shipyards to produce specialized warships with more guns than their Dutch or Spanish counterparts. In time, the reformed navy would officially adopt aggressive, line-ahead tactics as its main method of combat and take on strategic responsibilities like convoy protection, blockade, and long-term deployments to distant locales. In the eyes of Cromwell and his admirals, the navy's main task was to seek out and destroy the enemy wherever it might be. These naval reforms were launched and tested during a grueling series of wars at sea against the Dutch and the Spanish from the 1650s to the 1670s. The result was a navy forged into a force that would become the most formidable man-made enemy that ever attacked the ships and ports of the Spanish system of treasure fleets.

In 1654, Cromwell ended an inconclusive war with the Dutch that had been going on since 1652 and began to work with his advisers on a plan to strike at Spain. Rather than merely raiding Spain's colonies, as Drake and Hawkins had done, Cromwell's ambition was to tap into the wealth of the Indies by permanently occupying some major portion of the Spanish Empire. Cromwell believed that the fact that Spain and France were still at war would give him an opportunity. He decided to target Santo Domingo, which had little intrinsic value but could serve as a base for an attack on the treasure fleets. To accomplish this mission, the English sent out a fleet of nearly 40 ships and more than 6,000 men under the command of General-at-Sea William Penn, father of the founder of Pennsylvania. Penn soon found, however, that the soldiers lacked training, supplies, and, as was so often the case for expeditions to the Caribbean, a means to combat tropical diseases. The effort to capture Santo Domingo was a dismal failure. Moreover, the treasure fleet had been alerted to the presence of the English, and Spain's ships remained safe in their Caribbean ports that year. These poor results provided an incentive to implement the reforms that Cromwell and his advisers had already begun contemplating to make the navy an effective long-distance fighting force.

Instead of returning empty-handed, the English expedition to the Caribbean seized the centrally located, but lightly defended, island of Jamaica in 1655 and turned it into a source of sugar and smuggling. The loss of Jamaica was the first time that foreigners made a lasting conquest of a large area in the heart of the Spanish Empire. By the end of the century, legal and illegal activities in Jamaica were generating over 750,000 pesos in silver a year for the English, about half of the silver the English East India Company needed for its trade with India.[9]

All the problems that plagued the treasure fleets in the era of Spain's decline came together in the mid-1650s, when the flow of treasure virtually stopped for several years. The initial difficulty, with what appeared to be a cursed shipment of silver from Peru, came in 1654 when a galleon carrying more than 3 million pesos ran aground near the mouth of the Guayaquil River, off what is now Ecuador. Some of the silver was salvaged and sent on to Panama to go with the following year's fleet, but shifting sands soon covered the considerable amount of silver that remained in the wreck. Because of the Spaniards' fear of the English forces that had just seized Jamaica, as well as delays in outfitting the ships, no galleons sailed in 1655, and the silver shipment remained in Panama.

In 1656, the New Spain fleet stayed in Veracruz rather than risk capture by the English, but the Tierra Firme fleet, heavily laden with three years of production from the mines, including some of the "cursed" shipment from Peru, managed to evade English patrols operating out of Jamaica. In the strait between Florida and the Bahamas, two of the Spanish ships collided because of poor seamanship, and one, the Nuestra Señora de las Maravillas, went down with 5 million pesos on board. This was one of the largest single cargoes lost during the colonial period. Over the next several years the Spanish sent out a number of salvage expeditions, which were able to retrieve about 1.5 million pesos. Tragedy continued to haunt this load of silver, though, and in 1657, two of the salvage vessels, with a cargo of recovered treasure on board, were sunk in a storm off Gorda Cay.[10]

Cromwell had not given up his dream of capturing a treasure fleet, and he dispatched another fleet under General-at-Sea Robert Blake to cruise off the Spanish coast. Blake was the prototype of the professional naval officer that would make the Royal Navy such a formidable force in the following centuries. He was a master seaman, like the sea dogs of the previous century, but he also valued discipline and had a grasp of strategic priorities. His main limitation was that he did not always have the resources to make his talents more effective. Nonetheless, Blake scored impressive successes against the treasure fleets. His preferred technique was to keep his ships on continuous blockade duty off the Spanish coast, even though this caused great wear and tear on his ships and it was extremely difficult to provide supplies for such a long and distant deployment.

Blake's persistence paid off when, in 1656, he caught the remaining ships of the trouble-plagued *Tierra Firme* fleet when they were only a few miles away from safety in Cadiz. These vessels were the survivors of the collision off Florida earlier that year, and they were carrying some of the doomed 1654 shipment from Peru. The English were unaware that the Spanish still put treasure on small, fast ships, and they let two minor ships pass, one of which was carrying a large amount of silver. Instead, Blake concentrated on the galleons and captured two of them, including the Spanish flagship with over 2 million pesos aboard. Two other ships, loaded with another 9 million pesos, were sunk. Even the stern and principled Blake was unable to restrain the delirious officers and crews, who pilfered more than half the treasure before it could be turned over to Cromwell's officials.

Blake was not satisfied with seizing one treasure fleet and kept his ships on station in the hope of being able to catch another one. The following year, in 1657, the treasure fleet that had been held at Veracruz finally sailed and made it as far as the Canary Islands. Spanish officials instructed it to wait there until either Blake gave up his blockade or an escort fleet could be sent from Cadiz. Blake's officers urged him to leave his post off the Spanish coast and sail for the Canaries, but he was reluctant to take his fleet so far from English waters as long as a strong Spanish force remained in Cadiz. Only when he was convinced that the Spanish fleet had no plans to sail to either England or the Canaries did he give the order to head south with 23 ships.

After arriving in the Canaries, he immediately attacked the Spanish fleet, which was anchored in the heavily fortified harbor of Santa Cruz, on the island of Tenerife. Blake's forces destroyed or captured every one of the 16 Spanish ships present. Although several of Blake's ships were badly damaged, none of them were sunk by the Spanish. Blake was unable to capture any of the treasure, however, because local officials had taken the precaution of removing the 10 million pesos carried by the fleet and storing it in the harbor's fortress. Because Blake did not have the troops necessary for land operations, he was unable to capture the fortress and seize the silver. Nonetheless, by destroying the treasure fleet he had denied the Spanish government the use of the silver. It was the second time in less than 30 years that all the galleons in a treasure fleet had been destroyed or captured. For the next two years, the Spanish dared not risk sending another convoy. The battle at Santa Cruz was also one of the few times when a fleet was able to be so successful in the face of well-prepared stone fortifications ashore.[11]

In the months that followed, the shortage of funds, because of the disruption of the treasure fleets, was a major reason for Spain's growing weakness. The French again crushed the Spanish army at the Battle of the Dunes, outside Dunkirk, in 1658. Defeated and impoverished, Spain finally made peace with France with the Peace of the Pyrenees in 1659. As a result of this treaty, Spain gave up part of the Spanish Netherlands, made important commercial concessions, and provided a Spanish princess as a bride for the young French king, Louis XIV. It was now clear to all that Spain had fallen from the first rank of the European states.

In the meantime, the English were trying other means to keep the pressure on Spain. As an alternative to sending large numbers of regular troops to the disease-ridden Caribbean, the English tried using local forces recruited from the buccaneers. Buccaneers were outcasts, such as escaped prisoners, castaways, and misfits, who lived in rough-and-tumble, self-governing communities on small Caribbean islands, well away from the centers of Spanish power. The buccaneers normally made their living by slaughtering wild animals and trading the meat and hides for supplies from passing ships. They were also willing, from time to time, to join an expedition in search of plunder. Although the buccaneers were experienced in the use of firearms and could be fierce fighters, they lacked discipline. Sometimes the English were able to influence the time and place of the buccaneers' attacks, but usually the disorderly rabble were difficult to control.[12]

The most dangerous of the buccaneer leaders was Henry Morgan, and the success of his depredations against some of the main ports of the Spanish Empire were yet another sign of Spanish weakness in the late seventeenth century. Morgan was a former army officer who owned a plantation on Jamaica and had an uncanny ability to command the loyalty and obedience of the ragtag buccaneers through skillful use of two main tools: military victory and financial profit.

Although England and Spain were technically not at war, there was suspicion and tension in the Caribbean, and colonial forces often clashed while the mother countries were at peace in Europe. In 1668, Morgan and several hundred buccaneers, encouraged by the English governor of Jamaica, captured Porto Bello, where they alleged that a plot to invade Jamaica was being hatched.

A savage sack of the town followed, and the local Spanish authorities paid Morgan and his men 250,000 pesos to prevent complete destruction of their city.

Later that same year, with a larger force of 10 ships and 800 men, Morgan pillaged cities along the coast of the Bay of Maracaibo. The haul from this series of attacks was another 250,000 pesos in cash and large amounts of other booty. In 1671, Morgan carried out his last and boldest attack when he led a force of 1,000 men across the Isthmus and looted Panama City of 400,000 pesos' worth of treasure and merchandise. Morgan brought so many pesos back to Jamaica that English officials on the island had to recognize Spanish pieces of eight as legal tender.

But with the capture of Panama City, Morgan had gone too far, and he was arrested and sent back to England. Morgan's arrest was part of an effort to mend fences with Spain so that the English could concentrate on the French. Officials in London now saw the rising power of France, rather than the declining threat from Spain, as the main enemy in the Caribbean, and the British were eager to make peace with the Spanish. As a result, in the 1670 Treaty of Madrid, the English agreed to stop supporting the buccaneers in return for Spanish recognition of England's possession of Jamaica. Nonetheless, the anti-Catholic, anti-Spanish lobby was still influential in London, and the government was forced to release Morgan in response to a surge of sentiment in his favor. In a further ironic turn of events, Morgan was later granted a knighthood and sent back to Jamaica as lieutenant governor. None of Morgan's attacks involved great losses or a sustained interruption of the operation of the treasure fleets, but they were a tremendous embarrassment to Spain and encouraged attacks by others.[13]

In the 1660s, King Louis XIV of France launched a campaign to make his country the greatest power in Europe, and taking control of the wealth of the Spanish Empire was an integral part of fulfilling these ambitions. France, united, prosperous, and militarily powerful, again became the main threat to Spain's grip on the gold and silver of the Indies. Because the Spanish did not produce the manufactured goods their colonists wanted, French merchants already provided most of the merchandise for the westbound Spanish fleets; and it was the French who received much of the silver that came back on the ships. But this only whetted the appetite of Louis and his advisers.

Louis' finance minister, Jean-Baptiste Colbert, was the chief French proponent of mercantilism. He believed that the government should be actively involved in promoting the economy, and that precious metals were the preeminent form of wealth. Moreover, Colbert thought that an activist colonial policy was one of the best ways to generate a favorable balance of trade. In 1664, he founded the French East India Company so that France could participate in the lucrative Asian trade. France's version of a great colonial trading company benefited from more government funds and tax breaks than its English or Dutch counterparts, and perhaps this was a reason why the French East India Company was usually less well managed and less successful than its rivals.

Colbert also argued successfully for a major buildup of the French navy. The French had a powerful war fleet by the 1690s, but suffered a series of defeats and never fulfilled Colbert's ambitions. King Louis lacked an understanding of sea power, and gave a higher priority to maintaining a large army for conquests along France's extensive land frontiers. As a result, France lagged behind the Dutch and English in the maritime competition of the seventeenth century, and Louis XIV derived only limited benefits from the wealth being generated by colonial trade. Nonetheless, the French did have some successes overseas, often at Spain's expense, including their incremental takeover of St. Domingue, the western half of the island of Hispaniola, in the 1660s.[14]

Like England, France harassed the Spanish in the Caribbean by encouraging the buccaneers. France continued to use the buccaneers as tools against the Spanish even after the English had quit, and in 1683 the French incited the buccaneers to attack Veracruz. An outlaw fleet of 8 ships, carrying 1,000 men, seized and ruthlessly pillaged New Spain's main Caribbean port. The annual Spanish fleet arrived during the battle, but the commanders were too intimidated to take on the vicious and well-armed brigands. The capture of Veracruz was probably the most lucrative of the buccaneers' expeditions, and netted them about 800,000 pesos in silver and large quantities of merchandise. In typical buccaneer fashion, they went to a nearby island to divide the loot and promptly began fighting among themselves over the spoils.[15]

The last of the great buccaneer attacks was their joint expedition with French regular forces against Cartagena in 1697. Louis XIV hoped to knock Spain out of the coalition then fighting France and to recoup much of the expense of the war through captured gold and silver. The attack was a success, and the citizens of Cartagena paid a spectacular indemnity of about 8 million pesos to save their city from destruction. French regular troops quickly took control of the loot and apportioned only about 40,000 pesos for the buccaneers. The buccaneers responded with a furious mutiny. Faced with disorderly buccaneers, along with an outbreak of tropical disease, the commanders of the regulars decided to withdraw and take the booty with them. Feeling cheated and angry, the buccaneers looted the city a second time on their own. The regular troops, too sickened and disorganized to attack any other targets in the Caribbean, soon returned to France. After the victory at Cartagena, French officials concluded that alliances with the buccaneers had become too difficult to handle. In the Treaty of Ryswyck, signed later in 1697, Louis XIV agreed to

Map 6.
Possessions of the European Powers
in the Americas in 1700

stop sponsoring buccaneer attacks in return for Spain's acceptance of French possession of St. Domingue, the western half of Hispaniola.[16]

By the end of the seventeenth century, Spain's naval and military weakness in the face of its more dynamic rivals meant that it had to abandon its effort to protect the gold and silver mines by claiming a colonial monopoly in the Western Hemisphere. Numerous foreign settlements were now firmly planted in the Caribbean and North America. Another result of the various treaties Spain signed during the late seventeenth century was a consensus that peace would prevail in the Caribbean as long as there was peace in Europe. The diplomatic convention, which went back to the Treaty of Câteau-Cambrésis in 1559, that the West Indies were outside normal diplomatic agreements and that conflict there was not linked to diplomacy in Europe, was no longer in effect. A worldwide political system was now in place under which the same rules applied everywhere, including the routes of the treasure fleets.

During this period, attack by pirates was not a serious threat to the treasure fleets, even though the last decade of the seventeenth century and the early decades of the eighteenth were the golden age of piracy. Demobilized sailors, buccaneers without government sponsors, and escaped slaves, along with other castoffs from the colonial wars of the time, were prime candidates for recruitment into a pirate crew. But Captain Kidd, Blackbeard, and others preferred low-risk ventures like seizing single ships. Pirates never directly attacked the well-armed treasure fleets, even when the fleets were at their weakest.

One adventurer did manage to make an impressive haul of Spanish treasure during this period, but it was in a most unusual way. For years, a Boston ship captain, William Phips, had heard tales that there were sunken galleons in the Caribbean, with millions of pesos on board that the Spanish had not been able to recover. Based on knowledge gained from his travels in the West Indies and some experience with salvage operations, he believed he could find treasure in one of the wrecks. In 1682, the fast-talking and self-confident Phips got King Charles II of England to provide a Royal Navy ship for an effort to locate and salvage lost Spanish treasure in the Caribbean. Phips picked up some ideas about where lost treasure might be when he talked to a survivor from the galleon *Nuestra Señora de la Concepción*, which had gone down in 1641 with 4 million pesos on board. But the crew Phips had recruited for the salvage operation turned out to be too mutinous to be reliable, and he returned to England empty-handed.

In 1686, Phips put together another expedition, this time financed by private investors. Through a combination of systematic searching, patience, and luck, he was able to locate the remains of the *Concepción*. His crew brought up nearly 30 tons of gold and silver worth about 1 million pesos. Phips returned to England in triumph and instantly became a celebrity. Ten percent of the treasure went to the English crown, the backers got back more than 17 times what they had invested, and members of the crew received bonuses of up to 500 pesos. The Spanish ambassador in London demanded that the silver be turned over to the government in Madrid, but British authorities ignored him.

Convinced there was still more silver on the wreck, Phips returned for a third salvage attempt in 1687. By this time, however, word of the treasure had spread and other salvors were at work on the site. The results of the third voyage were a disappointment, but Phips believed that there was still a vast quantity of silver underneath the hard coral crust that had grown up over much of the wreck. Phips returned to Boston a wealthy man, and in 1691 the British monarchs, King William and Queen Mary, appointed him governor of Massachusetts. He was the first native-born American to be named a British colonial governor. The Salem witch trials took place during Phips's tenure as governor, and he was the one who ended the trials after his wife was accused of being a witch.[17]

Falling Silver Production
Spain's weakness in the seventeenth century was not only due to military and naval defeats. At the same time, the very foundations of her power, the control of the wealth of the Indies, was slipping away. One of the most important and dangerous symptoms of Spanish decline was falling silver production. The output of the mines at Potosí, for example, peaked around 1600 at about 9 million pesos a year and then began a slow decline that lasted for more than a century. Because of an increase in illegal production and smuggling, total output probably did not fall as far as the official figures seemed to indicate. But what the government cared about was the legal production that it could monitor and tax.

There were a number of reasons for the drop in Peruvian silver production. For one thing, the richest and easiest-to-reach ores had already been exploited, and so costs began to rise. In addition, production of mercury, vital for processing the silver ore, was falling off at the Huancavélica mine. The Council of the Indies responded to reports of declining production of quicksilver by sending European mercury to Peru instead of New Spain, but this reduced silver production in New Spain without bringing much of an improvement in Peru.

Yet another problem was that the forced labor system in Peru, the *mita*, was producing fewer workers. War, famine, disease, and harsh treatment had led to a decline in the native population of Peru from more than 8 million at the time of the conquest to less than 2 million a century later. It was a demographic disaster of monumental proportions; and, in addition to reducing the labor force, it had a profound psychological effect. One knowledgeable old Inca told

Spanish officials, "The Indians seeing themselves dispossessed and robbed ... allow themselves to die and do not apply themselves to anything."

The colonial authorities, for their part, were hardly indifferent to the economic impact of the declining population. Having dramatically fewer laborers in the colony struck at the heart of their main mission, which was to ensure the greatest possible production of precious metals. One observer pointed out that "if the natives cease, the land is finished. I mean its wealth: for all the gold and silver that comes to Spain is extracted by means of these Indians." Mine owners had few solutions to offer, except to replace forced labor with miners who worked for wages; but this only added to the rising costs of production. Output from the other mines in Peru was not enough to compensate for the lower productivity at the silver mountain. By 1700, annual production at Potosí had fallen to only 2 million pesos' worth, and another 2 million came from the other mines in Peru.[18]

The increasing strains on the system of production in Peru were revealed by a major scandal at the Potosí mint. In the 1640s, officials in Spain began to realize that the silver merchants who supplied the mint were adding large amounts of copper to the bullion used for coinage. Apparently many local officials in Peru knew about the adulteration of the silver, but in the prevailing atmosphere of greed and corruption such peculations were often overlooked. Moreover, the silver merchants were powerful men and a vital source of capital in the community, and local authorities were reluctant to challenge them. On the other hand, the dishonest silver merchants had become shockingly brazen in their crime, and by the 1640s they had increased the copper content of the bullion to about 25 percent. Since this undermined royal authority and business confidence, not to mention the acceptability of the pieces of eight that were so essential for Spain's international payments, officials in Madrid decided to intervene.

In 1647, the Council of the Indies sent a former inquisitor, Francisco de Nestares Marín, on a special mission to Potosí with full authority to do whatever was necessary to clean up the corruption. He took up the responsibility with a vigor and ruthlessness that shocked even the hardened residents of Potosí. First, Nestares dismissed several senior mint officials and levied fines of over 1 million pesos on dishonest silver merchants. Then Nestares claimed that one of the silver merchants was trying to poison him, and he ordered the local authorities to arrest the hapless merchant and execute him along with a corrupt mint official. When Nestares decreed that yet another prominent merchant should be arrested, the businessman's friends broke into the prison, released their colleague, and hid him in a monastery. In response, Nestares culminated his campaign against corruption by ordering local authorities to violate the

New design for Peruvian pesos after the scandal at the mint. To reassure the public about the integrity of the mint and its product, the Peruvian government took firm action in 1652. Officials ordered that all coins recently made at Potosí be returned to the mint, where they were punched with a  *distinctive counterstamp so that they could be easily recognized. Next, mint officials began issuing new coins with the regulation 93 percent purity. In order to even more clearly differentiate the new coins from their debased predecessors, mint officials changed the design of the coins and returned to a variation of the pillar motif used on the first colonial coins in New Spain. (Photo from the author's collection)*

sanctuary of the monastery to recapture the accused individual. This ruthless approach set in motion the process of restoring high standards at the mint.[19]

The slump in production at Potosí was so serious that it canceled out improvements in production elsewhere, and the total official output of precious metals in the Indies declined by almost a third, to about 11 million pesos a year, during the seventeenth century. In New Spain, silver production was affected by similar problems. Like Peru, New Spain suffered a sharp drop in the native population, but the losses were even more horrific. From over 20 million natives in Moctezuma's time, the population dwindled to only about 1 million a century later. This was probably the greatest demographic disaster in history. The response on the part of the mine owners was to increase the number of men working for a wage. Although this raised the cost of production, for the long term it turned out to be a source of strength, because, unlike Peru, there were still rich, untapped sources of ore in New Spain.

The great potential production of silver in New Spain remained unrealized, however, because of the diversion of vital supplies of mercury to Peru. The output at Zacatecas, for example, fell from 1 million pesos a year in the 1630s to about 500,000 pesos 30 years later. Nonetheless, because of the opening of new mines, overall production in New Spain remained at the same level of about 4 million pesos a year. The situation began to improve during the 1680s as the colonists continued to open even more new mines, and by the 1690s, the northern colony had overtaken Peru as the most important source of silver in the world. Output also increased in the gold fields of New Granada, and by the end of the seventeenth century about 1.7 million pesos a year came from there. Rising gold output led to the foundation in 1622 of a mint at Bogotá, where gold coins with the value of 1 and 2 *escudos*, were produced.[20]

The decline in registered production of precious metals for most of the seventeenth century was a source of concern, of course, but even more troubling was the fact that the amount sent to Spain fell even faster than overall production. By far the largest single drain on the government's share, the *quinto*, was the expenditure for local defense, especially the massive fortifications at the main ports. By the 1680s, defense costs were absorbing a third of the royal revenues from the Indies. About 45 percent of the income from Peru had been shipped to Spain early in the century; only 5 percent could be spared by the end. This meant that the crown's income from Peru shrank from almost 4 million pesos a year at the beginning of the century to less than 2.5 million in the 1680s. There was a similar pattern in New Spain, where 50 percent of the *quinto* went to Spain at the beginning of the seventeenth century, but 100 years later only 25 percent or less was left after local expenses had been paid.

Silver drained away into other channels as well. Although shipments of silver to the Far East declined, they were still sizable. In addition, the Dutch and English continued to smuggle out large amounts. Wealthy miners and merchants in the New World also preferred to invest their money locally rather than risk losing it through taxes and confiscations if they sent it to Spain. As a result, during the second half of the seventeenth century, although official production averaged approximately 11 million pesos a year, the crown usually received less than 1 million pesos of that total.[21]

The Deterioration of Spanish Shipping

Spain's commercial shipping network, once the greatest in the world, also fell on hard times in the seventeenth century. Besides losses in war, the main reason it ceased to be competitive was its high costs. Ships purchased from the Dutch or built in the colonies were cheaper and of higher quality, and by 1650 only about a third of the ships used in Spain's Atlantic trade had been built in Spain. Even after purchases abroad, the overall number of ships under Spanish control decreased dramatically, and by 1650 the Spanish had only half the carrying capacity they had just 30 years before. By the end of the seventeenth century, only about 20 Spanish ships a year sailed to the Indies, less than a fifth of the size of the merchant fleets of a century earlier.

Frantic efforts were made to cut costs. In 1645, the commander of an outgoing fleet discovered that his food stores were left over from the provisions for a fleet seven years earlier. Despite his complaints, officials from the *Casa de Contratación* forced him to take the rotten supplies, and over 100 seamen died of food poisoning. Another way to cut costs was to have shipbuilders make galleons larger, in an effort to carry more goods with smaller crews. This meant, however, that many ships could no longer make it over the sandbar at the mouth of the Guadalquivir River that led to Seville.[22]

Seville's fate was linked to the health of the colonial trade. The city had prospered during the period of commercial and industrial growth in the sixteenth century, and it slipped into decline with the economic troubles of the period that followed. A devastating plague killed about half the population in the middle of the seventeenth century, exacerbating the city's woes. In 1680, the Spanish government moved the terminus of the Indies trade to Cadiz, although the administrative machinery of the *Casa* remained in Seville. Even though Cadiz was vulnerable, and foreign fleets had attacked it on several occasions, the city's large and deep harbor was now essential to the operation of the treasure fleets.[23]

In the Pacific there were fewer changes, and the rhythms of trade established in the previous century continued with little interruption. Dutch fleets attacked the Philippines in 1646 and 1647, but local Spanish forces successfully repulsed them. As was the case in the Atlantic, storms and navigational errors were the most common reasons for disruption of the treasure fleets. Galleons full of silver from New Spain were lost in the Pacific in 1639 and 1690. Because the trade between Manila and Acapulco was carried on only 1 or 2 large ships a year, the number of vessels in service was not cut as drastically as in the Atlantic. Nevertheless, the long Pacific voyage continued to be one of the most harrowing maritime challenges in the world. In 1657, one of the eastbound galleons, which had left Manila 14 months before, was found adrift south of Acapulco; everyone on board had died of either disease or hunger.[24]

Another sign of weakness was Spain's inability to satisfy the economic needs of its own colonies. As a result of the dominant role of the English, Dutch, and French in the Atlantic economy, most of the profits of Spain's colonial commerce flowed right through Cadiz and Seville or never even entered the country. Because the Spanish could not produce most of the manufactured goods the colonies wanted, it was Frenchmen, working through Spanish merchants in Seville and Cadiz, who provided the majority of the legal cargo shipped to the colonies. Many other foreign merchants, especially the Dutch and English, skipped the Spanish brokers entirely and smuggled their goods directly to the Indies.

The colonists were happy to do business with the smugglers because it meant quality goods at cheaper prices and on a more flexible schedule than the annual fleets. In addition, the colonists found that, unlike Spanish merchants, the smugglers would take unregistered silver in payment. In the second half of the seventeenth century, it became increasingly hard to maintain the annual schedule of fleets because of war and the shortage of goods and ships. Between 1650 and 1699, the New Spain fleet sailed only 25 times and the *Tierra Firme* fleet just 16 times.[25]

The cost of protecting the fleets had also gotten out of control. With a smaller number of ships sailing, each vessel had to pay a higher *averia* tax to finance the galleon escort. By the 1630s, the *averia* rate was 35 percent, which was in addition to 17.5 percent in customs duties on outbound cargoes and the 20 percent tax on bullion traveling eastbound. These tax rates of over 70 percent meant that there was little incentive to increase the volume of goods that shipped, so prices remained high to cover costs. The staggering tax burden also increased the potential return on smuggling.

In addition to fiscal difficulties, other problems with financing the treasure fleets continued to mount. In 1641, the *Consulado* refused to continue its assistance in administering the *averia*, and royal authorities had to start providing the money for operating the galleons from general revenues. The government had so much difficulty paying to protect the treasure fleets that in 1661, it had to accept the humiliating alternative of having the Dutch provide an escort. The Dutch were happy to comply because most of the silver was coming to them in any event.[26]

Spain's commercial failure was registered in international law through a series of treaties in which Madrid made important trade concessions to foreign powers. In 1648, Spain recognized the independence of the Netherlands and granted some trade concessions that gave Dutch merchants increased access to trade with Spain, but not the colonies. Similar treaties followed with France in 1659 and England in 1667. By the end of the seventeenth century, Spain's claims to a monopoly of the Atlantic trade no longer existed in either fact or theory. Allowing foreigners to bring goods to Spain for onward shipment to the colonies meant abandoning the trade monopoly once enjoyed by the treasure fleets. It also meant, of course, that Spain had lost control of an important way to earn silver from the colonies. As profits from trade declined, Spain relied more and more on keeping tax levels high.[27]

Aside from smuggling, the greatest single threat to the flow of silver continued to be destruction through storms at sea and poor seamanship. In addition to the *Concepción*, carrying 4 million pesos, and the *Maravillas*, with 5 million on board (both of which have already been noted), there were other maritime disasters in the first half of the seventeenth century that resulted in huge losses of treasure. Three galleons of the *Tierra Firme* fleet went down in a storm near the Florida Keys in 1622. Spanish crews salvaged most of the cargo from two of them in the years that followed, but severe weather and shifting sands wiped out clues to the location of the remaining wreck, the *Nuestra Señora de Atocha*, which had a cargo of silver worth one million pesos. The *Atocha* was one of the few cases in which no treasure was recovered from a shipwreck. In 1624, two more ships, each carrying 1 million pesos, were destroyed at sea. Most of the ships of the New Spain fleet, and more than 3 million pesos in treasure, were lost north of Veracruz in 1631. That same year, another galleon loaded with silver sank off Panama City.[28]

Spain's Decline in Europe

Spain's losses of territory during its era of decline were not limited to the colonies. Because Habsburg lands surrounded France, Louis XIV's aggressive campaigns in Europe inevitably involved Spanish territory, and successful French attacks completed the dismantling of the Habsburgs' territorial and strategic system dating back to the time of Charles V. The key to Spain's power had been the Spanish Road, the string of possessions and allies that stretched between Italy and the Low Countries. This had been the main route for sending troops and money to the fighting fronts in the Netherlands, France, and the Holy Roman Empire. As long as it was open, the Spanish were able to dominate western Europe.

King Louis understood all too well that expansion to the north and east would not only add to French territory but also would break the ring of Spanish power that had surrounded his country. In the late seventeenth century, after decades of naval and military defeats, Spain was in no position to block Louis XIV's ambitions. After the Peace of the Pyrenees in 1659, which had cost territory in the Spanish Netherlands, one loss followed another in rapid succession: Louis nibbled off more of the Spanish Netherlands in 1668, the French took Franche-Comté in 1678, and France forced Spain to give up Luxembourg in 1684.

The decline of colonial silver production and the deterioration of the Atlantic trade were linked to other problems in Spain itself. The country was slipping farther and farther behind economically and politically as her rivals, France, England, and the United Provinces, moved forward. One symptom of weakness was a drop in the Spanish population, which ironically paralleled the demographic catastrophe in the colonies. As a result of war, plague, famine, and emigration to the colonies, by 1700 the population of Spain dropped to about 6 million, which was 2 million less than in 1500. This meant that Spain's population was less than half that of France and roughly equal to Germany and Italy.

Another shortcoming in the Spanish economy was that so many essential goods, even food and cannons, had to be imported, which meant that higher and higher percentages of the shrinking imports of silver had to be used to pay for such goods. Unproductive uses of money, like foreign wars, the large church establishment, ostentatious luxury, an extensive bureaucracy, and the state debt, absorbed badly needed resources. The government had expelled commercially oriented groups like the Jews and Moriscos (Muslims who had ostensibly converted to Christianity), and much of the rest of the population valued pride and piety over productive work. Moreover, the administration was staffed largely by lawyers, landed aristocrats, clerics, and military officers, who were incapable of formulating an economic policy that could have modernized and strengthened the country.[29]

One of the most striking aspects of Spain's economic decline was the continued manipulation of the coinage. During the seventeenth century, tampering with the currency reached absurd proportions and showed that the fabulous wealth brought to Spain by the treasure fleets had been almost completely squandered. Although the government tried on several occasions to reduce the assigned value of copper *vellón* back to something approaching its intrinsic value, in the end, officials always succumbed to the temptation to raise the value of the copper coins.

After Spain entered the Thirty Years' War in 1621, the government again issued overvalued *vellón*, and over the next six years the operation netted the royal treasury a profit of some 30 million pesos. Authorities were again attempting to create a fiat currency, one whose value was based on government decree rather the amount of precious metals it contained. But the government, too, suffered from the debasement of coinage because the resulting inflation drove up expenses and officials had to accept the copper coins for taxes. In 1628, there was a massive deflation as the government reversed policy, reduced the value of the copper coins by half, and promised to stop minting them. After France entered the Thirty Years' War in 1635, expenses quickly rose, and the following year the government broke its promise and resumed the minting of copper. Copper coins were arbitrarily revalued upward twice in 1641 and again in 1651.[30]

By the time King Charles II came to the throne in 1665, silver had virtually disappeared from circulation, and over 90 percent of the transactions in Spain were being carried out in the debased coinage. In the 1670s, Spain was flooded with *vellón* and dealing in money became ridiculous. It took 6 pounds of copper coins to purchase 10 pounds of cheese and over 2 pounds of coins to buy 1 pound of wax candles. In 1679, payments in silver were worth a 275 percent premium. Ironically, for such a backward country, the most advanced machinery was a German-made press that mass-produced copper coins at the Segovia mint.

It is worth re-emphasizing that this collapse in the national currency took place in the country whose colonies contained the world's greatest sources of precious metals. Tampering extended even to the hitherto sacrosanct silver coinage. In 1642, the government decided to reduce the weight of the silver coins in Spain by 20 percent while still marking them at their original value. Pieces of eight in Spain were now worth 10 reales instead of 8. This was the first time the silver coinage had been debased since the time of Ferdinand and Isabella.

Manipulating the currency meant that inflation continued in Spain in the seventeenth century long after it had moderated elsewhere in Europe. Spanish officials maintained the integrity of the pesos minted in the colonies, however, because the pieces of eight were essential for international payments. Thus the Spanish Empire operated on two coinage systems, one in Spain and one in the colonies and abroad, which only added to the economic confusion and weakness.[31]

Some Spaniards did understand what the problems were and offered alternatives. In a 1686 report to Charles II, one observer noted that "the most precious of metals, the most indispensable, the most excellent, and the most reliable that ever has been or ever will be, is the sweat that glistens on the brow. It is the only wealth that can support a powerful state. For where it is lacking gold and silver will not long remain. For it alone is the coinage that all the world over possesses the highest value." Wise recommendations such as this, combined with the clear failure of traditional policies, led to efforts at reform, even in the midst of Spain's decline.[32]

Manipulation of the coinage was so detrimental to the Spanish economy that in 1680 the government was finally forced to take action. Coinage of pure copper *vellón* was stopped and new coins were issued that were made from an alloy of copper and silver and marked at approximately their intrinsic value. There was a short-term disruption of trade, finance, and tax collection as a result, but the sharp swings of inflation and deflation ended. Next, the Count of Oropesa, the chief minister, launched a program of reducing taxes and spending in an effort to revive the economy. In 1686, he also confirmed the 1642 reduction of value of the silver coins. This brought silver coins closer to their market value, and they began to return to circulation.

The manipulation of Spanish coinage that had gone on since 1599 ended at last, although there was still confusion because there was a different valuation of silver in Spain and in the colonies. Unfortunately, resistance from vested interests limited the impact of Oropesa's reforms, but his tenure in office laid the foundation for later efforts.[33]

Economic and financial problems during the seventeenth century meant that it remained impossible to balance the budget. When Philip IV became king in 1621, expenditures were being held at about 11 million pesos a year; but income had fallen to about 5.5 million pesos, which included about 1.4 million from the Indies. Almost immediately after coming to the throne, Philip took Spain into the Thirty Years' War, assuming that the necessary money would come from the Indies. It was just at that time, however, that legal production of silver began to drop. Even after the slump in the government's share of silver production became obvious, the Spanish continued to pursue the war effort. The government's actions were not based on financial concerns, and the political requirements of prestige and security outweighed any economic calculation. A senior financial official expressed a typical view when he said that "the lack of money is serious, but it is more important to preserve reputation." To cover the difference between income and expenditure, the government resorted to an old remedy and increased its borrowing on the international money market. By the mid-1620s, the government needed over 10 million pesos a year for debt repayment.[34]

With declining silver shipments and a decaying economy, royal receipts could not keep up with expenditures, and in 1627 the Spanish government yet again suspended payments on its short-term *asiento* debts to bankers. This suspension was different, however, in that most of the Genoese bankers, who had been instrumental in arranging royal finances since the first suspension of payments in 1557, gave up in disgust and stopped loaning money to the Spanish government. The risks and losses had become too great for the Genoese to bear, and for the next 20 years Portuguese bankers took over as the main financiers of the Spanish royal government.

Expenditures, mainly for war, continued to rise, and by 1647 the Spanish government expected outlays to be more than 17.5 million pesos while receipts were less than half that. The crown tried a variety of desperate expedients, in addition to manipulating the coinage, to raise money. At least six times between 1621 and 1649, royal officials seized large amounts of private funds from the treasure fleets. In 1647, with the total income for the next four years already promised to the bankers, there was the inevitable suspension of payments. This time it was the Portuguese bankers who bore the brunt of the losses; then they, like the Genoese, withdrew from the business of loaning money to the Spanish government.[35]

Unlike past financial crises, the 1647 suspension of payments did not have much of an impact in the rest of Europe because Spain no longer played a large role in the international financial market. Since foreigners were less and less willing to loan money to the Spanish government, the funds increasingly had to come from domestic sources. It was a burden that a declining economy was ill prepared to bear. Financial exhaustion was one of the main reasons the

Spanish government finally made peace with the United Provinces in 1648, after 80 years of fighting, and at last recognized Dutch independence. The end of the war with the Dutch brought some relief for the Spanish budget, but the war with France continued until 1659. There were further suspensions of payments in 1652 and 1662, and by the time Philip IV died in 1665, the short-term royal debt was nearly 30 million pesos and another 300 million was owed to holders of *juros*.

During the reign of Charles II, from 1665 to 1700, the same dreary cycle of loans and suspensions continued. Spain's relations with foreign bankers finally came to an end in the 1690s after the government bestowed a title of nobility on a Genoese banker in gratitude for a rare loan. The deal horrified the proud aristocrats at court, and the uproar forced the government to stop doing business with one of the few foreigners who would still loan Spain money. To make matters even worse, the government tried to make the Italian banker the scapegoat for the whole wretched affair, and royal authorities seized his assets in Spain as compensation for the trouble he had caused. The upshot of the scandal was that no foreign banker would loan money to the Spanish government. After two centuries of massive foreign loans, Spain's borrowing abroad finally came to an end.[36]

Silver and the World Trade System
In the seventeenth century, little of the silver of the Indies remained in Spain, and the sizable amounts that were still being produced found their way into the international economy through a variety of channels. Spain's unfavorable trade balance, foreign loans, and wars meant that large amounts of silver had to be sent abroad legally. With the political, economic, and military decline of the seventeenth century, illegal exports, which had always existed, also became a major drain. Dutch and English traders drew off large amounts of silver through smuggling. French merchants provided most of the legal merchandise that went to the Spanish colonies, and they sometimes took the silver they earned directly off the galleons before the treasure fleets even landed in Cadiz. As a result of all of these factors, there was no need for other powers to conquer the Spanish Empire to control the flow of gold and silver from its mines. As a German commentator of the time said, "Spain kept the cow and the rest of Europe drank the milk."[37]

The seventeenth century was the greatest era of Dutch prosperity and power. Because of the success of the Dutch commercial and financial networks, Amsterdam became the capital of international finance, and much of the Spanish silver found its way there. In the early 1640s, nearly 7 million pesos a year was flowing from Spain to Amsterdam, where it was used to support the operations of the Bank of Amsterdam. From Amsterdam, the silver flowed in two large and roughly equal streams to finance Dutch trade in the Far East and the Baltic. Around 1700, the Dutch were sending about 2 million pesos a year along each of these routes.

Another indication of Dutch commercial supremacy was the size of their fleet, which contained 1,000 large ships that could be used for either trade or war. The Dutch East India Company alone had 150 ships, more than the entire Spanish fleet, at its command. One of the most important components of Dutch success was their great trading company's control of most of the trade with Asia. At first, the Dutch East India Company concentrated on replacing the Portuguese as masters of the lucrative spice trade. As time passed, however, there was a new trend that would eventually mean dramatic changes in the lives of the majority of people in Europe and its colonies.

This new development was the Dutch policy of using their commercial skill and Spanish silver to expand their trade beyond a few luxury items. Instead of shipping limited amounts of spices and other luxuries for a small, elite market, they increasingly dealt in large volumes of a wide variety of exotic foreign products, like sugar, tobacco, and tea. This revolution in Dutch commercial policy made such colonial products into household items for millions of customers. The Dutch could not rest on their laurels, though, because others were also using new financial techniques.[38]

A Swedish bank was the first European financial institution to issue paper money that could be redeemed in precious metals, in 1661. This eventually turned into an effort to create a fiat currency, however, with many parallels to the manipulations of the coinage by the Spanish government at roughly the same time (and also with fascinating similarities to Chinese experiments with paper money 300 years earlier). As time passed, the Swedish bankers became greedy and issued more paper currency than the gold and silver they had on deposit. The reliability and acceptability of the Swedish paper money became suspect, and after seven years the bank decided the experiment had been a failure and stopped issuing the bank notes.

By the end of the seventeenth century, it was the English who were the most successful at harnessing the power of new financial techniques by creating a successful European paper money and long-term national debt. Unlike its Swedish predecessor, the Bank of England, the main institution for managing the country's paper currency and national debt, was rock solid. It was founded in 1694 to help finance the wars against Louis XIV. Besides issuing paper money and making loans to the government, the bank also assisted in collecting taxes and transferring money abroad. Although there was some inflation as a result of its operations, the Bank of England carefully managed the issuance of paper currency and long-term loans with an eye toward inspiring the confidence of investors.

One tool the bank used for managing paper money was to issue only limited numbers of high-denomination bank notes that circulated almost exclusively in the rarefied world of London's financial community, where the top bankers, businessmen, and government officials knew and trusted one another. Another technique that inspired confidence was to redeem Bank of England notes readily in gold. Moreover, the bank's debts, unlike those of the Spanish government, were repaid promptly and fully. As a result, the English government could command unrivaled financial resources. A French attempt, a few years later, to duplicate the achievements of the Bank of England was a failure, and France did not have a national bank until early in the nineteenth century.

The English were also increasingly active in commerce with Asia. With the Dutch firmly ensconced in the Spice Islands, the English East India Company looked to India as its main source of trade goods, such as cotton textiles. By the end of the seventeenth century, the English were exporting almost as much silver to Asia as the Dutch.[39]

As successful as the Dutch and the English were in taking over the Asian seaborne trade from the Portuguese and the Spanish and gaining control of the flow of silver to the east, they still were subject to many of the same difficulties as their Iberian rivals. Bad weather and ignorance of local hazards to navigation could wreck ships in the Indian Ocean and the Pacific just as they could in the Atlantic or the Caribbean. Although the Dutch and the English were generally better seamen and seem to have lost fewer ships, they still had some disasters. In 1656, for example, the Dutch ship *Vergulde Draeck* loaded with almost 200,000 pesos for the Far East trade, struck a reef and sank off western Australia. A few survivors managed to sail one of the ship's boats all the way to Batavia, but the salvage expedition they sent back could not locate either the wreck or the rest of the crew. A few years later, in 1682, the English vessel *Joanna*, also carrying silver for purchases in Asia, went down off the coast of South Africa.[40]

The Dutch, English, and French, with their much larger overseas commerce, were encroaching on all three main segments of the worldwide flow of precious metals. They had the most impact on the eastward route around Africa and on to Asia, where traders from all three countries operated openly. By a combination of force and skill, the three countries replaced the Portuguese as the main power in the trade with Asia during the seventeenth century. In addition, the Dutch and the English were infringing on a second component, the flow of silver across the Atlantic, through smuggling rather than legitimate trade. The only portion of the flow of precious metals that the Spanish still

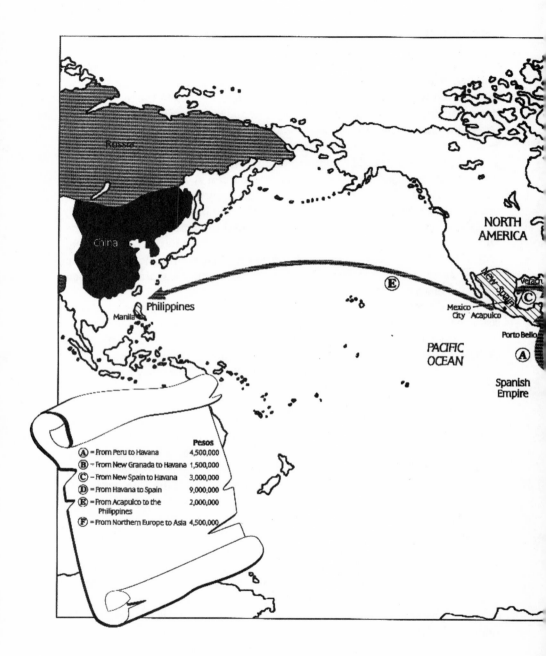

		Pesos
Ⓐ	= From Peru to Havana	4,500,000
Ⓑ	= From New Granada to Havana	1,500,000
Ⓒ	= From New Spain to Havana	3,000,000
Ⓓ	= From Havana to Spain	9,000,000
Ⓔ	= From Acapulco to the Philippines	2,000,000
Ⓕ	= From Northern Europe to Asia	4,500,000

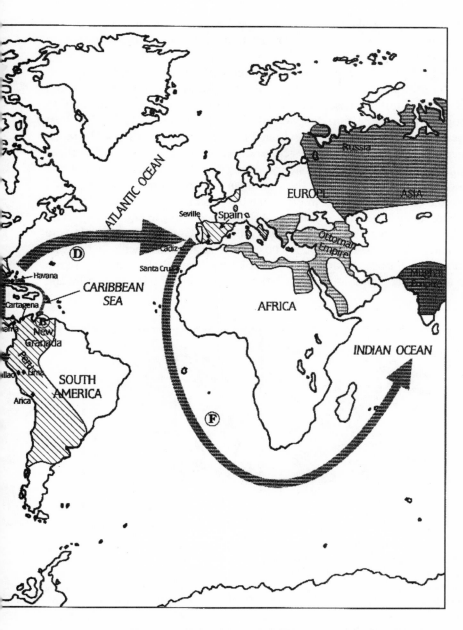

Map 7. The Spanish Empire and Global Flows of Precious Metals in 1700

controlled was the transpacific trade of the Manila galleons, and this was declining in the face of government restrictions and superior competition from the Dutch and English.

By 1700, official production of precious metals in the Indies was down to about 11 million pesos a year (in contrast to 16 million a century before), and only about 9 million pesos went across the Atlantic as legal shipments to Europe. At the same time, exports of silver from Europe to the Far East increased to 4.5 million pesos (up from 2 million a century earlier). The much larger shipments to Asia in the seventeenth century meant there was less silver available for the European economy. Along with the extended warfare and natural disasters, like plagues, the slowdown in silver from the Indies helped make the economy sluggish in Europe in the seventeenth century.[41]

This much larger flow of silver to Asia was beginning to have an important political and economic impact, especially in China. Government officials were becoming accustomed to collecting taxes in silver and were increasing assessments to pay for wars against barbarian tribes in the north. But the new wealth was also producing inflation, speculation, unequal distribution of wealth, and

Chopmarked seventeenth-century peso. In the seventeenth century there was a dramatic growth in trade between Europe and Asia. This brought an increase in the number of Western-style coins, which were used to settle Europe's unfavorable trade balance with Asia. As a result, the convenient and well-known peso coins became more common as a circulating currency, especially in the southern ports of China. Many of them, like this example originally from the mint in Mexico City, acquired numerous chopmarks from the Chinese merchants who handled them. The stream of silver from the West could be erratic, however, and the use of coins made from precious metals did not become firmly established in the Far East during this period. (Photo from the author's collection)

spanish treasure fleets

the disruption of traditional patterns of trade. Moreover, the fighting between the European powers as they tried to control the trade routes to Asia, such as the unsuccessful Dutch attacks on Manila in 1621 and 1623 and their capture of the Portuguese port of Malacca in 1641, meant there could be serious fluctuations in the level of silver imports. Now that China was becoming more integrated into the world economy, it was vulnerable to these changing conditions.

In response to such uncertainties, wealthy Chinese went back to hoarding their silver. With less silver in circulation, it became more difficult for the peasants to pay their taxes. These economic difficulties, combined with bad weather that brought flood and famine, undermined the Ming dynasty. In 1644, the Manchu tribe was able to sweep in from the north, seize control of the government, and found the new Qing dynasty.[42]

During the 1690s, the reign of silver as the main precious metal in international trade began coming to an end because the Portuguese discovered extremely productive gold mines deep in the interior of Brazil. By the early eighteenth century, large amounts of gold were being exported from Brazil, and this began slowly to shift the relative value of gold and silver in international trade. This reversed a process that had taken place a century and a half earlier, when the torrent of silver from the Spanish colonies began. Through their close trade relations with Portugal, the British drew off about three-quarters of the Portuguese gold, some 8 million pesos' worth a year, and laid the foundations for adopting the gold standard in Britain. The French and Dutch, on the other hand, continued to earn silver from the Spanish colonies and stayed on a silver standard. Another result of the increasing gold production in Brazil was that the relative value of silver increased, and this stimulated a rise in Mexican silver production toward the end of the seventeenth century.[43]

The War of Spanish Succession
The political, financial, and strategic weakness of Spain reached its nadir during the War of Spanish Succession. King Charles II was sickly and childless, and the question of who would succeed him was complicated by a tangled web of marriage contracts, treaties, and wills. The issue was whether the Austrian Habsburgs or the French Bourbons, both of whom had family ties to the Spanish ruling family, would inherit Spain and its empire. At stake in this contest between the Habsburgs and the Bourbons was the potential to establish political and economic hegemony over Europe and the Indies. France, England, and the United Provinces had signed a treaty in 1698 in which they agreed on a scheme that would partition the Spanish Empire and keep any one of them from inheriting all of Spain's possessions, thus preventing a single power from becoming overwhelmingly stronger than the others.

Charles II and many Spaniards wanted to keep the Spanish Empire together, however, and when the king died in 1700 his will left his entire empire to Louis XIV's grandson, who was proclaimed King Philip V. Louis decided to accept the will rather than the treaty and began moving troops into the Spanish Netherlands to improve his strategic position, a move which immediately alarmed the Dutch. The French king also foolishly alienated the English by openly backing the Catholic claimant to the English throne. Moreover, England, Austria, and the United Provinces shared a common fear that having Bourbons on the throne in both Paris and Madrid would upset the balance of power in Europe, and they quickly united to support the claimant from the Austrian Habsburgs.

The English and Dutch decision to go to war was also motivated by concerns about control of the precious metals coming from the Americas. French power and dynamism might give the Spanish the tools they needed to reassert their command of the flow of gold and silver. England's and the United Provinces' share of the precious metals from the Indies, which came through illegal trade that did not require them to go to the expense of actually conquering and administering the Indies, might come to an end. These fears in London and Amsterdam were well-founded, because Louis XIV had, in fact, formulated plans to have France take over control of the treasure fleets. Louis and his advisers wanted to strengthen Spanish and French control over the flow of precious metals by providing troops and ships to reduce the smuggling that diverted so much of the precious metals to England and the United Provinces. In sum, Louis XIV proclaimed, "The main object of the present war is the Indies trade and the wealth it produces."

As soon as Charles II died, the new Spanish king, Philip V, took steps to retain control of the treasure from the Indies, and ordered the New Spain fleet to remain in the Caribbean rather than risk a crossing. By 1701 it was safe enough for the fleet to slip through; and its successful transit, just as Philip arrived in Spain to claim the crown, was a powerful boost for the Bourbon cause.[44]

The following year, in 1702, rather than leave anything to chance, the treasure fleet was escorted by French warships under the command of Admiral François de Rousselet, the Marquis of Châteaurenault. Because a joint British and Dutch fleet was attacking Cadiz at the time, the Spanish and French ships went instead to Vigo, in northwestern Spain. The treasure of over 13 million pesos was not immediately unloaded from the ships, though, because the officials from the *Casa de Contratación* in Seville were reluctant to see the income from the customs duties go to the local authorities in Vigo. Eventually, after much bickering, agreement was reached and the unloading of the silver by

English shilling made from silver captured at Vigo Bay. Over 2 tons of silver seized during the battle was later turned over to Sir Isaac Newton, Master of the Mint in London at the time. Newton was overseeing a reform of the English coinage that involved producing coins that were of consistent weight and purity and that, unlike the Spanish cobs, were machine-made with milled edges to discourage clipping. Under Newton's direction, the Royal Mint struck coins in the new style from the captured silver and marked them "Vigo" to commemorate the battle. (Photo from the author's collection)

the French and Spanish crews began.

In the meantime, the English and Dutch had broken off their attack on Cadiz and pulled into Lagos, in neutral Portugal, for supplies. An English chaplain, while pausing for refreshment in a tavern, overheard that the silver fleet was in Vigo. The alert chaplain quickly passed the word to the fleet commander, and Admiral Sir George Rooke ordered the allied warships to set sail immediately. Soon after arriving, the British and Dutch attacked, sinking or capturing all of the Franco-Spanish fleet.

Despite the stunning success of the British and Dutch in the battle of Vigo Bay, the Spanish government ended up getting most of the huge amount of silver brought by the 1702 treasure fleet. To begin with, much of the silver had been unloaded before the battle. Once the treasure was ashore, Philip V's officials, eager to raise money for the war, confiscated the share of the treasure destined for English and Dutch merchants in Cadiz as well as some that belonged to Spanish shippers. The royal share was further increased by the fact that the well-practiced machinery for smuggling, which usually drained off a sizable portion of the treasure at Cadiz, had been bypassed. Nonetheless, an undetermined amount of treasure ended up on the bottom of the bay. All in all, the crown's take from the cargo landed at Vigo was about 7 million pesos, which was a record for a single fleet up to that time.

The victory at Vigo Bay also had an important political impact because it convinced Portugal to sign an alliance with Britain the following year. This reconfirmed the long-standing close ties between London and Lisbon. It strengthened an economic and political partnership that provided valuable benefits for both sides, with Britain tapping into the gold from the Portuguese colony of Brazil while using its power to assure Portuguese independence.[45]

The War of Spanish Succession did not go well for the Bourbons, however, and the conflict brought a long list of Spanish humiliations. For the first time

Relation veritable de la Victoire remportée à Vigos en Gallice fur les Flottes de France & d'Efpagne jointes enfemble, par celle d'Angleterre & de Hollande, le 22, le 23 & le 24 d'Octobre 1702.

The Battle of Vigo Bay, 1702. This vivid print gives an idea of the magnitude and confusion of the battle. As a first step, the English and Dutch put troops ashore and stormed the forts at the narrow entrance of Vigo Bay. Then, as shown on the map, the 50 large English and Dutch fighting ships sailed in and crashed through a boom suspended across the narrowest part of the bay. Châteaurenault put up a stiff resistance, but with only 18 warships under his

S HOLLANDOIS A VIGOS.

KUST VAN VIGOS
CIEN.

arachtig bericht van de bevochten verwinning te Vigos, in Galicien, op de Fraanfe Oorlogs-hepen en Spaanfe Silver Vlooten behaald, door de Engelfe Hollandfe Zeemachten, den 22, 23 en 24 October 1702.

command, he was hopelessly outnumbered. After a sharp fight, the English and Dutch fleets captured six French escort ships and five Spanish galleons. Twenty-three other French and Spanish vessels were destroyed, and an undetermined amount of silver went to the bottom of the bay with them. Nonetheless, the English managed to capture a considerable amount of silver and other booty. This was the third, and last, time that hostile forces sank or captured all the ships of a treasure fleet. (Photo courtesy of Robert F. Marx) in centuries there was extensive fighting on Spanish soil, and, for a few months in 1706, foreign armies occupied Madrid. In addition, the British were able to capture Minorca, in the Balearic Islands, and Gibraltar, at the entrance to the Mediterranean Sea. These conquests gave Britain strategically important permanent bases on Spanish soil and fulfilled a goal set by Essex more than 100 years earlier. British ships based on Minorca could keep an eye on the Spanish and French Mediterranean ports. Even more crucial was Gibraltar, where a British squadron could keep the gateway to the Mediterranean open for their own ships while making it difficult for the Spanish and French Mediterranean fleets to link up with their Atlantic counterparts.

Success at Vigo Bay did not dampen the English appetite for Spanish gold and silver, and the English also tried to capture the Spanish treasure fleets on the high seas. In 1708, a squadron commanded by Commodore Sir Charles Wager intercepted the *Tierra Firme* fleet off Cartagena. Most of the Spanish merchantmen and one treasure galleon managed to make it safely to Cartagena, but the English seized one of the escort galleons and sank another. The British Admiralty later court-martialed two British captains because they did not continue on into Cartagena harbor and capture the rest of the fleet. In keeping with the Royal Navy's aggressive outlook, Wager agreed with the Admiralty's decision to punish the officers. Wager fulminated, "A man who will not fight for treasure will not fight for anything." In the Pacific, Spanish ships fended off an attack on the Manila galleon in 1704; but in 1709 two English privateers managed to capture the *Encarnación*, an eastbound ship loaded with goods from the Orient, off California.[46]

With French assistance, annual treasure fleets got through more times than not during the fighting. Most of the treasure came from New Spain, and the *Tierra Firme* fleet, which brought precious metals from Peru and New Granada, sailed only once during the conflict. During the War of Spanish Succession, the Spanish received approximately 75 million pesos, or an average of more than 6 million pesos a year. This was less than the 9 million pesos that had been coming in annually just before the war broke out, but was still an impressive sum. The crown's share of the total, including what was saved from the Battle of Vigo Bay, was about 13 million pesos.

Large as these sums were, they were only a fraction of the more than 10 million pesos' worth of precious metals being produced annually in the colonies. Diversions were large because the French were achieving some success in their plans to gain control of most of the precious metals from the Spanish colonies. On two occasions, treasure fleets trying to escape the English and the Dutch actually ended up in France, where most of the silver was removed. These exceptional wartime movements of silver were in addition to

The destruction of the **San José**. *The galleon destroyed in the battle off Cartagena, the* San José, *was carrying about 7 million pesos' worth of gold and silver. This was probably the largest cargo of treasure ever carried on a single ship. The* San José *went down in deep water and has never been salvaged. (Photo courtesy of the National Maritime Museum, London)*

expenditures necessary to finance Spain's unfavorable balance of trade. Shipments were disrupted by the war, but the Spanish normally sent about 4 million pesos a year to France to pay for imports. Moreover, large amounts of silver were drawn off directly from the colonies. In 1709, at the peak of French wartime trade with the Spanish colonies, French merchants operating in the Indies sent more than 30 million pesos in silver to France. All these French gains at the expense of Spain produced growing concern among the Spanish about the wisdom of having a king from France.[47]

Spanish suspicions were also aroused by French military moves, such as when they learned about Louis XIV's proposals to put French garrisons into some ports of the Spanish Empire to ensure that these locations remained under the control of King Philip. The British captured documents concerning these plans, and to sow discord among the Bourbon forces, they made sure the papers found their way into Spanish hands. As a result, when the French offered troops to serve in the Indies, the Spanish declined them. By 1706, Spanish mistrust of their allies was so great that officials in Havana refused to allow French forces to come ashore, and there was even some fighting between French and Spanish troops.[48]

The Dutch and English also continued to drain off silver from the Indies. The victory at Vigo Bay was only one example. Spain normally sent about 6 million pesos a year to Amsterdam to help finance its trade deficit. Although the war interfered with these shipments, the Dutch, and even more so the English, profited by the confusion of the struggle to continue their smuggling operations.

Exact figures are uncertain because of the turmoil associated with the War of Spanish Succession, but it appears that during the conflict there may well have been more silver leaving Spain than was coming into the country. For the first time in two centuries, Spain had virtually lost control of the precious metals produced by its colonies. The mother country's skewed and ill-managed economic and political systems had finally succeeded in wasting even the fabulous wealth of the Indies.

The financial strain of the war forced Philip V to adopt some of the worst practices of his Habsburg predecessors and debase the currency. In 1707, the fineness of the silver coins used in Spain was reduced again, although an increase in the weight of the coins softened the blow somewhat. Two years later, the government issued orders to reduce the silver content of the colonial peso, but it appears that this measure never went into effect.[49]

The War of Spanish Succession was brought to an end by the Treaty of Utrecht with Britain and the United Provinces, in 1713, and the Treaty of Rastatt with Austria the following year. To make sure that neither Vienna nor Paris would be in position to upset the balance of power, the major states of Europe agreed in these treaties that Spain and its empire would remain independent from both Austria and France.

Under the provisions of the treaties that applied to Spain, the major powers recognized Philip V as king, and all agreed that the crowns of Spain and France would never be held by the same person. The British were allowed to trade legally and directly with the Spanish colonies for the first time, and Spain gave up the Spanish Netherlands and its holdings in Italy. British possession of Gibraltar, Minorca, St. Kitts, and parts of Canada also was confirmed. As a result, Spain lost its place as a major power in Europe, and Madrid's focus shifted to the empire overseas and the partnership with France as the main sources of its strength.

France, for its part, had failed in its bid to take over the Spanish Empire and the treasure fleets. Louis XIV's decision to give priority to his army and conquests on land had meant that, despite some successes, France never had the resources needed for a decisive victory at sea.[50]

One last disaster capped this sad period in Spanish history. The entire 1715

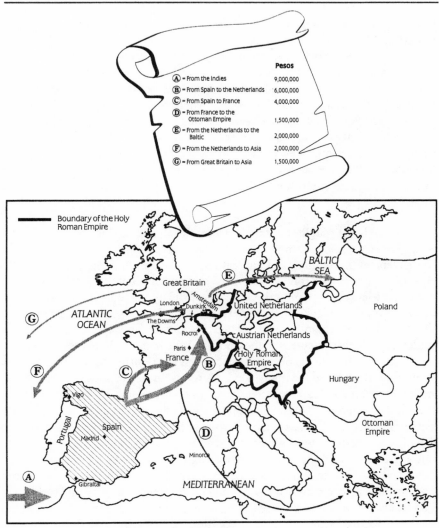

		Pesos
Ⓐ	= From the Indies	9,000,000
Ⓑ	= From Spain to the Netherlands	6,000,000
Ⓒ	= From Spain to France	4,000,000
Ⓓ	= From France to the Ottoman Empire	1,500,000
Ⓔ	= From the Netherlands to the Baltic	2,000,000
Ⓕ	= From the Netherlands to Asia	2,000,000
Ⓖ	= From Great Britain to Asia	1,500,000

Map 8.
Spanish Possessions in Europe and the
Flow of Precious Metals in 1715

treasure fleet, carrying the first major shipment after the end of the war, was lost in a storm off the Florida coast. A fleet of 11 Spanish ships, carrying 7 million pesos in treasure, crashed ashore along a lengthy stretch of Florida shoreline; almost half of the 2,500 people aboard were lost. The Spanish immediately began a salvage operation, and over the next few months recovered more than 4 million pesos from the shallow waters where the ships had gone down.

Word of the mountains of silver on the beaches of Florida spread quickly, and pirates from all over North America and the Caribbean descended on the scene. One raider managed to carry off 90,000 pesos. Although much of the treasure eventually got to Spain, millions of pesos were left on the ocean bottom because salvagers could not find them using the primitive techniques of the time.[51]

The riches brought by the treasure fleets had given the Spanish an exaggerated sense of complacency, and they made little effort to modernize in the seventeenth century. But indications of weakness long present in the Spanish Empire took on new importance as the century wore on. Spain remained a largely agricultural economy with an outdated financial system and an excessive dependence on foreigners. Once the flow of gold and silver slowed down and Spain's enemies surged ahead in wealth and power, the Spanish came under unbearable pressure, and their political and economic position collapsed.

These developments began to change the relationship between Spain and its empire. Because of the many demands on its limited resources, Madrid had never been able to fill all the bureaucratic posts in the empire with people from the mother country. This meant that local residents assumed considerable power and began to develop their own viewpoints and interests. In addition, Spanish authorities could never afford to keep a separate army and navy to enforce their will in the Indies, even though protection of the mines and sea lanes was essential to Spanish prosperity and power. Finally, Spain's economy had not been able to supply the wants and needs of the colonists, and foreigners had taken over much of the trade of the empire and had drawn off much of the profits. Once the War of Spanish Succession was over, the new Bourbon rulers would have to turn their attention to providing remedies for some of these problems.

The wars of the second half of the seventeenth century showed that the existence of an integrated, worldwide political and economic system had become accepted as a commonplace aspect of international relations. The agreement of Câteau-Cambrésis, which stipulated that fighting in the Indies would remain isolated from the international politics of Europe, was replaced by agreements, such as the Treaties of Ryswyck and Utrecht, in which territorial settlements in the Indies were important parts of European diplomatic settlements.

As a result of the War of Spanish Succession, Spain lost her position as a leading power in Europe and others took over the global system that Spain and Portugal had pioneered. During the late seventeenth century and early eighteenth century, the Spanish government also exhausted financial tools such as foreign loans and manipulation of the currency that it had long used to compensate for the uncertainties of the flow of treasure from the Indies.

Although Spain's chief asset, control of the mines in the Indies that produced precious metals, remained intact, it was not enough to secure a leading place in a more competitive international environment. Spain controlled the sources of gold and silver, but the mechanisms for circulating that wealth around the world were increasingly in foreign hands. As a result, the Spanish treasure fleets were no longer the main method of controlling precious metals.

Britain had now become the predominant sea power. Unlike Spain, it had built a decisive tool for dominating the sea. This was its large, professional navy, made up of heavily armed, specialized warships owned by the state and commanded by well-trained officers. Such a fleet was a far cry from the privately financed English expeditions of the sixteenth century. Private profit, through opportunities such as corruption and sale of prizes, remained important in the Royal Navy; but from the late seventeenth century on, there was an increasing emphasis in the navy on achieving public purposes as well. It was England's professional, aggressive, and wide-ranging navy that provided the prototype for modern naval forces. Although this superior naval force had originally been built up by Cromwell, England's monarchs found it too valuable to disband after they returned to the throne.

Other players were still important on the international scene, however. France, although weakened, was clearly still the greatest land power in Europe and had a respectable number of colonies. The Dutch were also somewhat weakened but still a major commercial power. As the eighteenth century began, the struggle for wealth and power in Europe, and the wider world, had entered a different phase that would present Spain's new Bourbon dynasty with a formidable series of challenges.

5. RECOVERY,
1716–1790

he kings of the new Bourbon dynasty were acutely aware of Spain's relative weakness compared to the power of Britain and France. After the War of Spanish Succession, Spain's last major asset outside the Iberian Peninsula was the wealth of the Americas, and the Bourbon monarchs were determined to manage it more effectively. Inside Spain, the choices facing Philip V were whether to use traditional Spanish methods or adopt more modern techniques based on French and other foreign models. In the wider world, he would have to decide how active a role Spain should play.

Early Bourbon Reforms
Spain's unwieldy administrative system was one of the first targets of the Bourbon reformers. Philip V wanted a uniform administrative structure, so he ended Aragon's existence as a separate kingdom and abolished that province's separate coinage and customs barriers. Instead of retaining the system of overlapping councils that was the traditional Habsburg method of managing affairs, Philip V appointed individual ministers, based on French administrative models, who took responsibility for well-defined areas. In 1714, for example, the government set up a Ministry of Marine and Indies.

Philip also preferred ministers who came from the minor nobility rather than haughty and independent grandees, who had virtually monopolized senior posts in the previous century and who had not depended on the crown for wealth and honors. The new breed of ministers gave the monarch more control because they were retained and promoted on the basis of their ability and loyalty. Philip also made reforms in colonial policy by founding trading companies, over a century after the Dutch and English had begun such operations.[1]

In 1717, Philip named José Patiño as president of the *Casa de Contratación* and commander of the naval facilities at Cadiz. Patiño moved the *Casa* and the merchants' *Consulado* from Seville to Cadiz, where the ships of the Indies trade had been calling since 1680, and started rebuilding the navy. He became Secretary of the Navy and Indies in 1726, and later took over the war and finance ministries.

Philip's and Patiño's goal was to stimulate industry and commerce in order to increase royal revenues, in the hope that this would again make it possible for Spain to be one of the leading states of Europe. Although some of the staff at the colonial ministry suggested that the government could also stimulate trade by lowering taxes, the need for revenue was too great and assessments remained at high levels.[2]

One of Patiño's chief methods for again making Spain a power to be reckoned with was to rebuild the Spanish navy. He began by founding up-to-date dockyards and arsenals as well as a training academy for officers. During the early years of his ministry, Patiño had to purchase modern ships from France to replace the old galleons, but in time the Spanish were able to produce their own vessels. Patiño also re-established the Caribbean squadron, a key part of Menéndez's original maritime defense strategy that had been abandoned during the seventeenth century.[3]

In conjunction with the rebuilding of the navy, Patiño believed it would be important to revive the treasure fleets, which had languished since the war. He hoped a vibrant system of convoys would spur growth in the colonies and make it possible to recover control of the flow of precious metals and improve royal revenues. As was the case with his other reforms, Patiño was a cautious innovator when dealing with the treasure fleets. His basic technique for rejuvenating the fleets was to return to the traditional system of privately owned vessels traveling in tightly controlled fleets. The government wanted the more or less predictable revenues derived from regular sailings of the fleets, and the merchants' *Consulado* supported the plan in the hope of again earning high profits through a controlled market. In 1720, the government ordered that the New Spain and *Tierra Firme* fleets should again sail once a year.[4]

It turned out, however, that although production of precious metals in the colonies was rising, the fleet system could not be reconstructed on the old basis. It was no longer profitable to carry manufactured goods on the outbound ships, because Spanish merchants were constantly undercut by the lower prices of their foreign rivals, especially the British. Moreover, the colonies had become more self-sufficient and there was not much of a market for staples from Spain, such as flour or olive oil. As a result, the fleets became less and less a private commercial operation and instead concentrated on servicing the silver trade for the crown.

In the eighteenth century, westbound ships carried mainly mercury, still a government monopoly and essential for separating silver from ore, along with official correspondence and passengers. The eastbound ships carried mostly silver. This more-restricted traffic required fewer ships, and during the 1720s and 1730s, fleets sailed only every two or three years instead of once a year, with single ships filling the gaps in between. The 1721 New Spain fleet, the first to sail after the 1720 order reviving the fleets, returned to Spain with 10 million pesos. This was about the average for the occasional New Spain and *Tierra Firme* fleets that sailed over the next 20 years.[5]

In 1740, the War of Austrian Succession broke out when the major European powers began fighting over who would inherit the Habsburg lands in central Europe. Spain's response to the start of the conflict was to suspend the treasure fleets rather than risk having them captured by the British. Although the New Spain fleet returned to service with the coming of peace in the 1750s, the *Tierra Firme* fleet never sailed again. Instead, only single ships sailed to the southern colonies, and those vessels sailed around Cape Horn and directly to Peru instead of picking up goods and silver transported across the Isthmus of Panama. In any event, in the second half of the eighteenth century, there was little need for secure transport from the ports of Arica and Callao because the cost of local administration and defense absorbed virtually all the royal revenues from Peru. There was virtually no treasure left to ship to the mother country.[6]

The main type of ship used in the Spanish treasure fleets of the eighteenth century was the frigate, usually based on French designs of the time. Frigates were larger and better armed than galleons, and their more trim lines enabled them to sail faster. Although still dependent on the vagaries of the wind, they were an efficient means of moving heavy cargoes, like silver, over long distances. A typical frigate was 125 feet long and 25 feet wide, had a cargo capacity about twice that of a galleon, and carried up to 50 cannon.

The greatest threat to the Spanish treasure fleets after their revival in the 1720s continued to be the weather. Even the vigorous Bourbon reforms could not change this age-old problem. In 1730, the frigate *Nuestra Señora del*

Carmen, with 3 million pesos on board, went down in a hurricane south of Jamaica. Local Spanish authorities managed to salvage only about half the cargo before the sea demolished the wreck and drifting sand covered what remained. Three years later, most of the ships in the New Spain fleet, a total of 22 ships carrying more than 11 million pesos, were lost in a hurricane in the Florida Keys. Colonial officials quickly salvaged much of the treasure and sent it to Spain the following year. Another hurricane hit the 1750 fleet when it was off the coast of North Carolina, and four ships were lost. English colonists managed to get their hands on some of the silver, and the crew on one of the damaged ships mutinied and carried off more of the treasure. Most of the ships were repaired, however, and they made it to Spain with the bulk of the treasure.[7]

Philip V and his ministers did not confine their reforms to maritime matters, and in 1728 the Spanish government also made improvements in the mints and coinage. For a start, the colonial mints, which had been operated by private contractors for centuries, were taken over by the government and run directly by royal officials. Moreover, the weight and purity of the coins was reduced for the first time since the beginning of the minting of colonial pesos in the 1570s. The new pesos weighed about 27 grams and were about 92 percent pure silver, while the old ones had been almost 27.5 grams and 93 percent pure silver. Even so, the new coins were a great improvement over the traditional cobs. The higher quality of these coins, along with the rising production of silver in the eighteenth century, reinforced the peso's role as a world standard. These new pieces of eight were an appropriate symbol of a revived and reformed empire. The reform of the colonial mints took effect in New Spain in the early 1730s, but it was another 15 years before the measures were enacted in the distant and sleepy backwater of Peru.[8]

Although the reforms of Philip V were not always a daring departure from past practices, they did bring considerable improvement when compared to the last years of the Habsburgs. One key indicator of progress was that Philip V's government was in much better financial shape than its predecessors. Revenues increased and expenses were kept under control, which meant that for the first time in centuries the Spanish treasury had a surplus and there was no need for foreign loans. The problem, however, was that Britain and France were moving ahead even faster. Despite the Bourbons' efforts, Spain remained only a secondary power.[9]

Attacks on the Fleet System

Spain's attempts to rebuild its naval and commercial power did not escape the attention of Great Britain, which was determined to defend its newly acquired dominance at sea. When Philip V sent an army to Italy in a bid to recapture

Machine-made peso from the Mexico City mint. One of the most visible results of the Bourbon reforms was a striking change in the appearance of the pieces of eight that made up the bulk

of the cargoes of the treasure fleets. Starting in 1732, colonial mints used machinery, instead of manual labor, to produce more uniform coins. These perfectly round coins, with their milled edges, discouraged attempts to clip off small pieces of silver and pass underweight coins, and the more intricate and precise designs helped foil counterfeiters. These new pesos were among the most attractive coins in history and had the distinctive pillar motif long associated with colonial coinage as a prominent feature. (Photo from the author's collection)

Spanish influence there, officials in London responded quickly. Britain sought assistance from Austria and France and sent a fleet to the Mediterranean, where it defeated the Spanish in 1718. A few years later, when Madrid offered the Austrians commercial access to the Spanish Empire, the British reaction was again prompt and firm. Without formally declaring war, the British launched a somewhat misguided effort to punish Spain, blockading Porto Bello from 1725 to 1727. This had only a limited financial effect, because so little treasure was coming through Panama, but it was a potent symbol of Britain's ability to exert its sea power deep within the Spanish Empire.[10]

The real tests of the early Bourbon reforms, however, were the great worldwide wars of the mid-eighteenth century. As had been the case so often in the past, the treasure fleets were one of the main targets of Spain's enemies once a war began. As a weaker power, Spain had little choice but to adopt a restrained and defensive strategy, which stressed maintaining fortifications and avoiding the risks of battles at sea. The goal was to save ships from destruction rather than to try to control the seas. This caution was a result of the fact that by the middle of the eighteenth century the Spanish fleet was only the third-largest in the world, after Britain and France. Diplomatically, Spain's main strategy was to ally itself with France, and throughout much of the eighteenth century a series of family compacts linked the Bourbon rulers in Madrid and Paris.[11]

In 1738, a British sea captain named Robert Jenkins made a sensational appearance in the English Parliament, displaying what he claimed was his ear, which had been cut off by Spanish coast guards in the Caribbean. There were many other colonial disputes between London and Madrid, but Jenkins' complaint was the catalyst that led the following year to a British declaration of war on Spain and the beginning of what became known as the War of Jenkins' Ear. In 1740, this colonial struggle merged into the larger European conflict of the War of Austrian Succession. As had become commonplace, because of the growth of fleets and colonies, major European wars meant there would be fighting all over the globe.

Even before the war started, the British dispatched a fleet under Admiral Edward Vernon to the Caribbean with orders to attack the treasure fleets. Vernon faced the classic strategic problem that had bedeviled English naval commanders in the Caribbean for almost 200 years. One option was to strike at the treasure fleets by attacking their bases. These ports were static and easy to find, but they were often heavily fortified and there was no guarantee there would be ships or treasure present. The other possibility was to seek out the fleets on the high seas, where at least some of the eastbound Spanish ships were bound to be carrying treasure. But there were drawbacks to this approach as well. Although sailing times were generally limited to certain seasons because of weather conditions, it was hard to come by accurate and timely information about the exact departure dates of the treasure fleets. Moreover, once the convoys were on the high seas, it was virtually impossible to locate them.

After mulling over these factors, Vernon recommended trying to capture the treasure fleets at sea, but the Admiralty overruled him and issued orders to attack the ports. The admiral complied. His first target was Porto Bello, which had once been the transit point for the riches of Peru and the scene of one of the main commercial fairs in the Western Hemisphere but was of little consequence in the mid-eighteenth century.

Vernon then sailed to Cartagena and laid siege to that city. Reinforcements arrived from the American colonies and from Britain, but after several months it became clear that Vernon still did not have enough strength to capture the fortress, and he withdrew. George Washington's older half brother, Lawrence, served in the expedition to Cartagena and named his Virginia plantation, Mount Vernon, which George later inherited, in honor of his commander. While the English were distracted at Porto Bello and Cartagena, the New Spain fleet managed to leave Veracruz and slip back to Spain. Vernon's campaign achieved none of its goals, and although there was some desultory fighting in the West Indies later in the war, the focus of the conflict moved elsewhere.[12]

In the meantime, the British Admiralty had sent a second fleet, under Commodore George Anson, around Cape Horn and into the Pacific. Anson was supposed to strike Panama City from the west at the same time that Vernon was

Vernon's attack on Porto Bello, 1739. Although he was successful in capturing the town, the British admiral found no treasure there. Little silver passed this way in the 1730s because most of Peru's production remained in the colony to pay administrative expenses. The small amounts of treasure that did go to Spain were picked up by single, fast frigates that traveled around Cape Horn. Vernon's destruction of the city was so thorough, however, that it brought to an end what limited use the Spanish still made of the port. The city's once great fairs, which were a losing proposition for Spanish merchants in the eighteenth century, were never revived. (Photo courtesy of the National Maritime Museum, London)

attacking Porto Bello from the east. Both Anson's plan to attack Panama and Vernon's seizure of Porto Bello were misguided and based on an out-of-date conception of the operations of the treasure fleets. By the 1740s, little silver was being shipped from Peru to Panama, and it was Veracruz and Havana that were the main transit points.

After losing several ships in a storm and hearing that Vernon was bogged down at Cartagena, Anson decided he lacked the strength to take Panama City on his own, so he concentrated on seizing Spanish shipping in the Pacific. This was potentially a much more fruitful strategy, because the Manila galleons were still sailing. But Anson missed the eastbound ship from Manila, and then the westbound vessel also eluded him because the colonial authorities kept the ship in Acapulco rather than run the risk of losing it at sea. With only one ship left, Anson headed westward across the Pacific, where he finally captured a treasure-laden Spanish ship. After this success, Anson made the first visit by an English warship to China and then headed for home. He became the first English

Anson's capture of a Manila galleon, 1743. After failing to catch any of the Manila galleons along the Pacific coast of New Spain, Anson decided to try to intercept one of the Spanish ships near Manila, the western terminus of their route. When nothing was heard of Anson for months, the authorities in New Spain, believing that he had gone home or been wrecked, released the ship loaded with silver that they had been holding in Acapulco. Months later, as the Nuestra Señora de Covadonga *approached the Philippines, Anson captured her. The* Covadonga *was carrying over 1.3 million pesos in coins and more than a ton of silver bullion. (Photo courtesy of the National Maritime Museum, London)*

As the War of Austrian Succession dragged on, the operations of the Spanish treasure fleets were seriously disrupted, with convoys getting through only in 1740 and 1744. In 1748, a fleet tried to make a run for Spain, but a British squadron caught it off Havana.

French and Spanish ships also tried to make the Atlantic crossing successfully by traveling alone or in small groups, and some of them were also captured by the British. In 1745, for example, British privateers seized two French ships loaded with pesos. An average of only about 5 million pesos a year reached Spain during the war. Because of such risks, the Spanish stored huge amounts of treasure in the Indies rather than expose it to possible capture. In the first two years of peace the fleets brought over 60 million pesos to Spain.[14]

Despite the fighting in the Caribbean and Pacific, Spain was only a secondary player in the War of Austrian Succession, which was mainly a worldwide struggle between the major colonial powers, Britain and France. In

British attack on the treasure fleet off Cuba, 1748. *This battle in 1748 was the only fleet action of the war in which the Spanish were involved and showed that protecting the treasure ships was the sole cause for which the cautious Spanish naval commanders would risk a fight. After a short clash, the British captured one Spanish ship and forced ashore another one that was carrying 10 million pesos. The Spanish crew then blew up the beached ship and scattered millions of coins over a wide area in a desperate move that kept the British from capturing the treasure. (Photo courtesy of the National Maritime Museum, London)*

British crown made from captured Spanish silver. *As they had done after the battle of Vigo Bay, the English triumphantly celebrated their capture of Spanish treasure ships in the War of Austrian Succession by turning some of the booty into their own currency. The British melted down the captured Spanish pesos, which were from the mint in Lima, and reminted them into English coins marked "Lima" to commemorate the victory. (Photo from the author's collection)*

addition to considerable fighting on land in Europe, North America, and India, there were clashes between British and French fleets in the Atlantic, the Mediterranean, the Caribbean, and the Indian Ocean. The British were generally able to establish naval superiority everywhere, but France remained the supreme power on land in the central theater of Europe. As a result, the war eventually became an exhausting standoff.[15]

King Ferdinand VI, who inherited the Spanish crown in 1746, was glad to make peace. The Treaty of Aix-la-Chapelle in 1748, which ended the War of Austrian Succession, was a return to the pre-war situation as far as Spain was concerned, as she neither gained nor lost anything. Britain and France were not able to achieve a decisive result in their conflict either. France returned conquests she had made in India in exchange for the Canadian fortress of Louisbourg, which the British had captured. Such an inconclusive result could only be a truce until the exhausted European powers recovered the financial, military, and diplomatic means to resume the struggle. The War of Austrian Succession had been so discouraging that Ferdinand was reluctant to become involved when another world war loomed a few years later, and Spain stayed on the sidelines as Britain and France again moved down the path toward war in the mid-1750s.

Like the War of Austrian Succession, the Seven Years' War was a global struggle with origins in colonial rivalries. The conflict began in 1754, when French and British forces clashed in North America, and two years later the fighting spread to Europe. After an embarrassing series of early defeats, William Pitt took over control of British policy and put into place a successful strategy that linked the diplomatic, financial, and naval struggles against France on a worldwide basis. Pitt was faced with the same strategic problems that had faced England's wartime leaders since the days of the Elizabethan sea dogs: how to manage allies, blockades, and money. In time, he found ways to solve all these interrelated challenges and to carry out an integrated strategy with ruthless efficiency.

First, Pitt strengthened Britain's alliance with Prussia by sending money and troops to the continent, which kept France preoccupied with fighting on land in Europe. Then he used a continuous blockade by part of the Royal Navy to confine the French fleet to European waters. A sustained blockade, lasting years at a time, was now possible because the British had developed the ships, discipline, and logistical support to conduct such extended operations.

With the French warships locked in their ports, the remainder of the British fleet had almost unimpeded access to the rest of the world, making it possible for the Royal Navy to capture lucrative colonies in North America, Africa, the Caribbean, and India. These victories overseas were a result of the fact that the

British had finally mastered the techniques of combined operations, in which the navy and army cooperated closely in sending large and well-equipped forces all over the world. The expanding overseas empire generated more trade, which enabled Pitt to finance the British fleet and the Prussian army with a handsome profit left over. Pitt also used the British government's solid financial reputation to raise loans, and the British national debt grew to the equivalent of about 500 million pesos during the war.[16]

When King Charles III came to the throne of Spain in 1759, his country was at peace, but the new monarch had much more wide-ranging ambitions and concerns than his predecessor. Charles wanted Spain to be a major power but realized that there were many difficulties in achieving this. For example, he was worried that if France lost the war against Britain in North America, a victorious and dynamic Britain would have new territory in the Mississippi Valley, dangerously close to Spain's possessions. The Spanish king was also sympathetic to his Bourbon relative, King Louis XV. In 1761, his concern about Britain and his sense of family loyalty led him to renew the family compact between Spain and France. Once Spain appeared ready to help France, war between Spain and Britain was almost inevitable.

Pitt's determination to deal forcefully with Spain cost him his job. The British leader was aware that the Spanish were moving closer to joining the French in the war, and his plan was to strike a crippling preemptive blow by capturing the Spanish treasure fleet. He acknowledged that taking on another enemy before France was defeated was risky, but he also believed that the year 1761, with British resources mobilized all over the world, was the best time to strike. In the fall of that year, he sent a fleet to cruise off Spain to intimidate Madrid and to be in a position to seize the treasure fleet if Spain declared war. When the rest of the British ministers objected to his belligerent policy, Pitt resigned.

Shortly afterward, the 1761 treasure fleet from New Spain, with 16 million pesos on board, made it safely to Spain, which convinced Charles that he could afford to fight. He refused to give the British details of the new family compact or to make concessions in the colonial arguments between London and Madrid, knowing his firm stance would mean war. During the first week of 1762, Britain responded by declaring war on Spain. Charles' decision to enter the conflict was a major miscalculation, however, because the British had become much more powerful, especially at sea, than even France and Spain combined.[17]

Spain's participation in the Seven Years' War was a disaster. She intervened on the losing side just when the British, still following Pitt's principles, were winning the war by conducting the most successful example of an integrated global strategy the world had yet seen. Within weeks of the outbreak of war, British forces were attacking two of Spain's most important colonial strongholds.

The first target was Havana, Spain's main base in the Caribbean. Royal Navy ships transported more than 10,000 soldiers to Havana and later brought more reinforcements from the North American colonies. After a siege of two months, the Spanish garrison of Havana surrendered, without realizing that the traditional ally of the defenders of Caribbean ports, tropical disease, was having a serious effect on the British forces. The victorious British were exhausted but mollified by capturing booty worth millions of pesos. It was the first time Havana had fallen to enemy forces in 200 years. Britain had now sealed the exit to the Caribbean and was in a position to completely cut off the Atlantic treasure fleets. A few weeks after the fall of Havana, British ships patrolling the Atlantic captured a Spanish frigate carrying 4 million pesos.[18]

Later that same year, the British moved against their second main target, Manila, by sending a small force from India to lay siege to the capital of the Philippines. After two weeks, the Spanish garrison gave up, and for the first

British attack on Havana, 1762. This painting shows the beginning of the final phase of the assault: an amphibious landing to capture the fortress known as El Morro (on the left), which guards the narrow entrance to the harbor. Inside the harbor are the 12 warships and 100 merchantmen, which was about one-third of the total Spanish fleet, that the British captured when the city fell. (Photo courtesy of the National Maritime Museum, London)

time, Manila was in the hands of a foreign enemy. To stave off a sack of the city, the population of Manila promised a 4-million-peso ransom. Because this was Spain's only possession in the Far East, its loss meant she now had no links to the lucrative Asian trade. A few weeks later, the British also captured both the inbound and the outbound Manila galleons, which had cargoes worth another 4 million pesos. Thus, within 10 months of the start of the war, Spain had lost her two most valuable overseas ports and millions of pesos' worth of merchandise and treasure. [19]

In the Peace of Paris, signed in 1763, Britain consolidated its position as the leading colonial power and the mistress of the seas. In addition to the defeats inflicted on the Spanish, British fleets and armies had conquered all of Canada, the province of Bengal in India (which became a fief of the East India Company), valuable sugar-producing islands in the Caribbean, and slave trading ports in Africa. The Spanish Empire was weakened but not destroyed, because Madrid still retained control of the vital mining centers in America. But Spain did have to give up Florida and Minorca in order to get Cuba and the Philippines back.

France was seriously crippled by the peace settlement, especially in the competition to control the wealth generated by overseas trade. The French gave half their territory in North America to Britain and turned the rest over to Spain as compensation for the loss of Florida and Minorca. This peace settlement fulfilled Charles III's nightmare by enlarging the British colonies and bringing them directly in touch with Spain's possessions.

After the peace, Spain renewed efforts to improve the defenses of the colonies. In the past, the Spanish government had always depended on local militias to provide most of the permanent military forces in the Indies. Now, for the first time, Madrid sent large garrisons of regular troops to the colonies. These forces were not only for protection from foreigners but could also be used to enforce Charles's efforts to extract more revenues from the empire. Although the government would have liked to station a permanent naval squadron in the Caribbean, there was never enough money to do this during the remainder of the colonial period.

Charles III and Further Reforms

The magnitude and speed of the Spanish defeats in 1762 convinced the king that further modernization was necessary, if Spain was to retain a place as one of the great powers. Charles and his ministers reexamined the Spanish government's mercantilist policies and concluded that rigid controls had become counterproductive and some liberalization was necessary. The new wave of reforms had an important impact on the operation of the treasure fleets because it included modernization of mining regulations, commercial policies, and government finance.

In 1765, Charles sent a trusted and experienced royal official, José de Gálvez, on a special inspection mission to New Spain to see what could be done to improve silver production. Gálvez agreed with the king that reforms in colonial administration were necessary so that there could be an increase in the royal revenues. He focused on mining, because he believed that precious metals were the main form of wealth. According to Gálvez, "Since mining is the origin and unique source of the metals which give spirit and movement to all human occupations and to the universal commerce of this globe, in justice it demands the principal attention of the government."[20]

Based on Gálvez's report, authorities in Madrid instituted several important reforms in the regulations governing mining in the colonies. First, the crown reduced taxes on silver and lowered the price of mercury and gunpowder in order to stimulate production. After Gálvez returned to Spain in 1771, reforms in the same vein continued, including the establishment of a mining guild to encourage new techniques, a special court to settle disputes, a new mining code, a bank to provide credit, and a technical school. After centuries of decline, the native population of New Spain was increasing in the eighteenth century, and good wages drew more workers to the silver mines.

As a result of these developments, silver production in New Spain rose to about 12 million pesos a year in the early 1770s, 18 million pesos by the end of the decade, and almost 30 million pesos a year in the 1780s. This represented more than half of total global production at the time. During this period, Guanajuato was the most productive silver mining area in the world, with an output of over 5 million pesos a year.

This new silver boom helped to revitalize the entire economy of New Spain, leading to growth in agriculture, ranching, and manufacturing. The large amounts of silver retained in New Spain and the other colonies to cover the costs of administration and defense helped create a prosperous, monetized economy and gave the colonists a growing sense of self-confidence. There was also a feeling of resentment that Spain, the mother country, was something of a parasite, feeding off the wealth produced in the Indies.

Besides addressing themselves to mining, Charles III's reforming ministers also tightened administrative procedures and improved communications by instituting a monthly mail service between Havana and Cadiz. The goal of all these new improvements was to increase control and revenues, but the reforms also alienated many colonists, who had become used to the weak government of the previous century.[21]

Similar reforms were tried in Peru, but with less success. Some of the methods used in New Spain, such as opening new mines, reducing costs, and implementing new mining laws, helped make the production of silver in Peru more efficient. The great mercury mine at Huancavélica was less and less productive, however, and the silver mines in New Spain, with their higher output, got priority for mercury shipments from Europe. Miners in Peru were not as successful as those in New Spain in adopting new technology or organizing sufficient credit. Peruvian production increased in the 1770s from 6 million pesos a year to 9 million, but this was still only half what was coming from New Spain. Gold production in New Granada also improved slowly during this period and averaged nearly 2 million pesos' worth a year in the eighteenth century.[22]

In the wake of the humiliating defeat in the Seven Years' War, Charles III devoted a great deal of energy to improving his navy, which was an essential tool for keeping the empire together and exerting influence in European diplomacy. Spain built high-quality ships, based on French models, but had great difficulty finding enough qualified officers or seaman. By working together, Spain and France could put as many ships at sea as the English; but because the Spanish king was not confident of the navy's fighting ability, he was always hesitant to risk his ships in combat.[23]

Spain also made efforts to restore the treasure fleet system, but these were not a success. An attempt was made in the 1760s to revive the annual convoys to New Spain at the request of merchants in both Cadiz and New Spain, but the experiment was a commercial failure because the markets in the Indies were flooded with low-cost, high-quality foreign goods. Because of these setbacks, a special royal commission in Madrid began re-examining the commercial policies of the Spanish Empire in 1764. The commission's report, issued a year later, was a scathing critique of the traditional Spanish colonial system. It concluded that the convoy system was bad for business because the fleets were slow, expensive, and delivered only a limited quantity of goods. Moreover, the commissioners criticized the high taxes levied on the fleets, asserting such taxes only encouraged smuggling.

To breathe new life into the system, the government declared an end to the Cadiz monopoly in 1765 and allowed eight Spanish cities to trade with much of the Caribbean. In 1776, Gálvez became Minister of the Indies, and one of his chief concerns was to continue this liberalization of trade. Two years later, the government further expanded the number of ports in Spain and the Indies that were permitted to trade with each other. This meant there was free trade within most of the Spanish Empire, but the colonies were still not permitted to have unrestricted commerce with the rest of the world.[24]

As part of his reform program, Charles III also turned his attention to the coinage. In a continuing effort to thwart counterfeiters and provide a unified currency, he ordered an empire-wide recoinage in 1772. Ostensibly the recoinage of 1772 was also an effort to end the century-old difference in purity between the coins circulating in Spain and the colonial coins. In order to make a profit on reminting the coins, however, Charles secretly ordered a reduction in the silver content of all the coins from the mints in both the colonies and Spain. New colonial pesos were now 90 percent silver, instead of 92 percent, and Spanish coins had an even lower silver content. This was only the second time the government had debased the colonial pesos since the founding of the mints in the New World in the sixteenth century.[25]

The constant efforts by Charles III and his ministers to increase royal revenues were extremely successful, and as long as Spain was at peace it was possible to keep income ahead of expenditures. By the 1780s, the crown's income was about 30 million pesos a year, almost double what it had been 20 years before. About 6 million pesos of the royal revenue was the surplus from New Spain, after the cost of local administration and defense had been paid. Spanish businessmen earned even larger sums by participating in the vibrant trade with New Spain, and this increased the tax base in Spain. In contrast, from the 1750s onward, the government in Madrid derived no revenue from Peru, where the costs of administration absorbed all the silver production.[26]

When fighting broke out between the British government and its colonies in North America, in 1775, Charles III faced a dilemma. The king hoped that encouraging the colonial uprising might weaken Britain and provide an opportunity to get back territories lost over the past century, such as Minorca, Gibraltar, and Jamaica. He was also interested in recovering Florida, still a vital

Redesigned peso with a portrait of King Charles III. For some time, the monarch's portrait had appeared on the obverse of coins minted in Spain, and now the colonial coins were redesigned to match. Colonial coins retained a distinctive reverse, however, with the traditional pillars flanking the royal arms. This example is from the mint in Mexico City. (Photo from the author's collection)

post on the route of the treasure ships. At the same time, Charles did not want to set a precedent of successful revolt that might inspire his own American colonies, nor did he want to expose the ships carrying treasure from his colonies to attack by the Royal Navy.

His cautious compromise was to support the North American rebels discreetly by selling them arms and providing bases for their privateers, while refusing to give the rebels any public diplomatic recognition. By 1779, this balancing act had become impossible to maintain, and Spain had to choose sides. Once that year's treasure ships were safely in Spain, Charles III openly joined France in the struggle against Britain.[27]

With both France and Spain in the war, Britain was at a strategic disadvantage because of the vast areas of land and sea and the large number of merchant ships it had to protect. In addition, London was not able to find a continental ally to tie down the French and Spanish with land warfare in Europe. Finally, there was no leader of Pitt's stature who could conceive and carry out a successful strategy. As a result, the French and Spanish were able to use their improved navies to make initial gains in the war. French and Spanish fleets patrolled the English Channel in 1779, causing an invasion scare in Britain. For years the allies also besieged Gibraltar by land and sea.

In addition, Spanish and French support was crucial to the success of the decisive Yorktown campaign. Wealthy merchants in Havana loaned Admiral François de Grasse about 250,000 pesos, so he could pay French troops in North America. De Grasse then shifted his fleet from the Caribbean to the Chesapeake Bay, where he sealed the fate of the British army at Yorktown.

The Bourbon allies were timid in pursuing their advantages, however, and except for reoccupying Florida and capturing Minorca, Spain and France were not able to turn Britain's weakness to their own advantage. Gibraltar withstood a three-year siege, and the Royal Navy delivered several stinging defeats to the French and Spanish fleets late in the conflict.[28]

Another war with the powerful global empire of Britain meant that Spain faced a financial crisis. Expenditures would have to go up; but with the Royal Navy controlling the Atlantic, revenues from the colonies were sharply reduced. To solve the problem, Charles returned to the Habsburg policy of borrowing money abroad and also issued Spain's first paper money.

In 1782, in another innovation, the king authorized the establishment of the *Banco de San Carlos*, Spain's first national bank, to manage the supply of paper money. When peace came in 1783, the regular flow of American treasure resumed and the government began redeeming the paper money issued during the war. In sum, although Spain's finances had been strained by the war, it had been able to find ways to survive the crisis.[29]

The peace after the American Revolution was also a political success, and showed that Spain could hold her own among the great powers. Under the Treaty of Versailles, in 1783, Spain was allowed to keep Florida and Minorca. This outcome was acceptable to Spain because the weakness of the new United States removed the threat of having a major European power as a neighbor in North America. The Spanish were also pleased to see that their ally France had put on a respectable performance and that their old enemy, Britain, had been humbled.

After the war, the Spanish government continued its reform program and dismantled the now-outdated system of treasure fleets that had existed for almost 300 years. Royal officials decided that more participation and competition in the commerce of the empire might lower prices and bring more silver back to Spain. Free trade was extended to the last exceptions, Venezuela and New Spain, in 1789. A consequence of this was an end to the last vestiges of the system of organized treasure fleets. Single ships now traveled back and forth freely as weather and commercial conditions dictated, and there were no more carefully controlled convoys.

In the Pacific, the Spanish government turned over management of the Manila galleons to a private company in 1785. Five years later, the crown ordered the *Casa de Contratación* closed and turned its building in Seville over to the Archives of the Indies, the repository of colonial records that had been founded in 1784. The closing of the *Casa* in 1790 showed that the era of the Spanish treasure fleets had come to an end.

The wisdom of removing the last restrictions on commerce within the empire was demonstrated by the fact that there was a quadrupling of trade between 1778 and 1790 and a commensurate increase in royal revenue. Moreover, silver production continued to increase until the Spanish Empire began to fall apart early in the nineteenth century.[30]

In the midst of all these changes, Charles III died in 1788, adding to the sense that an era was coming to an end. During his tenure, he had strengthened royal control over the colonies and improved Spain's strategic position. An important part of his policy had been to abandon old methods, such as the annual treasure fleets. But the efforts to increase royal revenues alienated many local interests in the colonies, and the success of the American Revolution provided a powerful model. Moreover, the new leadership in Spain — King Charles IV and Manuel Godoy — was more prone to disastrous mistakes than Charles III had been.

A great deal more than the Spanish treasure fleets were passing into history as the eighteenth century ended. With the outbreak of the French Revolution in 1789, the world was entering an era of political and economic upheaval that would completely transform the Spanish Empire and much of the rest of the world. The time when the Spanish colonies would revolt and stop sending their silver to Spain was fast approaching. Moreover, an international financial system based on transporting precious metals around the world on wooden sailing ships would soon be an anachronism. The transformation seemed so complete that it was worth wondering if any of the heritage of the treasure fleets would survive in the modern world.

Precious Metals in the World Economy

During the eighteenth century, Europeans encouraged a dramatic increase in the production of precious metals in their colonies, and every year they shipped tons of gold and silver home to the mother countries. Because Europeans used gold and silver in so many different ways, especially in finance, there never seemed to be enough of the precious metals. Early in the eighteenth century, Brazil produced an average of over 10 tons of gold a year and continued to be the world's leading source of the yellow metal. As it became more plentiful, gold, with its high value per unit of weight, became the preferred method of settling most international debts and trade balances in Europe. Because the island kingdom of Britain had a large stake in international commerce but only a small domestic market, it tended to rely more on gold and was moving toward a gold standard.

A large proportion of the new silver coming into Europe in the eighteenth century came from the Spanish colony of New Spain, which had taken over from Peru as the main producer. The mint in Mexico City, which was the largest in the world, was producing as many as 20 million pesos a year in the 1770s, with three-quarters of that total going to Spain to pay for taxes and imports. But because of Spain's negative trade balance, a similar amount, about 15 million pesos a year, was then shipped from Spain to France, the Netherlands, and Britain. Virtually none of the riches from the mines of the Indies remained in Spain. This flood of silver from New Spain, plus the fact that merchants and bankers in Europe usually dealt with shorter distances and smaller amounts of money than their British counterparts, meant that silver was still the predominant form of currency in Europe outside Britain.

The French, as the leading economic power on the continent, had a large domestic market and a relatively small international trade. As a result, France, along with the other continental countries, was effectively on a silver standard by the end of the eighteenth century. Although the English used gold as a standard of value, they also dealt in large amounts of silver, which they earned through the resale of colonial products in Europe and then transported to Asia to help finance their trade there.[31]

Even with the expanded production from New Spain, there was not enough silver to finance both a dynamic economy within Europe and a continuing expansion of world trade. So it became necessary to improve the ability to make payments without transferring precious metals. Paper forms of money and wealth, such as checks, paper currency, bills of exchange, stocks, and bonds were increasingly used in the eighteenth century, especially for large and distant transactions. The natural consequence of this was that a decreasing proportion of financial transfers had to be carried out using coins and bullion. Although there were occasional crises of confidence, the convenience and lower costs of dealing in financial paper outweighed the unquestioned acceptability of the bulky coins and bullion.

Another achievement of the eighteenth century was to expand the use of commercial paper outside Europe. The British, who had shown the way with the Bank of England, were the acknowledged experts in managing financial paper. As other countries followed this model, the use of such paper instruments in international trade grew even faster than the rising production of precious metals in Brazil and New Spain. Sugar, slaves, and tobacco made Atlantic commerce the most dynamic part of the world economy, and this trade was conducted largely through barter and paper instruments, with only limited amounts of cash changing hands.

In another example, the English East India Company brought India within the system of bills of exchange for the first time, reducing the need to send precious metals to settle an unfavorable trade balance with that part of Asia. As a result, imports of reasonably priced, high-quality Indian cotton boomed. International commerce was no longer a matter of shipping a small volume of high-priced goods. Instead, increased supplies and lower prices were making products such as pepper, coffee, tea, sugar, porcelain, and cotton textiles into mass-market items. In dramatic contrast to the situation 300 years before, only the poorest families could not afford items brought halfway across the world, and average people were now participating in the international economy. These expanding markets were discrediting the old tenets of mercantilism, which had assumed that trade involved a fixed and relatively small amount of goods.[32]

Precious metals were still important, however, because they served as the foundation for the system. The reliability of the increasing number of paper instruments was assured by making them readily redeemable in precious metals. Moreover, as noted earlier, gold was still the preferred method of settling trade balances in Europe, while silver remained the everyday currency there. Finally, silver was used to settle large unfavorable trade balances that European countries had with distant areas such as China, the Baltic region, and the Ottoman Empire.[33]

Outside Europe, the precious metals, especially silver, were vital for economic development in many places. Pieces of eight from New Spain and Peru were widely used by the British colonists in North America, where the coins were known as Spanish dollars. The British had not found any large-scale sources of precious metals in their colonies, and authorities in the mother country never sent many coins or authorized a mint. To fill the gap and keep business moving, authorities in London allowed foreign coins to circulate. Many of the pieces of eight minted in the Spanish colonies found their way northward because the British colonies in North America conducted a lively trade with the Caribbean, where pesos were widely used in all the European colonies. On the eve of the American Revolution, about half the coins used in the British North American colonies, some 4 million pesos worth, were pieces of eight from New Spain and Peru. These large sums were insufficient, however, even when combined with the British bills of exchange that were available, and the shortage of money threatened to hold back development of the colonial economy.

In response, the British colonies turned to paper money. Unlike the situation in England, the colonial paper currency was produced in small denominations and was widely used in everyday transactions. Although there was some inflation and doubt about whether it could be redeemed, the practicality of paper money outweighed these considerations. British North America was one of the first regions of the world to use paper money so widely. Once the American Revolution started in 1775, one of the first financial measures of the Continental Congress was to follow this precedent and issue paper money. The new national legislature promised the bills would be redeemed in what most people then considered the standard in reliable currency, pieces of eight.[34]

The greatest single need for silver in the late eighteenth century was for trade with China. European merchants continued to import Chinese luxury products like silk and porcelain, but the truly explosive growth came in the tea trade of the English East India Company. Tea became a popular drink in Europe during the first half of the eighteenth century, and the market for the dried leaves that produced the beverage continued to grow throughout the century.

The huge international trade in tea involved cooperation between two virtual monopolies: China and the English East India Company. China was the only area in the world where tea was produced at that time, and the English East India Company carried most of the tea to Europe. The Chinese exported over 2 million pounds of tea in 1760, 9 million in 1770, and 14 million by 1785. East India Company profits on the tea trade rose in tandem, to the equivalent of about 1 million pesos a year in the 1770s and double that a decade later.

The growth of the tea trade caused a dilemma for the Chinese authorities. Over the years, as the rulers of the Qing dynasty had become more secure, they had relaxed the ban on foreign commerce instituted by their predecessors in the Ming dynasty. As a result, the merchants and the government of China reaped increased profits and taxes from overseas trade. But the growth of the tea trade revived old fears about the negative impact of too much contact with the outside world. To cope with the problem, Chinese officials allowed the trade to expand but tried to retain control by restricting foreign trade to only two ports: Macao for the Portuguese and Canton for the British and all the others.

There was another age-old difficulty that restricted profits and tax revenues from the tea trade for both the Chinese and their Western trading partners: there were virtually no Western products that the Chinese wanted. As a result, Europeans always had a negative trade balance with China and could only afford to acquire as much tea as they could purchase with silver. The faster trade with China grew, the more desperate the Europeans were to find enough silver for both their own domestic use and foreign commerce. Rising production in New Spain and a booming international economy provided only partial relief.

The British, who had the greatest need for silver because of their dominance in the tea trade, could acquire the metal by smuggling goods to the Spanish colonies, where the mines were, or by reselling tea and other colonial products for silver in Europe. But these sources of silver proved insufficient for the growing volume of trade with China.

In the 1760s, 3 million pesos' worth of silver a year was flowing into China to pay for tea and other products. By 1790, shipments of silver from Europe to China had increased to about 7.5 million pesos annually. This latter figure was equivalent to over a third of the silver production of New Spain at that time and almost as much as had come from Peru during the peak years of production at the end of the sixteenth century. As had been the case for centuries, much of the silver shipped internationally was in the form of pieces of eight from the Spanish colonial mints. In the late eighteenth century, so many pesos were coming into China that the chopmarked versions became firmly established as a form of currency, especially in the region around Canton.

One benefit of the massive exports of silver to the Far East was that the expansion in silver output in the Western Hemisphere did not have the same inflationary impact it had had in the sixteenth century, and the eighteenth century was an era of more stable currencies. It was uncertain, however, whether there would continue to be enough silver to finance trade with China as well as to provide much of the basic currency in the Americas and Europe. As a crisis loomed, the British at last solved a centuries-old problem and found something instead of silver that the Chinese wanted and the West could provide.

The crucial product was opium.[35]

Opium smoking had been a minor problem in China since the early eighteenth century, but the great leap in imports came in the 1770s, when the demands on the silver supply were particularly acute. The fighting at sea associated with the American Revolution was disrupting exports of silver from New Spain, and the cash-strapped British government badly needed the taxes it derived from the tea trade.

East India Company officials realized that the conquest of Bengal in the Seven Years' War had given them control of a prime opium-growing region. Because officials in Beijing had decreed that it was illegal to import opium into their country, the British had to smuggle the drug through Canton. Once the opium was in China, British merchants sold it for silver, then used the silver to pay for tea and other products without having to import coins or bullion from the West. Illegal opium sales spurred the legitimate trade in Chinese goods and meant that more taxes were collected by the British government. Through rising profits, Chinese merchants acquired their share of the increased amounts of silver circulating, and Chinese officials took in higher tariffs as well as generous bribes to ignore the smuggling. In short, everyone gained — except for the growing number of opium addicts.[36]

The other major European trading powers were not as involved in the Chinese tea and opium trade as the British, but they still needed large amounts of precious metals, especially silver, for their worldwide commerce. Like the

Chopmarked eighteenth-century peso. Liquidity for the opium trade was provided by chopmarked pieces of eight from the Spanish colonial mints. This example is from the mint in Lima. These coins had long been regarded as a reliable currency in China, but the supply had been erratic. With increased silver production and growth of the tea trade in the late eighteenth century, pesos became available in China in increasing numbers. The high silver content of the 8-reales pieces and the fact that they were widely accepted around the world made them the favorite currency of opium traders. (Photo from the author's collection)

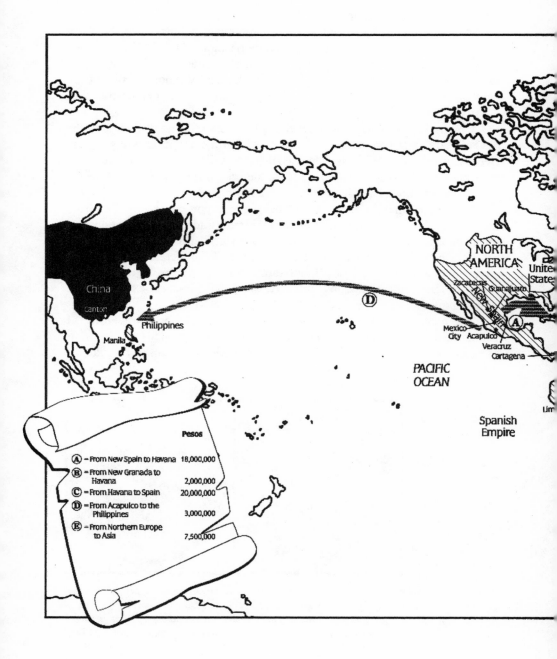

NORTH
AMERICA

United
State

Zacatecas Guanajuato
New Spain

China

Canton

Philippines

Manila

Mexico
City Acapulco

Veracruz

Cartagena

PACIFIC
OCEAN

Lim

Spanish
Empire

	Pesos
Ⓐ = From New Spain to Havana	18,000,000
Ⓑ = From New Granada to Havana	2,000,000
Ⓒ = From Havana to Spain	20,000,000
Ⓓ = From Acapulco to the Philippines	3,000,000
Ⓔ = From Northern Europe to Asia	7,500,000

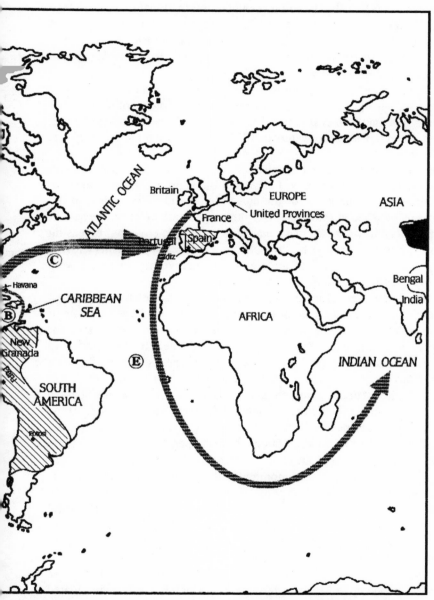

Map 9. The Spanish Empire and Global Flows
of Precious Metals in 1790

British, the Dutch got sizable amounts of silver from the Americas by smuggling. Amsterdam was still an important center of international finance, and the Dutch kept huge sums in silver at the Bank of Amsterdam to support its operations. In the early eighteenth century, the Bank of Amsterdam had over 120 million pesos' worth of silver in its vaults, probably the greatest treasure in one place anywhere in the world.

The Dutch needed about 3.5 million pesos' worth of silver a year for their trade with Asia. But not all their ships carrying cargoes of pieces of eight for the Far East trade reached their destination. Dutch ships with large cargoes of silver coins went down in European waters in 1735 and 1743, and another sank off South Africa in 1747.

Like the English, the Dutch were also active in the trade in naval stores with the Baltic countries. Timber, flax, hemp, and other products from northern Europe were much in demand for the construction and maintenance of the growing fleets of wooden sailing ships. In the eighteenth century, the sale of colonial products, like tobacco and sugar, was helping to cover an increasing proportion of western Europe's traditionally poor balance of payments with the Baltic region. But the amount of trade and the negative trade balance were growing even faster.

Northern and eastern Europe remained poor regions, relative to western Europe, and there was only a small elite who could afford large amounts of exotic goods. With exports from western Europe so limited and demand for naval stores so high, the net amount of the trade deficit skyrocketed to unprecedented amounts. In the 1780s, some 4 million pesos' worth of silver a year went from western Europe to the Baltic to pay for such goods.

The third and last of the major international users of silver from the Spanish colonies was France. Only the French, among the great trading powers of the eighteenth century, earned their silver through legal trade with the Spanish Empire. Although the French international traders operated on a smaller scale than their British counterparts, they still had many uses for the silver they earned from the Spanish colonies. France dominated the Mediterranean trade at this time, and shipped about 2.5 million pesos' worth of silver a year to the Ottoman Empire. In addition, the French sent about 2 million pesos annually to India and China.[37]

The Achievements of the Treasure Fleets

The most striking characteristic of world history in the 400 years after the Atlantic was opened up in 1492 was the extent to which Europeans dominated the rest of the planet through a system of seaborne political and economic linkages between continents. Europeans were able to achieve this unprecedented degree of control because of a number of factors, including a favorable geographic position which gave them access to the sea; a dynamic economy that used a wide range of resources efficiently and supported a growing population; an ability to generate scientific advances and apply them to practical problems; superior organizational skills in business, the military, and government; and the psychological advantage of a culture that valued individuality, competition, rational calculation, and a ruthless energy in pursuit of goals. In the sixteenth century, the Spanish had many, but not all, of these characteristics, and through the tool of the treasure fleets were able to lay the foundations of European dominance.

During the three centuries that the treasure fleets were in operation, the legal production of mines of New Spain, New Granada, and Peru was more than 4 billion pesos' worth of precious metals. This was about 80 percent of the world's silver production and 70 percent of the gold output in an era when precious metals were the most widely accepted international currency. Smugglers brought out additional millions of pesos' worth of unrecorded precious metals, which eventually found their way into the world economy.

The treasure fleets spread this economic lifeblood throughout the globe. Spanish ships carried about 2.5 billion pesos' worth of the total production of precious metals across the Atlantic to Europe, and perhaps 500 million pesos of that was then shipped around Africa and onward to Asia by other trading countries. Of the remaining 1.5 billion pesos, approximately 650 million went directly from Acapulco to the Far East, and 850 million pesos stayed in the Western Hemisphere.[38]

The treasure fleets gave Spain a measure of control over this fabulous wealth for centuries. This system of private vessels regulated by government action was one of the earliest ways in which the Europeans used sea power to establish their influence over virtually the entire planet. It's success was based, to a large extent, on the fleets' ability to elude attackers once the treasure ships were at sea.

Judged by the results, the convoy system was a considerable success at protecting the treasure from seizure. Hostile forces were able to capture or destroy entire fleets on only three occasions: 1628, 1657, and 1702. All these defeats were when the fleets were in or near ports, which was when they were most vulnerable. The treasure fleets were never intercepted on the high seas. Moreover, single ships or parts of convoys carrying treasure were only rarely captured. On land, the main ports, protected by massive fortifications, fell to Spain's enemies only occasionally and none was ever taken permanently. The success of the treasure fleets enabled a poor and backward country like Spain to play an economic, diplomatic, and military role as a great power that was considerably beyond its geographic and demographic resources.

Nonetheless, the system of treasure fleets also had its problems, and in commercial and financial terms it exhibited weaknesses almost from the beginning. The Spanish never found a way to defend successfully their claim to a monopoly of trade with their colonies, and smuggling drained off much of the production of the mines. In time, even the goods legally carried on the fleets came mostly from foreigners. Potential profits were also eaten up by the high costs of the galleons and the fortresses that were essential for protection.

Once the silver and gold reached Spain, most of it was wasted on wars rather than turned into productive investments. The Spanish government became so dependent on the mines of the Indies for income that it fell behind in developing alternative sources of wealth through commerce and industry. Government loans, manufactured goods, and even food had to be obtained abroad, and Spain's colonial wealth flowed out of the country in order to pay for them.

The Spanish reformed the system of the treasure fleets, which was expensive and had only limited flexibility, in the eighteenth century. But this was too late for Spain to re-establish control of the flow of precious metals from America. Despite considerable assets, such as fleets, ports, colonies, and occasionally inspired naval and colonial officials, Spain never became a true commercial nation. As time passed, the Spanish were unable to expand, or even maintain, their initial arsenal of skills, and Spain lost its commanding position.

Spain's loss was Europe's gain. Other Europeans, such as the French, the Dutch, and especially the English, built the banks, trading corporations, and professional navies, that enabled their countries to take control of the flow of precious metals from the Americas and forge a firmer hold on world leadership.

There were a number of factors behind the industrial revolution that began in Europe in the late eighteenth century. These included more productive farming, cheap and convenient transportation by water, a growing middle class, labor-saving inventions, the availability of key raw materials such as coal and iron, and the reorganization of work in factories. But one crucial factor was a reliable and widely available currency, and most of this was either gold and silver from the Spanish and Portuguese colonies in America or paper instruments backed by these precious metals.

An integrated and dynamic economic system, eventually managed by the British, pumped the precious metals from America throughout the world. What the treasure fleets achieved, above all, was to spread the European concept of money to the Western Hemisphere and the Far East. The wider use of European-style money spurred economic growth and brought the maximum amount of resources into play. The result was the foundation of an interlocking global economy that we know today.

Many people improved their lot as a result of this global system, through increased wealth and a better standard of living; many also suffered, through the violence, exploitation, and sometimes outright pillage that it generated. The most intelligent, sensitive, and creative individuals were not always the beneficiaries of a global economy; nor, to be fair, were they always the losers. Therefore, for better or worse, important elements of the world economic system that we take for granted today are due to the success of the Spanish treasure fleets.

6. Rediscovery,
1791-present

lthough the system of periodic treasure fleets came to an end in the late eighteenth century, the main cargo carried on those fleets, silver pieces of eight, continued to play a role in international commerce for more than a century afterward. Other forces set in motion by the treasure fleets, such as the opium trade, also remained an important part of the world economy. As the nineteenth century turned into the twentieth century, however, precious metals from the Americas had less and less impact on the world economy. Latin America lost its position as a leading producer of gold and silver, and the shift to forms of money not based on the precious metals continued. Nonetheless, memories of the riches of the Spanish treasure fleets remained alive in legend and literature, and people continued to wonder about what had happened to the millions of pesos lost at sea during the years the fleets had operated.

Pesos as Currency in the Nineteenth Century
When it became necessary to establish a currency for the new United States of America, attention focused on the pieces of eight because they were readily available and of high quality. The new country had an active domestic and foreign commerce, but there were no large-scale silver or gold mines within the

---

The origin of the dollar sign? The derivation of the symbol used for America's currency is obscure. One theory, based on the widespread use of pieces of eight in the United States in the late eighteenth century, is that the model for the symbol came from part of the design on these Spanish coins. Note, on the reverse of this coin from the Mexico City mint, the ribbon inscribed with the second half of the Habsburg motto, "Plus Ultra," and wrapped around the column on the right. (Photo from the author's collection)

borders of the United States in the 1780s. This meant that in the early years of the United States' existence many foreign coins circulated, and this foreign currency made up much of the new country's money supply. In 1782, Superintendent of Finance Robert Morris noted, "The various coins which have circulated in America have undergone different changes in their value, so that there is hardly any which can be considered as a general standard, unless it be Spanish dollars."

Two years later, Thomas Jefferson, as a delegate to the Congress then acting as a national legislature under the Articles of Confederation, recommended that the new country adopt a coinage system in which the main silver coin would be modeled on the weight and purity of the Spanish peso but divided into multiples of ten, the decimal system, rather than eight. Jefferson's plan, with a few minor changes, was passed by Congress in 1786, and Congress also authorized the founding of a mint.

The government soon became preoccupied with drafting a new constitution, however, and Jefferson's plans for the new dollar did not go into effect. In 1791, Alexander Hamilton, Secretary of the Treasury under the new constitutional government, also proposed that the national currency be based on the Spanish dollar, and this measure was passed in 1792. The new United States dollar contained about the same amount of silver as the peso, but a bit more alloy was added to reduce wear, so the American coin was about the same size as the piece of eight, but the purity was slightly less.[1]

Foreign coins, including pieces of eight, were allowed to circulate as legal

Counterstamped peso issued by the Bank of England. *The counterstamped pesos of 1797 gave rise to numerous witticisms that reflected the unpopularity of the aging King George III, such as, "The Bank to make their Spanish dollars pass/Stamped the head of a fool on the neck of an ass" and "Two kings' heads are not worth a crown." (Photo from the author's collection)*

tender in the United States until 1857, and had a powerful impact on the way Americans thought about money. Quotations of the dollar value of stocks on the New York Stock Exchange, which was founded in 1792, were divided into eight, a system that was used for two centuries. The dollar sign ($) may have come from the symbol the Spanish used in financial records for "pesos," a "P" superimposed on an "S," or from part of the design on the pieces of eight. [2]

Pesos also continued to be an important currency in Europe. In 1797, during the war with revolutionary France, concern in Britain about a possible French invasion led to a run on the Bank of England. The Bank suspended its policy of redeeming its bank notes in gold, and coins began to disappear from circulation. To keep the economy functioning, the bank brought out of its vaults large numbers of pesos that had been captured over the years, counterstamped them with a small portrait of King George III, and issued them as legal tender.

Although the treasury assigned the coins a value slightly more than their intrinsic value, they were still worth less than the somewhat larger crown, the standard large silver coin of the British Isles. Because the counterstamped Spanish coins had value as legal tender in excess of their intrinsic value, it was profitable for counterfeiters to make copies even if they used the same silver content. After a few months, the country was flooded with counterfeits, and the Bank withdrew the counterstamped coins from circulation. [3]

In the early years of the nineteenth century, the output of silver from the Spanish colonies continued to increase, with New Spain producing about 30 million pesos a year. Ironically, just as production was reaching its all-time peak, war and revolution brought the most serious disruption of the flow of silver since the days of Columbus. When Napoleon replaced the Spanish monarch with his own brother in 1808, local leaders in the American colonies stepped into the vacuum left by the collapse of royal authority. The colonists did not throw themselves into the arms of the French during the Napoleonic wars, but they did remember old grievances about Spanish rule and kept their distance from the provisional Spanish government that conducted the resistance to the French. For the first time, the colonies were learning how to get along on their own.

After the Napoleonic wars and the restoration of the Bourbons in 1814, the Spanish government's efforts to regain control over the empire revived memories of the drive to reassert royal power and increase revenues in the eighteenth century. With newly found self-confidence, the colonists were reluctant to accept orders from Spain, and revolutions soon broke out in most of the colonies. As Charles III and other Spanish leaders had feared, the American and French revolutions had provided ideals and models for revolutions against unpopular royal governments. Among the revolutionaries' chief demands was the right to participate freely in the world economy.

Spain was too weak to hold onto its colonies, and one by one they freed themselves. Peru, which had long been a conservative backwater, was one of the last strongholds of the loyalist forces. In 1825, Simón Bolívar, the liberator of much of South America, proclaimed the independence of Peru from the top of the silver mountain at Potosí. This announcement symbolized that Spain's most coveted possession in the colonies, the greatest silver mine in the world, was gone. The loss of Potosí was the end of the Spanish Empire on the mainland of the Western Hemisphere. Only Cuba, Puerto Rico, and the distant Philippines remained under Madrid's control. New Spain became the independent country of Mexico, much of New Granada became Colombia, and a dozen other nations emerged from the ruins of the Spanish Empire in Latin America.[4]

The Spanish colonies' successful fight for independence meant that, after more than four centuries, the shipments of precious metals from the Americas to Spain came to an end. While the conflict with Napoleon was going on, the British navy controlled the Atlantic and kept any of the colonial gold and silver from going to France or Spain. Even after the return of peace, it became clear that, because of the massive disruption of production and shipment, it was impossible to revive large-scale deliveries in the short interval before Spain lost control of the colonies. In 1815, the last of the Manila galleons left Acapulco with a cargo of silver for Asia, and in 1820 the final shipload of silver bound for Spain left Veracruz.

During the Napoleonic wars and the struggle for liberation that followed in the Spanish colonies, Britain was able to establish economic hegemony in Latin America by providing manufactured goods for the populations of the new countries and loans for the revolutionary governments. As a result, most of the sharply reduced shipments of precious metals coming from the mines in Latin America were redirected to London. Stripped of its colonies and the wealth they produced, Spain became a minor country on the fringes of world political and economic developments. Spain continued to mint 8-*reales* coins, albeit in much smaller numbers, until 1848, when the government converted to decimal coinage.[5]

Even after independence, many Spanish traditions remained intact in Latin America, and several of the new countries adopted the peso as their monetary unit. The republican governments changed the designs to reflect their independence, but initially they kept the weight and purity of their silver coins the same as the familiar Spanish pieces of eight so their currencies would be honored in overseas trade. As time passed, however, the countries of Latin America converted to decimal monetary systems and reduced the silver content of their coins, so eventually there was little resemblance to the pieces of eight. Even so, some Latin American countries, such as Colombia and Mexico, continued to call their currency pesos.[6]

Mexico, with its large silver deposits, had one of the greatest stakes in maintaining the traditional stability of the Spanish colonial currency. After the recovery from the disruption of the wars of independence, Mexico again became one of the world's leading silver producers and used its silver pesos to conduct an extensive trade with China. Mexico tried to convert to decimal coinage in 1866, but the Chinese refused to accept the new coins and the Mexican government reverted to coins based on 8 *reales* to the peso in 1873.

In 1905 Mexico went on the gold standard but continued to mint large numbers of silver pesos for the China trade. Until 1914 the weight and fineness of the pesos remained at the standards set in 1772. Mexican mints suspended coinage of precious metals during World War I. Then, between 1918 and 1969, the government succumbed to the temptations of inflation and progressively reduced the silver content of its coins until the peso was made from a copper-nickel alloy and contained no silver at all.[7]

The collapse of most of Spain's empire in the Western Hemisphere was only part of the changes taking place in the nineteenth century. During this period, the conditions that had prevailed when the Spanish treasure fleets sailed changed beyond recognition. Iron vessels with coal-driven steam engines replaced wooden ships and canvas sails. As a result, transportation and war at sea were no longer dependent on the vagaries of winds and currents. Moreover, warships were now completely specialized craft, which meant they no longer closely resembled merchant vessels in appearance and function, as they had in the days of the galleon. On land, railroads were making ground transport of bulk cargoes as efficient, or even more so, than sending goods by sea. Telegraph wires and cables along the seabed made communications almost instantaneous. All these changes linked the continents more closely together. This globally integrated economic system was a process begun by the treasure fleets, but as the integration gathered momentum it made the sailing ships of the treasure fleets an anachronism.

China was where the silver pieces of eight remained in circulation the longest. During the early nineteenth century, the opium trade continued to grow and was probably the largest single sector of the world's commerce at the time. By the early nineteenth century, opium sales had become so huge that, for the first time, one of the fundamentals of international trade since ancient Rome was changing, and silver was flowing out of China. China exported 2 million pesos' worth of silver annually to pay for opium in the 1820s, and by the 1830s it was exporting 9 million pesos a year.

The disruptions caused by the opium trade weakened China and made it easier for the Western powers to fasten their hold on the country. Large flows of silver out of the country meant it was more difficult for the peasants to pay their taxes. Social dislocation, in turn, motivated more people to turn to opium for solace, which further weakened the country and created a vicious downward cycle. Chinese officials insisted that the trade in opium was morally repugnant and should be stopped. But Westerners saw things differently, and insisted that the principles of free trade required that the commerce in opium continue.

The combination of the opium and tea trades had become so lucrative that it was indispensable to the British government, which earned through taxes on tea the equivalent of over 12 million pesos annually, or about half the budget of the Royal Navy. When the Chinese tried to limit trade in opium, the British fought a war in 1841-1842 to establish their right to import whatever they wanted into China. A similar conflict, this time with Britain and France acting as allies, took place in 1856-1860. As the loser in these wars, the Chinese government had to pay huge indemnities in silver and open more ports to Western trade, concessions that only exacerbated China's weakness.

The economic and political troubles of China in the nineteenth century meant that the country was too troubled and subservient to have its own effective currency. During the great Taiping rebellion, in the 1850s and 1860s, the Chinese government debased the traditional coinage so thoroughly that foreign coins, such as the silver pesos, became the only reliable currency. But even the large number of pesos in circulation did not provide enough liquidity for the growing trade with foreigners. This situation prompted China's main commercial partners — Britain, France, the United States, and Japan — to manufacture special silver trade dollars, modeled on the peso, for use in China. In 1890, Chinese provincial governments began minting their own silver dollars, and in a move to assert national identity, the central government began producing almost identical coins 17 years later.

But there were not enough of the new Chinese silver dollars to satisfy demand, and foreign trade dollars and pesos continued to be widely employed. Foreign coins, including old chopmarked coins from Mexico and Peru, circulated in China until the 1930s, when silver went out of use because of wars and civil unrest. Large numbers of the old silver coins ended up in secret hoards,

Chopmarked nineteenth-century pesos. The huge traffic in opium provided a voracious appetite for the pieces of eight that had once been the main cargo of the treasure fleets. These examples came from the Mexico City mint toward the end of Spanish colonial rule. Such coins were the main financial link between two vastly different cultures and economies, the Chinese, who grew tea and smoked opium, and the British, who drank tea and smuggled opium. (Photos from the author's collection)

however, and still appear on the market from time to time.[8]

The most striking contrast between the era of the treasure fleets and the modern world, however, was the changing role of silver and gold in the international economy. As the wilderness of North America became better known in the nineteenth century, it turned out that the continent was an even greater storehouse of precious metals than Central and South America. Coronado had been right about the potential wealth of the area; he just had not been persistent enough in trying to find sources of gold and silver. In fact, the huge new silver discoveries in Nevada and elsewhere in the United States, along with the continued high output from Mexico, resulted in more silver than the international economy could absorb without affecting its value, and silver prices fell dramatically in the late nineteenth century.

At the same time, the volume of foreign trade was becoming so large that it was difficult to use bulky shipments of silver to settle international accounts. Rich discoveries of gold in California and the Yukon, along with other new mines in Australia and South Africa, provided enough of the yellow metal to support a growing global economy. The increased production of gold, with its higher value per unit of weight, help make silver less desirable as a means of financing international trade. Moreover, Britain was the world's greatest trading nation in the nineteenth century, and it had been officially on the gold standard since 1816. The result was that during the nineteenth century, the British gold sovereign, rather than the Spanish peso, became the most widely used international coin.

World production tripled in the decade after the gold rush in California in 1848, and this flood of gold again demonstrated the difficulty of having a monetary standard based on two precious metals, when different levels of production meant the ratio between them was constantly shifting. For centuries, economists, financiers, and international traders had known about the difficulties of trying to maintain a currency standard based on two different precious metals. With the rising supplies of gold, there were renewed calls to change to a system in which only one metal, gold, would be the standard of value.

The debate was especially lively in the United States. On one side were the politicians and mine owners from silver-producing states, who worried that they would face ruin if silver were no longer a monetary metal. The silver lobbyists found ardent allies among the farmers, who hoped an abundant silver currency would mean lower prices and would reduce the burden of their debts. Gold's defenders included the large-scale international bankers and businessmen, who argued that gold was more efficient and that, if the United States were to function effectively in the world economy, it would have to follow the Europeans and adopt the gold standard.

In the 1870s, the supporters of gold won the debate, and the United States and most of Europe adopted the gold standard, which meant their currencies were redeemable in gold and had a fixed exchange rate among them. As a result, silver ceased to be an international monetary metal for most of the world's trade, although it was still widely used domestically. Interestingly enough, Spain, which had once supplied precious metals for the entire world, was too economically weak to accept the discipline required by the gold standard, and never adopted it. The reign of gold was a short one, however, because it became necessary to suspend convertibility of paper money into gold with the start of World War I in 1914. Fitful efforts were made to return to the gold standard but they were never successful for long.

The twentieth century became an era in which the amount of currency in circulation no longer depended upon productivity of gold and silver mines or commercial skill in garnering the precious metals. Instead, governments sought a more practical money supply, which could be created from paper or even electronic impulses, enabling politicians to promote economic and social goals, such as high employment and economic growth.

The United States was the last country to maintain the promise to redeem its paper currency in gold, but even Washington cut the link to gold in 1971. For over 2,000 years the success of a currency had been based on two characteristics: the perceived intrinsic value of its content and a government guarantee of its acceptability. After 1971, only the government guarantee was left.[9]

Even though pieces of eight had gone out of circulation around the world, they remained alive in literature and legend. Jules Verne's Captain Nemo salvaged silver from the bottom of Vigo Bay in *20,000 Leagues under the Sea*, and a pirate's parrot chanted "Pieces of eight, pieces of eight" in Robert Louis Stevenson's *Treasure Island*. Edgar Allan Poe caught the elusive allure of a lost, golden paradise, in the Indies or anywhere else, in his poem, "Eldorado":

Gaily bedight,
A gallant knight,
In sunshine and in shadow,
Had journeyed long,
Singing a song,
In search of Eldorado.

But he grew old—
This knight so bold—
And o'er his heart a shadow
Fell as he found

Proof of El Dorado? *The discovery of this gold object along the shore of a lake in Colombia, just a few years after Poe's death in 1849, caused a sensation. It is a Muisca artifact only eight inches (20 centimeters) long that shows a large figure, which might be a ruler or a god, with smaller attendants on a raft. Is this evidence to prove the tales of a civilization, never discovered by the Spanish, where the ruler covered himself in gold as part of a religious ritual*

conducted on a raft in the middle of a lake? Might the mysterious and wealthy kingdom still exist somewhere in the still poorly known interior of South America? Anthropologists and archaeologists have been skeptical, but the old stories of lost treasure from the days of the conquistadores *continue to have the power to generate curiosity and greed. (Photo courtesy of Robert F. Marx)*

No spot of ground
That looked like Eldorado.
And, as his strength
Failed him a length,
He met a pilgrim shadow—
"Shadow," said he,
"Where can it be—
This land of Eldorado?"

"Over the mountains
Of the moon,
Down the valley of the shadow,
Ride, boldly ride,"
The shade replied,—
"If you seek for Eldorado!"

Just as entertaining, and perhaps more profitable than the fiction about gold and silver, were the real mysteries concerning lost treasure from the Spanish fleets. What had happened to the cargoes of silver and gold that had gone down in the great shipwrecks in the mid-seventeenth century, like the *Atocha*? Had Captain Phips recovered all the treasure from the *Concepción*? Was there still silver strewn across the bottom of Vigo Bay or along the shores of Florida, where whole fleets of treasure-laden galleons had gone down? The Spanish treasure fleets had stopped sailing, but some of their cargoes still existed on the bottom of the ocean and still intrigued people. Most of the interest in lost treasure focused on the waters off Florida, because the channel between Florida and the Bahamas had been the only practical way for sailing ships to leave the Caribbean, and the area's hurricanes had claimed so many victims over the years.

Divers Rediscover the Treasure Fleets
Anyone trying to recover the lost riches of the treasure fleets faces formidable challenges. Spanish ships full of precious metals were lost all over the world, and surviving records of the widely scattered locations of shipwrecks are often imprecise or inaccurate. Even when a potential site is identified, few clues to the exact position of the lost ship remain. Teredos long ago consumed the wood that made up the body of the ship, sand or coral often cover what little is left, and immersion in salt water turns the surface of silver ingots and coins into black sulfide. Before the recent computerization, documents in the Archives of the Indies in Seville were hard to find, and even when vital documents are located,

Files in the Archives of the Indies, Seville. The tens of thousands of legajos, or bundles of documents, in the archives are the main source of information about the treasure fleets. Inside the legajos are important clues about the possible locations of lost treasure, such as ship's manifests and accounts of shipwrecks. Moreover, there is a wealth of information that helps to reconstruct other aspects of daily life in the Spanish Empire. These tons of documents are also a kind of monument to the bureaucrats who meticulously, perhaps too meticulously, chronicled the operation of the empire for hundreds of years. (Photo courtesy of Rob Crandall, The Image Works, Inc.)

they often turn out to be written in an archaic script that is difficult to read.

Nonetheless, there are a few indicators of treasure for those who know what to look for on the ocean bottom. The largest and most obvious sign of a shipwreck from the colonial period is the virtually indestructible mound made up of tons of ballast stones that kept the galleons on an even keel. Moreover, large cannon often retain their general shape, even if covered with corrosion, and the long, straight lines of their barrels are a rarity on the sea floor that can be easily picked out by a skilled observer. Finally, if a searcher gets close enough to see it, gold, in keeping with its reputation for permanence and enchantment, retains its luster even after centuries under water.

Arthur McKee, Jr., a professional diver in Florida who was fascinated by tales of lost Spanish gold and silver, was the first person in the twentieth century to be successful in uncovering the almost-forgotten secrets of the treasure fleets. Beginning in the 1930s, McKee explored the waters of the Florida Keys using

Olive jars recovered from Spanish wrecks. Divers usually find only fragments of pottery jars like these at wreck sites. The jars were used to hold olive oil and other liquids and are a reliable indicator that a wreck probably is Spanish and therefore worth a second look by a treasure hunter. British, Dutch, and French ships, less likely to have a cargo of treasure, did not normally carry this type of container. (Photo courtesy of Robert F. Marx)

a large metal helmet, a full diving suit, and a hose connected to an air source on the surface. The equipment was cumbersome, but it did allow a diver to spend an almost unlimited amount of time on the bottom in the shallow waters where most wrecks occurred.

McKee was the first diver to use compressed air to create suction that could move the tons of sand that had accumulated on top of wrecks over the centuries. He also realized the value of solid research, and sought documents from the Archives of the Indies to help him locate wrecks where there might be treasure. Most of McKee's efforts were focused on the fleet that had gone down in the Florida Keys in 1733, and he was successful in locating several of the wrecks and bringing up some coins and artifacts. Mendel Peterson, from the Smithsonian Institution, helped McKee identify what was brought up and also advised on preservation techniques.

Because the items McKee recovered were within Florida's territorial waters, he had to give the state a 12.5 percent fee to obtain a salvage lease and to establish legal title to what he found. Even though McKee had brought up only a limited amount of gold and silver, publicity about his work touched off a rush of amateur divers, who tore apart the area off Plantation Key in search of treasure. Apparently none of the treasure seekers had done enough research to realize that most of the cargo of precious metals from the 1733 fleet had been salvaged by the Spanish long before. As a result, a potentially valuable archaeological site was ruined with little or no material or scientific gain for anyone. McKee tried to save what he could, and eventually he established a private museum that displayed artifacts from the 1733 fleet and other locations where he had dived.[10]

Another successful professional diver captivated by the treasure fleets was Edward "Teddy" Tucker of Bermuda, who found a Spanish wreck by accident while diving off his home island in the 1950s. Without using elaborate equipment, he was able to carry out the first large-scale recovery of Spanish treasure since Captain Phips' day, almost 300 years before. Tucker brought up cannons, jewelry, coins, bullion, and artifacts, which not only had considerable intrinsic value but also were of great archaeological and historical interest. The Smithsonian's Peterson heard about the discoveries and, as he would on many future occasions involving other divers, offered his assistance.

Like McKee, Tucker had to make an arrangement with the government about the disposition of his find. The upshot of the negotiation was that the Bermuda authorities took full control of everything Tucker salvaged, and he derived no personal profit from his efforts. Tucker turned all the items he salvaged over to Bermuda officials, who put aside some for a museum and then set prices for the sale of the rest.[11]

In the meantime, technology from World War II revolutionized diving methods and dramatically increased the chances of finding and recovering lost treasure. Scuba gear, for example, gave divers more mobility, although it did limit the time they could remain underwater without refilling their air tanks. Another new piece of gear was the magnetometer, which made it possible to locate the iron fittings, like anchors, that were associated with wrecks.

New technology did not solve all the problems of treasure diving, however. The new equipment was expensive, and it soon became clear that a technologically advanced expedition for treasure hunting required a large initial investment without any guarantee that the hunt would be successful. Moreover, the question of the finder's rights to keep any treasure was also unresolved. Even if he was successful, it might be years before a salvor would see any profit after satisfying rival claimants and the tax men. Despite these challenges, the lure of lost treasure was powerful and continued to draw people to the sunken remains of the treasure fleets.

In 1955, an American, John S. Potter, Jr., and a Belgian, Robert Sténuit, led an expedition to Vigo Bay in Spain. They had done extensive archival research on the Battle of Vigo Bay of 1702, and had the most modern equipment available. The two were uncertain about how much treasure remained on the bottom of the bay but hoped it might be a considerable amount. Their effort to bring up treasure was fruitless, however, because the wrecks were widely scattered and covered with deep mud. Potter and Sténuit sadly had to admit that there was probably little gold and silver that could be salvaged, and they concluded that most of the treasure had been removed from the Spanish ships before the battle.

Despite the disappointment, both men were hooked on treasure diving. Sténuit turned his attention to the Armada ships that had been wrecked along the Irish coast in 1588. In 1967, with plenty of research and luck, but little in the way of manpower or equipment, he was able to find coins, cannon, and other artifacts from the wreck of the galleass *Girona*, all of which he donated to the Ulster Museum, in Belfast, Northern Ireland. Work on other Armada wrecks in Ireland continues up to the present day.

Potter, for his part, immersed himself in the history of the treasure fleets. His book, *The Treasure Diver's Guide*, with its detailed information on how to locate and identify wrecks, became a classic reference for the treasure hunter.[12]

These early achievements motivated a whole generation of treasure divers to take advantage of the new underwater technology and to set out in search of treasure. In some ways they were like their sixteenth-century predecessors: fascinated by gold and silver and just as determined to grab control of their share of the wealth that had come from the mines of the Americas. Their true inspiration, however, was feisty Captain Phips rather than the bloodthirsty *conquistadores*.

The first of the large-scale treasure finds was made by Kip Wagner, a Florida building contractor. Wagner had spent years picking up coins that washed up on the Florida beaches after storms, and he often wondered whether they came from a treasure buried on land or from ships that had sunk offshore. In the 1950s, he sent to the Seville archives to find out more about the possible origins of the coins, all of which bore dates of 1715 or earlier. A friend of Wagner's, Kip Kelso, had done considerable research on lost treasure in Florida. He had located a book in the Library of Congress that contained a map showing where the 1715 fleet had smashed ashore south of Cape Canaveral.

Wagner was now convinced that the coins appearing on the beach were from a fleet of treasure ships that had gone down just offshore. In 1959, he organized a group of friends, several of whom were technicians from the nearby space center, into a search team and applied for a salvage lease from the state

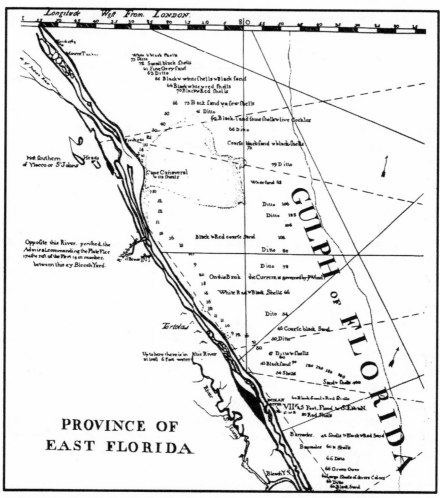

A real treasure map. This map, *from Bernard Romans'* A Concise Natural History of East and West Florida, *published in 1775, provided researcher Kip Kelso with the general location of the 1715 wrecks. Note the inscription, left of center: "Opposite this River, perished the Admiral commanding the Plate Fleet 1715, the rest of the fleet 14 in number, between this & y[e] Bleech Yard." The English often referred to a treasure fleet as "the plate fleet," apparently as a result of a hasty and inaccurate translation of* plata, *the Spanish word for silver. In fact, the fleets rarely carried treasure in the form of silver plate, except for whatever silver tableware the captain, officers, and wealthy passengers might have brought with them. Romans was slightly misinformed about the number of ships lost. There were, in fact, 11 Spanish ships in the 1715 fleet. The "Bleech Yard" is at the bottom of this portion of the map. (Photo from the author's collection)*

of Florida. The authorities in Tallahassee granted the lease in return for a 25 percent share of whatever Wagner and his colleagues found. Working on weekends, Wagner's group, all amateur divers, began a systematic survey.

Their first success was to locate the camp that had been used by the Spanish salvage teams in 1715. Calculating that the wrecks must be near the camp, they began an intensive search. Within a year, as result of luck, persistence, hard work, and appropriate equipment — such as using compressed air to move sand and magnetometers to locate wreck sites — they began to uncover the remains of the 1715 fleet. The coins, jewelry, and artifacts that Wagner and his partners brought up were worth millions of dollars and completely overshadowed the value of what McKee and Tucker had recovered. This was the first truly successful treasure salvage on a grand scale in the twentieth century.

Florida officials, mainly concerned that the state should receive its share of what Wagner and his colleagues recovered, did not get directly involved in either the salvage or the potential scientific aspects of the operation. Instead, they assigned an archaeologist, Carl Clausen, to observe the salvage and assure the accuracy of reports on the amount of treasure recovered. Neither Wagner nor the state government gave top priority to the archaeological potential of the shipwrecks, and valuable scientific material was almost certainly lost in the rush to bring up as much gold and silver as possible.

As Wagner and his colleagues continued their work, it became obvious that the task of salvaging the 1715 treasure fleet could not be handled by the means they had used up to this point. Financing, lawyers, special equipment, and large numbers of professional divers were all needed. To retain control, Wagner's team would have to become professional treasure salvors rather than just weekend hobbyists. They organized themselves as a business, the Real Eight Company, and began a systematic, large-scale salvage of the wrecks. The risks and expense of full-time treasure hunting eventually outweighed the gains, though, and Real Eight went bankrupt in the early 1970s.[13]

Wagner's work generated a tremendous amount of publicity and launched a new phase in the struggle to control the gold and silver of the Americas. Florida officials realized that they had been too lax in supervising Real Eight's work and that irreplaceable historical and archaeological information had been lost. Because of its location astride the exit from the Caribbean, Florida had the most treasure wrecks and the greatest responsibility for protecting them. New legislation was especially important because the regulations covering salvage of treasure were based on admiralty law, which encouraged the recovery of lost cargoes but had no provisions for safeguarding archaeologically important sites.

Proposals for new laws to regulate the salvage of treasure sparked a fierce debate between scholars and treasure hunters. On one hand, academic archaeologists insisted that private individuals could not claim the right to keep items of historical importance and that salvage techniques were often ecologically and archaeologically destructive. When wrecks were discovered, the scholars wanted to protect them until professional scientists could carefully collect and record the artifacts. Moreover, university-trained marine archaeologists believed that coins and other artifacts from wrecks should go to museums, where they would be available to the public.

For their part, the salvors maintained that it was their efforts that led to the discovery of wrecks, and therefore they should have the benefits. They preferred to define the issues in terms of private enterprise, with its commensurate risks and rewards. Treasure divers argued that selling coins or other items recovered from the wrecks, the vast majority of which were not historically or archaeologically unique, was necessary to raise funds for equipment and

Marine archaeologist mapping a wreck site. *Accurate measurement of the location of artifacts before they are removed is an essential part of the archaeological work at a wreck site. Detailed maps help reconstruct the ship and its cargo, as well as the circumstances in which the vessel was destroyed. This diver is using a transit, similar to what surveyors on land use, to establish a theoretical plane of reference as a basis for other measurements. (Photo courtesy of Robert F. Marx)*

personnel. Treasure divers claimed that universities and state governments had done little to locate or catalogue shipwrecks, and that existing lease arrangements and the generosity of salvors already meant that significant amounts of what was recovered went to museums. Florida officials generally came down on the side of the professional marine archaeologists in this debate, and the state legislature passed a variety of laws to regulate treasure hunting.

In the meantime, another important series of Spanish wrecks had been located in Texas, and officials there took a very different approach from their counterparts in Florida. In 1967, treasure hunters from out of state found the location of one of the ships that had been lost off Padre Island in 1554, and took valuable artifacts home with them. The incident generated considerable publicity as well as concern that the oldest known shipwrecks in the waters of the United States, an important part of Texas history, might be lost to the public. State authorities immediately stopped further private salvage at Padre Island and managed to get the artifacts returned to Texas.

In 1969, the Texas legislature passed a strict law to control future treasure

Diver's dream, archaeologist's nightmare. Although well-equipped treasure-hunting expeditions were beyond the means of most divers, it was still possible for amateurs, with more limited resources, to find and remove treasure. It is virtually impossible for authorities who are responsible for safeguarding wreck sites to stop such small-scale looting. (Photo courtesy of Robert F. Marx)

hunting, and the state set up its own organization, the Texas Antiquities Commission, to conduct archaeological work at Padre Island and other sites. The Institute of Nautical Archaeology, affiliated with Texas A&M University, became a leader in protecting and exploring sites that are important for nautical archaeology. Professor George F. Bass, from the institute, joined Peterson from the Smithsonian and a growing group of scholars in calling for a more scientific approach to dealing with shipwrecks.[14]

Not everyone agreed with the Texas approach, with its intense involvement on the part of the government and academics, and a whole generation of eager private treasure hunters preferred the methods used in the salvage of the 1715 fleet. Robert Marx, an underwater archaeologist, was one of the earliest and most active of the independent operators.

Marx was first attracted by the adventure of searching for lost underwater treasure, but in time he also became captivated by the history of the fleets. Unlike most other divers, he liked to do his own research, in Seville and other storehouses of information about the treasure fleets. Since the early 1950s, Marx had been discovering Spanish treasure ships, and in 1960 he began a systematic effort to locate the *Maravillas*, which had sunk 300 years before and was one of the richest lost treasures on record. He also spent more than three years working on the underwater excavation at Port Royal, Jamaica, the notorious smugglers' port that had sunk into the sea during an earthquake in 1692.

In 1968, Marx went to work for Real Eight, served as director of operations, and gained valuable experience in search and salvage techniques. But it was the *Maravillas* that continued to haunt him. One of Marx's favorite tools in his search for the lost galleon was the magnetometer, but research revealed that the cannon of the *Maravillas* had been bronze and so would produce no reading on the magnetometer, which detected only the presence of iron.

Like many other divers, Marx eventually found that his big break came by accident. In 1972, he pulled up ballast stones in the anchor of his search vessel and found that inadvertently he had been sitting right on top of the wreck of the *Maravillas*. Over a period of several months he was able to recover many coins and artifacts from the *Maravillas*, but disputes with rival treasure hunters and the Bahamian government kept him from recovering all the treasure. Marx ruefully acknowledges that most of the profits from his treasure hunting expeditions have gone to lawyers, outfitters, and bureaucrats and that the only way he has been able to make any real money from treasure hunting is through the many books he has written on the subject.[15]

Herbert Humphreys, Jr., a successful businessman from a prominent Memphis family, picked up where Marx had left off in the effort to salvage the

Divers at work on wreck sites. *Large objects containing iron, such as anchors and some cannon, can be readily located with magnetometers. This is one of the best techniques for pinpointing a sunken wreck. (Photos courtesy of Robert F. Marx)*

Maravillas. Humphreys had long been fascinated by underwater wrecks and had already successfully salvaged an eighteenth-century British warship. He heard about the *Maravillas* and founded his own company, Marine Archaeological Research, to conduct a more systematic effort to recover any riches in the wreck.

Using modern equipment and skilled divers, Humphreys was able to relocate the site where the ship went down. Moreover, he was shrewd and patient about protecting his interests and negotiated a salvage lease with the Bahamian government in 1986, which enabled him to recover treasure from the site in return for a 25 percent share.[16]

In 1976, Burt Webber, a professional treasure diver with little to show for his years of work, decided he needed to take a different approach. He had started out working with McKee and then had spent more than a decade making futile, small-scale searches all over the Caribbean for treasure wrecks, such as the fabled *Atocha* and his favorite target, the *Concepción*, which had sunk north of Hispaniola in 1641. Webber believed that Phips was right in his claims that there was still plenty of treasure to be recovered from *Concepción*. Jacques Cousteau and a number of other well-known divers had searched for the *Concepción*, but all had failed.

To be successful in finding the wreck, Webber believed he would have to organize financing, research, and legal work along the lines of a modern business. He and a group of associates set up a company called Seaquest International, raised $450,000 in working capital, and patiently worked to obtain the backing of the government of the Dominican Republic. The Dominicans agreed to support his claims in return for a 50 percent share, far more than even Philip II would have expected.

Seaquest followed what had become the classic recipe for successful treasure hunting by beginning with a search of the records at the archives in Seville. Then Webber and his associates applied high technology, such as aerial photographic surveys and magnetometers, to the problem.

After two years of failure, Webber got a lucky break when British author Peter Earle tipped him off about the location of Phips' log in a British archive. The log provided the more precise locating data Webber needed to narrow the search area. He designed a sensitive and submersible magnetometer that enabled him to locate the wreck precisely, despite the coating of coral that had hidden it from previous searchers. In 1978, Webber and his team found the remains of the *Concepción*; eventually they recovered more than 60,000 coins from the site.[17]

Not every government in the Caribbean was as cooperative with treasure hunters as those of the Bahamas and the Dominican Republic. Mexico, for instance, insisted that 100 percent of whatever was recovered in its waters had to be turned over to the government. Much of the underwater archaeological work along the coasts of Mexico was done by a Mexican diving club, known by its English initials CEDAM (Conservation, Exploration, Diving, Archaeology, and Museums). CEDAM was an avid proponent of careful scientific handling of wreck sites, and donated what it brought up from wrecks (such as the *Nuestra Señora de los Milagros*, which had gone down in 1741) to the club's Underwater Archaeological Museum in Mexico City. In 1967, CEDAM established an affiliate in the United States.

All of these expeditions were successes, but one prize that still eluded treasure hunters was the *Atocha*, the galleon that had gone down in the Florida Keys in 1622. The *Atocha* was famous in treasure-diving circles not only because of its large cargo of 1 million pesos' worth of coins and ingots, but also because, unlike most other wrecks, it had never been previously salvaged, and its large cargo was believed to be intact. Mel Fisher, one of the pioneers of scuba diving, had caught the treasure-hunting bug in the 1950s, and later went to work for Real Eight. He had looked for the *Concepción*, but Webber had found it first. In the 1960s, both Fisher and Webber turned their attention to the legendary, unspoiled wreck of the *Atocha*, and Fisher was determined that he would not be beaten again.

To increase the odds in favor of success, Fisher made use of a varied and talented team of assistants as well as some creative techniques. Eugene Lyon, a Florida historian who had mastered the old script used in the Spanish colonial records, spent years looking for information in the Archives of the Indies and helped Fisher determine the general area to search. Lyon's key contribution was to uncover that the names used to describe the Florida Keys had changed over the years. He advised a search based on seventeenth-century nomenclature rather than names used on twentieth-century maps.

To counter criticism that his methods disturbed valuable archaeological sites, Fisher hired a professional underwater archaeologist, Duncan Mathewson, to give scientific credibility to his work. Mathewson made strenuous efforts to ensure that enthusiastic divers did not destroy the archaeological value of the sites they were exploring. His careful mapping of the location of recovered artifacts revealed a trail that showed the direction in which the wind had pushed the stricken ship during its last journey. Fay Feild, a skilled electronics engineer, designed an improved magnetometer for underwater use, which also helped the search.

Once a promising site was identified, Fisher used a technique that he himself had developed: diverting the prop wash from the outboard motors of his search vessels down to the bottom. This involved using a large bent pipe, nicknamed the "mailbox," to produce a column of pressurized water. The diverted prop wash not only cleared away the sand that had accumulated over potential wreck sites, but also provided divers with clear water in which to work.

After more than a decade of effort, Fisher had recovered small amounts of treasure and artifacts, but there were still no signs of the main wreck. 1973 brought an important breakthrough, when Fisher's team discovered a silver bar with the usual Spanish markings, including a serial number. Lyon's research had turned up the *Atocha's* cargo manifest, which verified that the ingot was from the *Atocha*. At last the searchers, now incorporated as Treasure Salvors, appeared to be on the right track. As the search dragged on, four lives, including Fisher's own son and daughter-in-law, were lost through accidents.

Finally, in 1985, Fisher located the main wreck site and found that it contained over 30 tons of silver (969 ingots and over 160,000 coins), 200 pounds of gold in a variety of forms (including chains, coins, and ingots in various sizes and shapes), plus emeralds, jewelry, and thousands of artifacts. Nearby, Fisher's crew found a diver's spear, indicating that some anonymous sport diver had unknowingly come within a few yards of the fabulous treasure.

Like other salvors, Fisher found that competitors and state authorities, who had been indifferent to his work when it was producing no results, quickly took interest once success was assured. After a lengthy series of legal battles, Fisher was able to establish his right to most of the treasure of the *Atocha*.[18]

Although most of the Spanish wrecks, and therefore most of the salvage operations, have been in Florida waters, there have been important finds of ships' cargoes containing pieces of eight around the world. In 1963, local divers located the wreck of the *Vergulde Draeck*, a Dutch ship which had gone down in 1656 off the west coast of Australia. The following year, the Australian parliament passed legislation giving the government control over wreck sites, and authorities took over responsibility for recovery and preservation of the treasure and other artifacts from the *Vergulde Draeck*. (See frontispiece.) Another important discovery was in 1971, when English divers found the site off the Scilly Isles where the *Hollandia*, another Dutch ship bound for the Far East with a cargo of pieces of eight, had sunk in 1743.[19]

But with all their successes, the professional treasure divers like Fisher, Webber, and Marx have not located all the lost ships of the Spanish treasure fleets. A number of well-documented wrecks, with cargoes worth millions of dollars, remain to be found, including:

- The *La Magdalena*, which sank off Cape Canaveral, Florida, in 1573.
- The ships from the 1591 fleet that were destroyed by a storm in the Azores. Most of the treasure was salvaged shortly after the sinkings, but the loss was so large that a considerable amount should still remain.

Coins recovered from Spanish wrecks.
(Photos from the author's collection)

A Mexico City 2 reales *from the 1554 fleet*

A Potosi 8 reales *from the* Atocha

A Mexico City 8 reales *from the* Concepción

A Mexico City 8 reales *from the* Maravillas

A Mexico City 8 reales *from the 1715 fleet*

- The two ships captured by Dutch Admiral Heyn that went down in a storm off Grand Bahama Island in 1629. Some coins were found in 1965, but the bulk of the cargo remains on the bottom.
- The *San José*, sunk by the British off Cartagena in 1708. This is probably the largest single treasure that remains to be discovered.
- The *Carmen*, which went down in the open Caribbean south of Kingston, Jamaica, in 1730. Only half the cargo was salvaged at the time. McKee has worked this wreck, but large amounts of silver probably remain at the site.
- The ships of the 1750 fleet that were destroyed by a storm off Cape Hatteras, North Carolina.
- The Manila galleons that went down in the Pacific. A few have recently been salvaged, but a handful, each with 1 million pesos or more on board, are still waiting to be discovered.
- The numerous ships that sank off the main ports of the treasure fleets, including Veracruz and the mouth of the Quadalquivir River.

The mints no longer produce pieces of eight and the galleons no longer sail, but the history of the Spanish treasure fleets still exerts a fascination. If some elements of the story seem familiar, such as empires exhausting themselves through military spending, events on one continent having an effect on other continents thousands of miles away, debates over the role of government in the economy, and an intractable international drug trade, it is because our global political and economic system originated with the Spanish treasure fleets.

It is a system that has brought unprecedented prosperity to some parts of the world. But there is also a dark side to the story of the treasure fleets and the interconnected world system that took shape in their wake. The benefits of the global economic system have not been evenly distributed, and in both the past and the present, the heritage of the treasure fleets has included more than a little greed, ambition, and foolishness. Because large amounts of treasure remain to be found, the story of the Spanish treasure fleets is still unfolding; undoubtedly coming chapters will contain many of the same elements of greatness and folly that characterized earlier phases of the struggle to control the precious metals of the Western Hemisphere.

appendix a

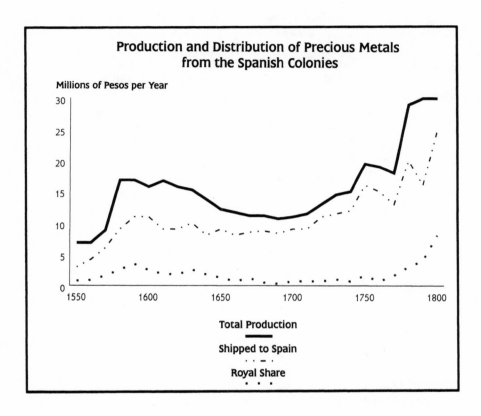

Production and Distribution of Precious Metals
from the Spanish Colonies

Millions of Pesos per Year

Total Production

Shipped to Spain

Royal Share

appendix B

Silver Content of Selected Coins
(figures have been rounded off)
1 troy ounce = 31.1 grams

	Date Minted	Gross Weight	Fineness	Net Silver Content
Spanish 8 *reales*				
	1497-1642	27.5 grams	.930	25.5 grams
	1642-1707	22	.930	20.3
	1707-1728	27.5	.917	25.2
	1728-1772	24	.833	20
	1772-1848	27	.812	22
Mexican 8 *reales*				
	1573-1728	27.5	.930	25.5
	1728-1772	27	.917	24.7
	1772-1914	27	.903	24.4
United States dollar				
	1794-1935	27	.900	24.3
Chinese dollar				
	1907-1934	27	.900	24.3

Dutch *Rijksdaalder*
(a trade coin widely used in the Baltic and the Far East)

	Date Minted	Gross Weight	Fineness	Net Silver Content
	1606-1700	27	.875	23.75

Austrian "Maria Theresa" taler
(a popular trade coin in the Middle East)

	Date Minted	Gross Weight	Fineness	Net Silver Content
	1781-1975	28	.833	23.3

appendix c

Resource Guide

Museums containing artifacts from the treasure fleets:
- The Corpus Christi Museum of Science and History in Texas displays the results of the archaeological work on the 1554 fleet.
- The St. Lucie County Historical Museum in Fort Pierce, Florida, has artifacts from the 1715 fleet. Additional treasure from 1715 is at the visitors' center at the Sebastian Inlet State Recreation Center in Vero Beach.
- The Museum of Florida History in Tallahassee has exhibits of some of the state of Florida's share of the various treasures found in Florida waters.
- Items from the *Atocha* are on display in two museums in Florida operated by Mel Fisher: his Maritime Heritage Society Museum in Key West and the Mel Fisher Center in Sebastian. More items from the *Atocha* are at the Treasures of the Sea Exhibit at the Delaware Technical and Community College in Georgetown, Delaware.
- Kimbell's Caribbean Shipwreck Museum, in Key Largo, Florida, contains material recovered from Florida and Caribbean wrecks.
- The Maritime Museum in Bermuda has items brought up by Tucker.
- The Museum of the Royal Houses in Santo Domingo, Dominican Republic, displays treasure from the *Concepción*.
- George Town, in the Cayman Islands, has two exhibits: the Cayman Maritime and Treasure Museum, with items found by Humphreys, and McKee's Treasure Museum, containing what is left of Art McKee's collection.
- The Ulster Museum, in Belfast, Northern Ireland, contains items from the *Girona* donated by Sténuit.

Book dealers specializing in works on the Spanish treasure fleets

Florida Classics Library
P.O. Box 1657
Port Salerno, FL 34992

Spyglass Publications
308-B West Marion Street
Chattahoochee, FL 32324

Organizations involved in maritime history and nautical archaeology

CEDAM International
One Fox Road
Croton-on-Hudson, NY 10520

Institute of Nautical Archaeology
P.O. Drawer AU
College Station, TX 77840

National Maritime Historical Society
5 John Walsh Blvd.
P.O. Box 68
Peekskill, NY 10566

Glossary of spanish terms

Asiento, "contract," was the way in which the Spanish government, with its limited manpower, conducted much of its business until the eighteenth century. Under royal supervision, private individuals performed some of the functions of government in return for cash payments and privileges. In the case of the treasure fleets, contractors provided services such as outfitting the ships and minting the coins that made up the cargo. The government also raised money through loan contracts, and much of the cargo of the fleets went to repaying these loans.

Avería, "average," was the tax levied on the cargo of the treasure fleets to pay for their protection. The tax was usually about 2 percent in the sixteenth century, although it could be three times that in time of war. By the seventeenth century, with the foreign threat to the treasure fleets increasing, it was sometimes 30 percent or more. Naturally, such a high tax rate discouraged legitimate trade and provided huge incentives for smuggling.

Casa de Contratación, or House of Trade, was located in Seville from 1503 to 1717 and in Cadiz from 1717 to 1790. It was the main government agency for supervising operation of the treasure fleets.

Consulado, or Merchants' Guild, was the organization that assisted in the administration of the fleets and also acted as the merchants' lobby at the royal court. It was made up of the businessmen who provided goods and services for the treasure fleets.

Escudo, "shield," was the basic Spanish denomination for gold coins. The double *escudo* was originally known as a doubloon, but eventually this term was loosely applied to all Spanish gold coins, which were minted in denominations of 1, 2, 4, and 8 *escudos*.

Juro, "annuity," was one of the Spanish government's chief sources of revenue. Private individuals loaned the crown a sum of money and then received interest back as a lifelong source of income.

Peso, "weight." Before the mints were established, there were few coins in circulation in the Spanish colonies. Payments were made with lumps of gold and silver of various weights and purity. After mints were established, coins became much more popular for payments because they had a uniform weight and purity. The standard silver coin, the 8 *reales* or piece or eight, which weighed one Spanish ounce, became known as the peso.

Quinto, "fifth," was the royal share of the precious metals that came from the mines. By law, all subsurface minerals belonged to the crown, but in practice, the government allowed private individuals to operate the mines in return for a 20 percent royalty.

Real, "royal," was the basic denomination for Spanish silver coinage. The largest silver coin was 8 *reales*, or the piece of eight, and there were also coins of 1/2, 1, 2, and 4 *reales*. This term is not to be confused with "royals," which is what numismatists call exceptionally high-quality cobs struck in limited numbers for presentation purposes.

Vellón, or Spanish copper coinage, was used for small transactions. Originally, the coins also included some silver, but in the seventeenth century the government reminted them without the silver but with their old face value. This contributed to inflation and was especially burdensome for the poor, who were the main users of small-denomination copper coins.

Zabra, also known as *gallizabra*, was a small, fast, and heavily armed ship, which carried treasure and traveled alone or in small groups. These were an alternative to the large and slow galleons of the treasure fleets.

notes

Chapter 1. Conquest 1492-1544

1. J.H. Parry, *The Discovery of the Sea* (Berkeley: University of California Press, 1981), pp. 17-23; Carlo M. Cipolla, *Guns, Sails, and Empires: Technological Innovations and the Early Phases of European Expansion, 1400-1700* (New York: Minerva Press, 1965), pp. 76-80; Fernand Braudel, *The Mediterranean and the Mediterranean World in the Age of Philip II*, 2 vols., translated by Sian Reynolds (New York: Harper & Row, 1972-1973), vol. I, pp. 299-300; J.H. Elliott, *Imperial Spain, 1469-1716* (New York: St. Martin's, 1964), pp. 27-31, 36-42; Richard W. Unger, ed., *Cogs, Caravels, and Galleons: The Sailing Ships, 1000-1650* (Annapolis: Naval Institute Press, 1993), *passim*; Roger C. Smith, *Vanguard of Empire: Ships of Exploration in the Age of Columbus* (New York: Oxford University Press, 1992), *passim*.

2. John Lynch, *Spain under the Habsburgs*, 2 vols., 2d ed. (New York: New York University Press, 1981), vol. I, pp. 156-158; James Lang, *Conquest and Commerce: Spain and England in the Americas* (New York: Academic Press, 1975), pp. 11-12; Elliott, *Imperial Spain*, pp. 31-34, 55-60.

3. Pierre Vilar, *A History of Gold and Money, 1450-1920*, translated by Judith White (London: NLB, 1976), pp. 69-74; Alan K. Smith, *Creating a World Economy: Merchant Capital, Colonialism, and World Trade, 1400-1825* (Boulder: Westview Press, 1991), pp. 54-56; Parry, *Discovery of the Sea*, pp. 30-34, 63-66, 145-150.

4. Angus McKay, *Money, Prices, and Politics in Fifteenth Century Castile* (London: Royal Historical Society, 1981), pp. 25-36; Immanuel Wallerstein, *The Modern World-System*, 3 vols. (New York: Academic Press, 1974-1989), vol. I, pp. 168-169; Frank C. Spooner, *The International Economy and Monetary Movements in France, 1493-1725* (Cambridge, Mass.: Harvard University Press, 1972), pp. 10-17; Harry A. Miskimin, *The Economy of Later Renaissance Europe, 1460-1600* (Cambridge: Cambridge University Press, 1977), pp. 32, 154; Joe Cribb, ed., *Money: From Cowrie Shells to Credit Cards* (London: British Museum Publications, 1986), p. 134; Richard Doty, *Money of the World* (New York: Grosset & Dunlap, 1978), p. 138; Vilar, *History of Gold and Money*, p. 62; Parry, *Discovery of the Sea*, pp. 74-79.

5. Earl J. Hamilton, *American Treasure and the Price Revolution in Spain, 1501-1650* (Cambridge, Mass.: Harvard University Press, 1934. Reprint. New York: Octagon Books, 1970), pp. 48-51; W.A. Shaw, *The History of Currency, 1252-1896*. 2d ed. (New York: G.P. Putnam's Sons, 1896. Reprint. New York: Augustus M. Kelley, 1967), pp. 328, 340.

6. Ralph Davis, *The Rise of the Atlantic Economies* (Ithaca: Cornell University Press, 1973), pp. 242-245; Charles P. Kindleberger, *A Financial*

History of Western Europe (London: George Allen & Unwin, 1984), p. 39.

7. Joe Cribb, et. al., *The Coin Atlas: The World of Coinage from Its Origins to the Present Day* (New York: Facts on File, 1990), pp. 136-137, 172-175; Smith, *Creating a World Economy*, pp. 23-30; Parry, *Discovery of the Sea*, pp. 71-74.

8. Yang Lien-Sheng, *Money and Credit in China: A Short History* (Cambridge, Mass.: Harvard University Press, 1952), pp. 5, 63-67; John King Fairbank, *China: A New History* (Cambridge, Mass.: Harvard University Press, 1992, pp. 134-137; Doty, *Money*, pp. 13, 35-37, 58; Cribb, *Money*, pp. 41, 122, 163.

9. Colin George Simkin, *The Traditional Trade of Asia* (London: Oxford University Press, 1968), pp. 142-145; Smith, *Creating a World Economy*, p. 30; Fairbank, *China*, pp. 137-139.

10. Carl O. Sauer, *The Early Spanish Main* (Berkeley: University of California Press, 1966), pp. 23-25, 138; Bailey W. Diffie, *Latin American Civilization: Colonial Period* (New York: Octagon Books, 1967), p. 142; Columbus, Christopher, *The Log of Christopher Columbus*, translated by Robert H. Fuson (Camden, Maine: International Marine Publishing, 1987), *passim*; Vilar, *History of Gold and Money*, pp. 63-64.

11. Samuel Eliot Morison, *Admiral of the Ocean Sea: A Life of Christopher Columbus* (Boston: Little, Brown and Co., 1942), p. 434.

12. Robert F. Marx, *Shipwrecks in the Americas*, rev. ed. (New York: Dover Publications, 1987), p. 367; Sauer, *Early Spanish Main*, pp. 104-106, 122; Morison, *Admiral of the Ocean Sea*, pp. 589-590.

13. C.H. Haring, *The Spanish Empire in America* (New York: Harcourt Brace & World, 1947), p. 11; Sauer, *Early Spanish Main*, pp. 197-198; Vilar, *History of Gold and Money*, pp. 66-67.

14. Sauer, *Early Spanish Main*, pp. 232-235.

15. William H. Prescott, *History of the Conquest of Mexico* and *History of the Conquest of Peru* (New York: Modern Library, 1930), pp. 164-166, 198-199.

16. John Hemming, *The Search for El Dorado* (New York: E.P. Dutton, 1978), p. 18; André Emmerich, *Sweat of the Sun and Tears of the Moon: Gold and Silver in Pre-Columbian Art* (Seattle: University of Washington Press, 1965), p. xx.

17. C.H. Haring, *Trade and Navigation Between Spain and the Indies in the Time of the Hapsburgs* (Gloucester, Mass.: P. Smith, 1964), pp. 69-71; A.P. Newton, *The European Nations in the West Indies, 1493-1688* (New York: Barnes and Noble, 1933), pp. 48-49, 57; Hamilton, *American Treasure*, p. 34.

18. Alberto F. Pradeau, *Numismatic History of Mexico: From the Pre-*

Columbian Epoch to 1823 (New York: Sanford J. Durst, 1978), pp. 23-36; Robert I. Nesmith, *The Coinage of the First Mint of the Americas at Mexico City, 1536-1572* (New York: American Numismatic Society, 1955), *passim*; Haring, *Spanish Empire*, pp. 244-245; Vilar, *History of Gold and Money*, p. 138.

19. Roger B. Merriman, *The Rise of the Spanish Empire in the Old World and the New*, 4 vols. (New York: Macmillan, 1918-1923), vol. III, pp. 562-567; F. A. Kirkpatrick, *The Spanish Conquistadores* (London: Adam and Charles Black, 1934), pp. 163-164; John Hemming, *The Conquest of the Incas* (New York: Harcourt Brace Jovanovich, 1970), pp. 73, 89, 565; Louis B. Wright, *Gold, Glory, and the Gospel: The Adventurous Lives and Times of the Renaissance Explorers* (New York: Atheneum, 1970), p. 229; Prescott, *Conquest of Peru*, pp. 947-948, 965-968, 995, 1008-1010; Vilar, *History of Gold and Money*, p. 116; Hamilton, *American Treasure*, p. 34.

20. Prescott, *Conquest of Peru*, pp. 957-958, 1103; Kirkpatrick, *Spanish Conquistadores*, pp. 194, 251.

21. Merriman, *Rise of Spanish Empire*, vol. III, pp. 578-586; Hemming, *Search for El Dorado*, pp. 70-96; Kirkpatrick, *Spanish Conquistadores*, pp. 313-325; Wright, *Gold, Glory, and the Gospel*, pp. 258-259.

22. Hemming, *Search for El Dorado, passim*; Wright, *Gold, Glory, and the Gospel*, pp. 262-263.

23. Paul E. Hoffman, *The Spanish Crown and the Defense of the Caribbean, 1535-1585* (Baton Rouge: Louisiana State University Press, 1980), pp. 20-21; Newton, *European Nations in the West Indies*, pp. 51-52; Haring, *Spanish Empire*, p. 304; Haring, *Trade and Navigation*, pp. 71, 201, 232-234; Hamilton, *American Treasure*, p. 34.

24. Haring, *Spanish Empire*, p. 7; Morison, *Admiral of the Ocean Sea*, pp. 368-373.

25. H.G. Koenigsberger, *The Habsburgs and Europe, 1516-1660* (Ithaca: Cornell University Press, 1971), pp. 20-23.

26. Karl Brandi, *The Emperor Charles V: The Growth and Destiny of a Man and of a World Empire*, translated by C.V. Wedgwood (London: Jonathan Cape, 1939), pp. 461-465; R. Trevor Davies, *The Golden Century of Spain, 1501-1621* (New York: Harper & Row, 1937), p. 81; Vilar, *History of Gold and Money*, p. 74; Lynch, *Spain*, vol. I, p. 41; Elliott, *Imperial Spain*, pp. 175, 198; Koenigsberger, *Habsburgs and Europe*, pp. 37-38.

27. Richard Ehrenberg, *Capital and Finance in the Age of the Renaissance*, translated by H.M. Lucas (New York: Harcourt Brace, 1928), p. 95; Henry Kamen, *Spain 1469-1714: A Society in Conflict* (London: Longman, 1983), pp. 49, 89; Lynch, *Spain*, vol. I, pp. 61-63.

28. Braudel, *Mediterranean*, vol. I, pp. 480-481; Wallerstein, *Modern World-System*, vol. I, pp. 173-176; Lynch, *Spain*, vol. I, pp. 288-289; Cipolla, *Guns, Sails, and Empires*, p. 36.

29. Merriman, *Rise of Spanish Empire*, vol. III, pp. 196-197; Haring, *Trade and Navigation*, p. 170; Vilar, *History of Gold and Money*, pp. 148-149; Brandi, *Emperor Charles V*, p. 465.

30. J.H. Parry, *The Spanish Seaborne Empire* (New York: Knopf, 1966), pp. 56-57; Hamilton, *American Treasure*, p. 14.

31. Ruth Pike, *Enterprise and Adventure: The Genoese in Seville and the Opening of the New World* (Ithaca: Cornell University Press, 1966), p. 20; Parry, *Spanish Seaborne Empire*, pp. 54-56.

32. Antonio Dominguez Ortiz, *The Golden Age of Spain, 1516-1659*, translated by James Casey (New York: Basic Books, 1971), p. 30.

33. Haring, *Spanish Empire*, pp. 95-100; Merriman, *Rise of Spanish Empire*, vol. III, pp. 619-621.

34. Robert S. Smith, *The Spanish Guild Merchant: A History of the Consulado, 1250-1700* (Durham: Duke University Press, 1940), pp. 95-96; Parry, *Spanish Seaborne Empire*, p. 125; Haring, *Trade and Navigation*, p. 137; Pike, *Enterprise*, pp. 9-11.

35. John R. McNeill, *Atlantic Empires of France and Spain: Louisbourg and Havana, 1700-1763* (Chapel Hill: University of North Carolina Press, 1985), pp. 46-50, 78; Haring, *Spanish Empire*, p. 293.

Chapter 2. Consolidation, 1545-1579

1. Arthur F. Zimmerman, *Francisco de Toledo, Fifth Viceroy of Peru* (Caldwell, Ohio: Caxton Printers, 1938), p. 131; Arthur P. Whitaker, *The Huancavélica Mercury Mine* (Westport, Conn.: Greenwood Press, 1941), pp. 9, 18-19; D.A. Brading, *Miners and Merchants in Bourbon Mexico, 1763-1810* (Cambridge: Cambridge University Press, 1971), p. 138; Eric Wolf, *Europe and the People Without History* (Berkeley: University of California Press, 1982), p. 136; Hemming, *Conquest of the Incas*, pp. 372, 405-408; Vilar, *History of Gold and Money*, pp. 121.

2. Haring, *Spanish Empire*, pp. 258-260; Hamilton, *American Treasure*, pp. 15-17.

3. Vilar, *History of Gold and Money*, p. 138; Doty, *Money*, pp. 161-163; Cribb, *Money*, p. 134.

4. Bartolomé Arzans de Orsua y Vela, *Tales of Potosí*, translated by Frances M. Lopez-Morillas (Providence: Brown University Press, 1975), pp. xiii-xiv; Zimmerman, *Francisco de Toledo*, pp. 132-133, 175.

5. Philip W. Powell, *Soldiers, Indians, and Silver: The Northward Advance*

of New Spain, 1550-1660 (Berkeley: University of California Press, 1969), pp. 10-11.

6. Davis, *Rise of Atlantic Economies*, p. 50; Diffie, *Latin American Civilization*, pp. 371-373.

7. J.F. Richards, ed. *Precious Metals in the Later Medieval and Early Modern Worlds* (Durham, N.C.: Carolina Academic Press, 1983), p. 409; Hamilton, *American Treasure*, p. 34; Miskimin, *Economy of Later Renaissance Europe*, p. 39.

8. Wright, *Gold, Glory, and the Gospel*, pp. 264-266; Hemming, *Search for El Dorado*, pp. 141-148.

9. Newton, *European Nations in the West Indies*, p. 58; Haring, *Trade and Navigation*, p. 203; Hoffman, *Spanish Crown and Defense*, pp. 47, 126.

10. Eugene Lyon, *The Enterprise of Florida: Pedro Menéndez de Avilés and the Spanish Conquest of 1565-1568* (Gainesville: University Presses of Florida, 1976), pp. 14-16, 27-28; Bartolomé de Barrientos, *Pedro Menéndez de Avilés, Founder of Florida*, translated by Anthony Kerrigan (Gainesville: University of Florida Press, 1965), pp. 19-21; Albert Manucy, *Menéndez: Pedro Menéndez de Avilés, Captain General of the Ocean Sea* (Sarasota: Pineapple Press, 1992), pp. 9-25.

11. Clark G. Reynolds, *Command of the Sea: The History and Strategy of Maritime Empires* (New York: William Morrow, 1974), p. 126; Mendel Peterson, *The Funnel of Gold: The Trials of the Spanish Treasure Fleets* (Boston: Little Brown, 1975), pp. 62-64; Oskar H.K. Spote, *The Spanish Lake* (Minneapolis: University of Minnesota Press, 1979), p. 214; Robert F. Marx, *The Treasure Fleets of the Spanish Main* (Cleveland: World, 1968), *passim*; Merriman, *Rise of Spanish Empire*, vol. IV, pp. 209-210; Haring, *Trade and Navigation*, pp. 189, 224.

12. Barrientos, *Pedro Menéndez*, pp. 63-66; Lyon, *Enterprise of Florida, passim*; Manucy, *Menéndez*, pp. 26-95; Haring, *Trade and Navigation*, pp. 252-253; Hoffman, *Spanish Crown and Defense*, pp. 139-140, 154-167; Peterson, *Funnel of Gold*, pp. 198, 206; Parry, *Spanish Seaborne Empire*, pp. 254-255.

13. Peter Kirsch, *The Galleon: The Great Ships of the Armada Era* (Annapolis: Naval Institute Press, 1990), *passim*; Carla Rahn Phillips, *Six Galleons for the King of Spain: Imperial Defense in the Early Seventeenth Century* (Baltimore: Johns Hopkins University Press, 1986), p. 146; Ruth Pike, *Aristocrats and Traders: Sevillian Society in the Sixteenth Century* (Ithaca: Cornell University Press, 1972), pp. 31-32; Geoffrey Parker, *The Military Revolution: Military Innovation and the Rise of the West, 1500-1800* (Cambridge: Cambridge University Press, 1988), pp. 89-95; Unger, *Cogs, Caravels, and Galleons, passim*; Lynch, *Spain*, vol. I, pp. 84, 125-127; Haring, *Trade and*

Navigation, pp. 264-265; Cipolla, *Guns, Sails, and Empires*, pp. 82-83; Reynolds, *Command of the Sea*, pp. 107-110.

14. Robert S. Weddle, *Spanish Sea: The Gulf of Mexico in North American Discovery, 1550-1685* (College Station, Texas: Texas A&M University Press, 1985), pp. 246-248; J. Barto Arnold and Robert S. Weddle, *The Nautical Archaeology of Padre Island: The Spanish Shipwrecks of 1554* (New York: Academic Press, 1978), pp. 13-48, 144; George F. Bass, ed., *Ships and Shipwrecks of the Americas: A History Based on Underwater Archaeology* (New York: Thames and Hudson, 1988), pp. 50-53; Marx, *Shipwrecks*, p. 279; Haring, *Trade and Navigation*, pp. 76-77, 327; Hamilton, *American Treasure*, p. 34; Merriman, *Rise of Spanish Empire*, vol. III, p. 632.

15. Haring, *Trade and Navigation*, p. 95; Hamilton, *American Treasure*, pp. 25-27; Phillips, *Six Galleons*, pp. 136-137.

16. Lyon, *Enterprise of Florida*, pp. 27-28.

17. I.A.A. Thompson, *War and Government in Habsburg Spain, 1560-1620* (London: Athlone, 1976), pp. 31-32, 185-189; Peterson, *Funnel of Gold*, p. 62.

18. Cipolla, *Guns, Sails, and Empires*, p. 108.

19. Artur Attman, *American Bullion in the European World Trade, 1600-1800* (Goteborg: Kungl. Vetenskaps-och Vitterhets Samhallet, 1986), p. 78; Artur Attman, *The Bullion Flow between Europe and the Far East, 1000-1750* (Goteborg: Kungl. Vetenskaps-och Vitterhets Samhallet, 1981), pp. 30-33.

20. W.L. Schurz, *The Manila Galleon* (New York: E.P. Dutton, 1959), pp. 22-25; Spote, *Spanish Lake*, pp. 101-103; Wallerstein, *Modern World-System*, vol. II, pp. 108-109.

21. Schurz, *Manila Galleon*, pp. 251-281, 371-375.

22. Haring, *Trade and Navigation*, p. 170; Ehrenberg, *Capital and Finance*, p. 114; Braudel, *Mediterranean*, vol. I, pp. 502-503; Wallerstein, *Modern World-System*, vol. I, pp. 214-215; Davies, *Golden Century*, pp. 180-181.

23. Newton, *European Nations in the West Indies*, p. 122.

24. Braudel, *Mediterranean*, vol. II, p. 1102; Reynolds, *Command of the Sea*, p. 121.

25. Koenigsberger, *Habsburgs and Europe*, pp. 120-138.

26. Geoffrey Parker, *The Army of Flanders and the Spanish Road, 1567-1659: The Logistics of Spanish Victory and Defeat in the Low Countries' Wars*, rev. ed. (Cambridge: Cambridge University Press, 1990), pp. 232-239; Jaime Vicens Vives, *An Economic History of Spain*, translated by Frances M. Lopez-Morillas (Princeton: Princeton University Press, 1969), p. 460; Geoffrey Parker, *Philip II* (Boston: Little, Brown and Co., 1978), pp. 121-124; Lynch,

Spain, vol. I, p. 147; Braudel, Mediterranean, vol. I, pp. 506-507, 533.

27. Spooner, International Economy, pp. 22-25.

28. Helen Hill Miller, Captains from Devon: The Great Elizabethan Seafarers Who Won the Ocean for England (Chapel Hill: Algonquin Books, 1985), pp. 4-9; John Sugden, Sir Francis Drake (New York: Henry Holt and Co., 1991), pp. 40-41.

29. Kenneth R. Andrews, Trade, Plunder, and Settlement: Maritime Enterprise and the Genesis of the British Empire, 1480-1630 (Cambridge: Cambridge University Press, 1984), pp. 126-127; Lynch, Spain, vol. I, pp. 311-312; Weddle, Spanish Sea, pp. 297-301; Sugden, Sir Francis Drake, pp. 31-41; Wright, Gold, Glory, and the Gospel, pp. 304-305; Parker, Army of Flanders, pp. 57-59.

30. Newton, European Nations in the West Indies, pp. 84-93; Peterson, Funnel of Gold, pp. 140-151; Andrews, Trade, Plunder, and Settlement, pp. 130-132; Spote, Spanish Lake, p. 235; Sugden, Sir Francis Drake, pp. 54-73.

31. Andrews, Trade, Plunder, and Settlement, pp. 133-140; Spote, Spanish Lake, pp. 236-237; Lynch, Spain, vol. I, p. 318.

32. Henry R. Wagner, Sir Francis Drake's Voyage Around the World: Its Aims and Achievements (San Francisco: John Howell, 1926), passim; Peter T. Bradley, The Lure of Peru: Maritime Intrusion into the South Sea, 1598-1701 (New York: St. Martin's, 1989), p. 2; Spote, Spanish Lake, pp. 241-263; Andrews, Trade, Plunder, and Settlement, pp. 154-155; Sugden, Sir Francis Drake, pp. 124-152.

Chapter 3. Ascendancy 1580-1620

1. Peter J. Bakewell, Silver and Entrepreneurship in Seventeenth-Century Potosí: The Life and Times of Antonio Lopez de Quiroga (Albuquerque: University of New Mexico Press, 1988), pp. 24-25, 191; Lewis Hanke, The Imperial City of Potosí (The Hague: Martinus Nijhoff, 1956), passim; Arzans, Tales of Potosí, p. xxv; Lynch, Spain, vol. II, pp. 238-239.

2. Peter J. Bakewell, Silver Mining and Society in Colonial Mexico: Zacatecas, 1546-1700 (Cambridge: Cambridge University Press, 1971), pp. 221-222; Michel Morineau, Incroyables gazettes et fabuleux métaux: Les retours des trésors américains d'après les gazettes hollandaises (XVIe-XVIIIe siècles) (Cambridge: Cambridge University Press, 1985), p. 250; Richards, Precious Metals, pp. 409-410; Hamilton, American Treasure, p. 34.

3. Charles Howard Carter, The Secret Diplomacy of the Habsburgs, 1598-1625 (New York: Columbia University Press, 1964), p. 56; Fernand Braudel, Civilization and Capitalism, 15-18th Century, 3 vols., translated by Sian Reynolds (New York: Harper and Row, 1981-1984), vol. II, p. 545; Reynolds,

Command of the Sea, p. 140; Parry, *Spanish Seaborne Empire*, pp. 242-243; Haring, *Spanish Empire*, p. 250.

4. John S. Potter Jr., *The Treasure Diver's Guide* (Garden City, N.J.: Doubleday, 1972. Reprint. Port Salerno, Fla.: Florida Classics Library, 1988), *passim*; Marx, *Shipwrecks*, p. 415.

5. Dominguez Ortiz, *Golden Age*, pp. 135, 147; Pike, *Aristocrats*, pp. 1, 19; Braudel, *Civilization and Capitalism*, vol. III, p. 31.

6. Hamilton, *American Treasure*, pp. 34, 42; Lynch, *Spain*, vol. I, pp. 132-135; Vicens Vives, *Economic History of Spain*, pp. 377-380.

7. Parker, *Army of Flanders*, pp. 18, 237-242; Parker, *Military Revolution*, pp. 61-62.

8. Parker, *Army of Flanders*, pp. 146-154.

9. Winston Graham, *The Spanish Armadas* (London: Collins, 1987), pp. 95-98; Peter Padfield, *Tide of Empires: Decisive Naval Campaigns in the Rise of the West*, 2 vols. (London: Routledge & Kegan Paul, 1979-1982) vol. I, pp. 112-113; Miller, *Captains from Devon*, pp. 32-43; Parker, *Military Revolution*, pp. 94-95.

10. Wright, *Gold, Glory, and the Gospel*, pp. 268-273; Miller, *Captains from Devon, passim*.

11. Colin S. Gray and Roger W. Barnett, eds., *Seapower and Strategy* (Annapolis: Naval Institute Press, 1989), pp. 146-147; Felipe Fernandez-Armesto, *The Spanish Armada: The Experience of War in 1588* (Oxford: Oxford University Press, 1988), pp. 78-82; Graham, *Spanish Armadas*, pp. 61-62; Sugden, *Sir Francis Drake*, pp. 176-177.

12. Parry, *Spanish Seaborne Empire*, pp. 255-256; Lynch, *Spain*, vol. I, pp. 332-333; Newton, *European Nations in the West Indies*, pp. 99-105; Sugden, *Sir Francis Drake*, pp. 177-199.

13. Lyle N. McAlister, *Spain and Portugal in the New World, 1492-1700* (Minneapolis: University of Minnesota Press, 1984), p. 432.

14. Schurz, *Manila Galleon*, pp. 306-308; Spote, *Spanish Lake*, pp. 281-282.

15. Gray and Barnett, *Seapower and Strategy*, pp. 147-148; Lynch, *Spain*, vol. I, p. 339; Sugden, *Sir Francis Drake*, pp. 205-217; Graham, *Spanish Armadas*, pp. 69-74.

16. Andrews, *Trade, Plunder, and Settlement*, p. 281; Lynch, *Spain*, vol. I, p. 167.

17. Colin Martin and Geoffrey Parker, *The Spanish Armada* (New York: W.W. Norton & Co., 1988), p. 135; Fernandez-Armesto, *Spanish Armada*, pp. 8-13.

18. Fernandez-Armesto, *Spanish Armada, passim*; Graham, *Spanish Ar-*

madas, pp. 86-142; Sugden, *Sir Francis Drake*, pp. 231-258; Thompson, *War and Government*, pp. 69-70.

19. Gray and Barnett, *Seapower and Strategy*, pp. 153-154; Graham, *Spanish Armadas*, pp. 173-185; Sugden, *Sir Francis Drake*, pp. 267-281.

20. Koenigsberger, *Habsburgs in Europe*, pp. 175, 193-198.

21. Graham, *Spanish Armadas*, pp. 169-171, 193; Thompson, *War and Government*, pp. 189-192; Kamen, *Spain 1469-1714*, p. 163; Dominguez Ortiz, *Golden Age*, p. 42.

22. Andrews, *Trade, Plunder, and Settlement*, pp. 239-240; Lynch, *Spain*, vol. I, p. 147; Marx, *Treasure Fleets*, pp. 93-104; Miller, *Captains from Devon*, pp. 88-90; Graham, *Spanish Armadas*, pp. 193-198.

23. Fernandez-Armesto, *Spanish Armada*, pp. 269-270; Parry, *Spanish Seaborne Empire*, pp. 256-257; Newton, *European Nations in the West Indies*, pp. 110-114; Spote, *Spanish Lake*, p. 212; Marx, *Treasure Fleets*, pp. 106-108; Graham, *Spanish Armadas*, pp. 207-209; Sugden, *Sir Francis Drake*, pp. 303-315.

24. Wright, *Gold, Glory, and the Gospel*, pp. 268-274; Hemming, *Search for El Dorado*, pp. 165-172; Miller, *Captains from Devon*, pp. 176-178; Newton, *European Nations in the West Indies*, pp. 115-117.

25. Gray and Barnett, *Seapower and Strategy*, p. 155; Miller, *Captains from Devon*, pp. 178-182; Graham, *Spanish Armadas*, pp. 210-216; Marx, *Treasure Fleets*, p. 110.

26. Graham, *Spanish Armadas*, pp. 217-265; Koenigsberger, *Habsburgs in Europe*, pp. 200-201; Gray and Barnett, *Seapower and Strategy*, p. 153; Thompson, *War and Government*, pp. 241-250.

27. C.R. Boxer, *The Dutch Seaborne Empire* (New York: Alfred A. Knopf, 1965), pp. 189, 295-296.

28. Miller, *Captains from Devon*, pp. 195-208; Hemming, *Search for El Dorado*, pp. 184-189; Wright, *Gold, Glory, and the Gospel, pp. 282-285.*

29. Thompson, *War and Government*, pp. 68-72; Kamen, *Spain 1469-1714*, pp. 167-168; Elliott, *Imperial Spain*, pp. 279-281; Lynch, *Spain*, vol. I, pp. 136-137, 174-175; Hamilton, *American Treasure*, p. 34.

30. Elliott, *Imperial Spain*, pp. 281-282; Davis, *Rise of the Atlantic Economies*, pp. 68-69; Dominguez Ortiz, *Golden Age*, pp. 32, 139.

31. R. Trevor Davies, *Spain in Decline, 1621-1700* (London: Macmillan, 1965), pp. 93-95; Spooner, *International Economy*, p. 48; Lynch, *Spain*, vol. II, p. 36.

32. Braudel, *Mediterranean*, vol. I, pp. 495-496; Boxer, *Dutch Seaborne Empire*, pp. 23-25.

33. Wallerstein, *Modern World-System*, vol. I, pp. 212-213; Vilar, *History*

of Gold and Money, pp. 206-209; Smith, *Creating a World Economy*, p. 127.

34. Hermann Kellenbenz, ed., *Precious Metals in the Age of Expansion* (Stuttgart: Klett-Cotta, 1981), pp. 266-267; Spooner, *International Economy*, p. 77; Schurz, *Manila Galleon*, pp. 63-64; Potter, *Treasure Diver's Guide*, pp. 441-442; Yang, *Money and Credit in China*, pp. 3, 45-48; Fairbank, *China*, p. 135.

35. Attman, *American Bullion in the European World Trade, passim*; Attman, *Bullion Flow between Europe and the Far East, passim*; Vilar, *History of Gold and Money*, pp. 204-205.

36. Parry, *Spanish Seaborne Empire*, pp. 131-133; Spote, *Spanish Lake*, pp. 201-202; Lynch, *Spain*, vol. II, p. 246; Schurz, *Manila Galleon*, pp. 155, 193; Simkin, *Traditional Trade of Asia*, p. 188.

Chapter 4. Decline 1621-1715

1. Elliott, *Imperial Spain*, pp. 321-323; Lynch, *Spain*, vol. II, pp. 75-82; Thompson, *War and Government*, pp. 198-200; Parker, *Army of Flanders*, pp. 129-131.

2. Koenigsberger, *Habsburgs and Europe*, pp. 257-258; Elliott, *Imperial Spain*, pp. 325-329.

3. P.A. Means, *The Spanish Main: Focus of Envy, 1492-1700* (New York: Charles Scribner's Sons, 1935), pp. 154-164; Cornelis C. Goslinga, *The Dutch in the Caribbean and the Wild Coast, 1580-1680* (Gainesville: University of Florida Press, 1971), pp. 267-274; Jonathan I. Israel, *The Dutch Republic and the Hispanic World, 1606-61* (Oxford: Clarendon Press, 1982), pp. 273-274; Newton, *European Nations in the West Indies*, pp. 129-147; Andrews, *Trade, Plunder, and Settlement*, p. 301; Haring, *Trade and Navigation*, pp. 119-120; Boxer, *Dutch Seaborne Empire*, pp. 25-26.

4. Goslinga, *Dutch in the Caribbean*, pp. 176-182; Haring, *Trade and Navigation*, pp. 237-238.

5. Robert F. Marx, *The Capture of the Treasure Fleet: The Story of Piet Heyn* (New York: McKay, 1977), pp. 180-181, 215, 233-239; Phillips, *Six Galleons*, pp. 4-5; Goslinga, *Dutch in the Caribbean*, pp. 188-195; Marx, *Shipwrecks*, p. 315.

6. Israel, *Dutch Republic and the Hispanic World*, pp. 197-198; Lynch, *Spain*, vol. II, p. 82; Goslinga, *Dutch in the Caribbean*, pp. 199, 284; Marx, *Capture of the Treasure Fleet*, pp. 249, 259-260.

7. Phillips, *Six Galleons*, pp. 106-116, 184-194; Parry, *Spanish Seaborne Empire*, p. 262; Haring, *Trade and Navigation*, p. 242; Weddle, *Spanish Sea*, pp. 380-381.

8. Phillips, *Six Galleons*, pp. 214-219; Israel, *Dutch Republic and the*

Hispanic World, pp. 268-270; Reynolds, *Command of the Sea*, p. 169; Parker, *Military Revolution*, pp. 99-100; Padfield, *Tide of Empires*, vol. I, pp. 171-179; Parker, *Army of Flanders*, pp. 77-78.

9. Means, *Spanish Main*, pp. 192-194; Padfield, *Tide of Empires*, vol. II, pp. 8-9; Wolf, *Europe and the People Without History*, p. 153; Lang, *Conquest and Commerce*, p. 57.

10. Marx, *Shipwrecks*, pp. 316, 439.

11. Michael Baumber, *General-at-Sea: Robert Blake and the Seventeenth-Century Revolution in Naval Tactics* (London: John Murray, 1989), pp. 223-235; Newton, *European Nations in the West Indies*, pp. 221-223; Reynolds, *Command of the Sea*, p. 183; Haring, *Trade and Navigation*, pp. 245-246; Lynch, *Spain*, vol. II, pp. 132-133; Padfield, *Tide of Empires*, vol. II, pp. 9-13.

12. C.H. Haring, *The Buccaneers in the West Indies in the XVII Century* (Hamden, Conn.: Archon Books, 1966), *passim*; Newton, *European Nations in the West Indies*, pp. 237-238; Parry, *Spanish Seaborne Empire*, pp. 265-266.

13. Dudley Pope, *The Buccaneer King: The Biography of Sir Henry Morgan, 1635-1688* (New York: Dodd, Mead & Co., 1977), *passim*; Newton, *European Nations in the West Indies*, pp. 232-233, 263-265, 337-338; Peterson, *Funnel of Gold*, pp. 320-323; Means, *Spanish Main*, pp. 208-217.

14. Holden Furber, *Rival Empires of Trade in the Orient, 1600-1800* (Minneapolis: University of Minnesota Press, 1976), pp. 103-105, 124; Padfield, *Tide of Empires*, vol. II, pp. 67-71; Kindleberger, *Financial History of Western Europe*, pp. 31-33.

15. N.M. Crouse, *The French Struggle for the West Indies, 1665-1713* (New York: Columbia University Press, 1943. Reprint. New York: Octagon Books, 1966), pp. 129-147; Newton, *European Nations in the West Indies*, pp. 325-338; Weddle, *Spanish Sea*, pp. 399-400.

16. Crouse, *French Struggle for the West Indies*, pp. 215-239; J.H. Parry, *Trade and Dominion: The European Overseas Empires in the Eighteenth Century* (London: Weidenfeld and Nicolson, 1971), pp. 18-19; Parry, *Spanish Seaborne Empire*, p. 267; Padfield, *Tide of Empires*, vol. II, p. 152.

17. Peter Earle, *The Treasure of the Concepcion: The Wreck of the Almiranta* (New York: Viking Press, 1980), *passim*; Marx, *Shipwrecks*, pp. 204, 315; Bass, *Ships and Shipwrecks*, p. 94.

18. Kenneth J. Andrien, *Crisis and Decline: The Viceroyalty of Peru in the Seventeenth Century* (Albuquerque: University of New Mexico Press, 1985), p. 14; Bakewell, *Silver and Entrepreneurship*, pp. 17-20; Braudel, *Mediterranean*, vol. I, pp. 536-538; Richards, *Precious Metals*, p. 409; Morineau, *Incroyables gazettes*, pp. 237, 289; Smith, *Creating a World Economy*, pp. 158-159; Hemming, *Conquest of the Incas*, pp. 348-350.

19. Haring, *Spanish Empire*, p. 291; Hamilton, *American Treasure*, pp. 68-70; Bakewell, *Silver and Entrepreneurship*, pp. 36-43.

20. Lynch, *Spain*, vol. II, pp. 220-227; Spote, *Spanish Lake*, pp. 178-179; Bakewell, *Silver Mining*, pp. 195, 246, 259; Richards, *Precious Metals*, p. 410; Morineau, *Incroyables gazettes*, pp. 237, 289.

21. Lynch, *Spain*, vol. II, pp. 207-213; Lang, *Conquest and Commerce*, pp. 60-63; Haring, *Spanish Empire*, pp. 250-257; Bradley, *Lure of Peru*, p. 193; Andrien, *Crisis and Decline*, p. 34; Richards, *Precious Metals*, pp. 428-430.

22. Lynch, *Spain*, vol. II, p. 165; Vicens Vives, *Economic History of Spain*, pp. 400-404; Marx, *Treasure Fleets*, p. 120.

23. Geoffrey J. Walker, *Spanish Politics and Imperial Trade, 1707-1789* (Bloomington: Indiana University Press, 1979), p. 102; Dominguez Ortiz, *Golden Age*, pp. 134-135.

24. Schurz, *Manila Galleon*, pp. 265-266, 355-356; Potter, *Treasure Diver's Guide*, pp. 443-444.

25. Richard Pares, *War and Trade in the West Indies, 1730-63* (London: Oxford University Press, 1936), pp. 5-6; Lynch, *Spain*, vol. I, p. 208.

26. Haring, *Spanish Empire*, pp. 305-306; Lynch, *Spain*, vol. II, pp. 177-178; Lang, *Conquest and Commerce*, p. 52; Smith, *Spanish Guild Merchant*, pp. 99-100; Haring, *Trade and Navigation*, p. 65.

27. Lynch, *Spain*, vol. II, p. 171; Vicens Vives, *Economic History of Spain*, vol. II, p. 435; Newton, *European Nations in the West Indies*, pp. 268-271.

28. Eugene Lyon, *The Search for the Atocha* (New York: Harper and Row, 1979), pp. 53-58, 78; Marx, *Shipwrecks*, *passim*; Potter, *Treasure Diver's Guide*, *passim;* Lynch, *Spain*, vol. II, pp. 190-191.

29. Dominguez Ortiz, *Golden Age*, pp. 175-176; Vicens Vives, *Economic History of Spain*, vol. II, pp. 463-464; Elliott, *Imperial Spain*, pp. 190-199.

30. Davis, *Rise of Atlantic Economies*, pp. 144-146; Davies, *Spain in Decline*, pp. 96-97; Spooner, *International Economy*, p. 51.

31. Earl J. Hamilton, *War and Prices in Spain, 1651-1800* (Cambridge, Mass.: Harvard University Press, 1947), pp. 10-11; Henry Kamen, *Spain in the Later Seventeenth Century, 1665-1700* (London: Longman, 1986), p. 102; Lynch, *Spain*, vol. II, pp. 285-286; Vilar, *History of Gold and Money*, p. 233; Hamilton, *American Treasure*, p. 65.

32. Davies, *Spain in Decline*, p. 152.

33. Spooner, *International Economy*, p. 52; Lynch, *Spain*, vol. II, pp. 286-287; Kamen, *Spain in the Later Seventeenth Century*, pp. 103-104, 365; Davies, *Spain in Decline*, pp. 150-152; Hamilton, *War and Prices*, p. 22.

34. R.A. Stradling, *Europe and the Decline of Spain: A Study of the Spanish System, 1580-1720* (London: George Allen & Unwin, 1981), pp. 65, 116; Paul

Kennedy, ed., *Grand Strategies in War and Peace* (New Haven: Yale University Press, 1991), p. 96; Lynch, *Spain*, vol. II, p. 91; Elliott, *Imperial Spain*, pp. 321-322.

35. James C. Boyajian, *Portuguese Bankers and the Court of Spain, 1626-1650* (New Brunswick, N.J.: Rutgers University Press, 1983), *passim*; Stradling, *Europe and the Decline of Spain*, pp. 99, 127; Lynch, *Spain*, vol. II, p. 128.

36. Kamen, *Spain 1469-1714*, p. 218; Lynch, *Spain*, vol. II, p. 134; Stradling, *Europe and the Decline of Spain*, p. 184; Kamen, *Spain in the Later Seventeenth Century*, pp. 360-367.

37. Lynch, *Spain*, vol. II, p. 208; Kamen, *Spain in the Later Seventeenth Century*, pp. 138-139; Wallerstein, *Modern World-System*, vol. III, p. 213.

38. Jonathan I. Israel, *Dutch Primacy in World Trade, 1585-1740* (Oxford: Clarendon Press, 1989), pp. 177, 203, 338; Boyajian, *Portuguese Bankers and the Court of Spain*, pp. 91-93, 144-145; Attman, *Bullion Flow between Europe and the East*, pp. 42-52; Boxer, *Dutch Seaborne Empire*, pp. 69, 199-201.

39. Doty, *Money*, p. 116; Cribb, *Money*, p. 168; Kindleberger, *Financial History of Western Europe*, pp. 50-53; Vilar, *History of Gold and Money*, pp. 215-216; Furber, *Rival Empires of Trade*, pp. 88-92; Attman, *Bullion Flow between Europe and the East*, pp. 51-52.

40. Potter, *Treasure Diver's Guide*, p. 424.

41. Davis, *Rise of Atlantic Economies*, pp. 96-97; Attman, *American Bullion in European World Trade, passim*.

42. Wallerstein, *Modern World-System*, vol. II, p. 166; Parry, *Trade and Dominion*, pp. 39-40; Smith, *Creating a World Economy*, pp. 181-182; Fairbank, *China*, p. 196.

43. Spence, *Search for Modern China*, pp. 20-21.

44. John Lynch, *Bourbon Spain, 1700-1808* (Oxford: Basil Blackwood, 1989), p. 54; Henry Kamen, *The War of Succession in Spain, 1700-15* (Bloomington: Indiana University Press, 1969), pp. 178-179; Parry, *Trade and Dominion*, pp. 94-96.

45. John S. Potter Jr., *The Treasure Divers of Vigo Bay* (Garden City: Doubleday, 1958), pp. 21-55; Peter Seaby, *The Story of British Coinage* (London: Seaby, 1985), p. 132; Padfield, *Tide of Empires*, vol. II, pp. 160-163; Kamen, *War of Succession*, pp. 179-181; Spote, *Spanish Lake*, p. 207.

46. Walker, *Spanish Politics*, pp. 44-46; Kamen, *War of Succession*, p. 185; Marx, *Shipwrecks*, pp. 431-432; Potter, *Treasure Diver's Guide*, p. 184; Schurz, *Manila Galleon*, pp. 321-327.

47. Walker, *Spanish Politics*, p. 48; Kamen, *War of Succession*, pp. 151, 181-191; Morineau, *Incroyables gazettes*, pp. 310-312.

48. Walker, *Spanish Politics*, pp. 31-32.

49. Hamilton, *War and Prices*, pp. 39-40.

50. Walker, *Spanish Politics*, pp. 87-88.

51. Robert F. Burgess and Carl J. Clausen, *Gold, Galleons, and Archaeology* (New York: Bobbs-Merrill, 1976), pp. 5-6, 40-41, 68-70; Peterson, *Funnel of Gold*, pp. 362-369; Bass, *Ships and Shipwrecks*, p. 96; Marx, *Shipwrecks*, pp. 206-209.

Chapter 5. Recovery 1715-1790

1. Kamen, *War of Succession*, pp. 113-115; Kamen, *Spain 1469-1714*, pp. 269-270; Vicens Vives, *Economic History of Spain*, vol. II, pp. 581-582.

2. Jean McLachlan, *Trade and Peace with Old Spain, 1667-1750* (Cambridge: Cambridge University Press, 1940), pp. 147-150; Lynch, *Bourbon Spain*, pp. 90-91.

3. McNeill, *Atlantic Empires*, pp. 53-54, 87; Walker, *Spanish Politics*, pp. 94-97; Stradling, *Europe and the Decline of Spain*, p. 206; Lynch, *Bourbon Spain*, pp. 128-129.

4. Parry, *Spanish Seaborne Empire*, pp. 285-286; Haring, *Spanish Empire*, pp. 315-316; McLachlan, *Trade and Peace*, pp. 150-152; Walker, *Spanish Politics, passim.*

5. McLachlan, *Trade and Peace*, pp. 176-177; Lynch, *Bourbon Spain*, pp. 155-156; Walker, *Spanish Politics*, pp. 128-129.

6. Lynch, *Bourbon Spain*, p. 153.

7. J. Leitch Wright Jr., *Anglo-Spanish Rivalry in North America* (Athens: University of Georgia Press, 1971), p. 104; David L. Horner, *The Treasure Galleons: Clues to Millions in Sunken Gold and Silver* (Port Salerno, Fla.: Florida Classics Library, 1990), pp. 182-186; Marx, *Shipwrecks*, pp. 167, 209-215; Peterson, *Funnel of Gold,* pp. 379-385.

8. Hamilton, *War and Prices*, pp. 45-47; Haring, *Spanish Empire*, p. 291; Parry, *Spanish Seaborne Empire*, pp. 283-284.

9. McNeill, *Atlantic Empires*, p. 70; Lynch, *Bourbon Spain*, p. 112.

10. Paul M.Kennedy, *The Rise and Fall of British Naval Mastery* (New York: Charles Scribner's Sons, 1976), pp. 88-89; Wright, *Anglo-Spanish Rivalry.* p. 78.

11. McNeill, *Atlantic Empires*, pp. 78-79; Wright, *Anglo-Spanish Rivalry*, p. 104.

12. Walker, *Spanish Politics*, pp. 207-209; Wright, *Anglo-Spanish Rivalry*, pp. 89-94; Reynolds, *Command of the Sea*, pp. 228-230; Padfield, *Tide of Empires*, vol. II, pp. 198-199.

13. Schurz, *Manila Galleon*, pp. 332-335; Reynolds, *Command of the Sea*, p. 229; Parry, *Trade and Dominion*, p. 111.

14. Pares, *War and Trade*, pp. 110-114; McNeill, *Atlantic Empires*, p. 98; Seaby, *Story of British Coinage*, pp. 136-137; Morineau, *Incroyables gazettes*, pp. 373-374, 391; Marx, *Shipwrecks*, p. 354.

15. Kennedy, *Rise and Fall of British Naval Mastery*, pp. 90-94.

16. Richard Middleton, *The Bells of Victory: The Pitt-Newcastle Ministry and the Conduct of the Seven Years' War, 1757-1762* (Cambridge: Cambridge University Press, 1985), *passim*; Stanley Ayling, *The Elder Pitt, Earl of Chatham* (New York: David McKay, 1976), *passim*; Gray and Barnett, *Seapower and Strategy*, pp. 174-177; Kennedy, *Rise and Fall of British Naval Mastery,* pp. 99-107.

17. Lynch, *Bourbon Spain*, pp. 317-318; Wright, *Anglo-Spanish Rivalry*, p. 107; Pares, *War and Trade*, pp. 582-584.

18. McNeill, *Atlantic Empires*, pp. 103-104; Padfield, *Tide of Empires*, vol. II, p. 248.

19. Schurz, *Manila Galleon*, pp. 194-197; Reynolds, *Command of the Sea*, p. 246.

20. Brading, *Miners and Merchants*, p. 28.

21. Herbert I. Priestley, *José de Gálvez, Visitor-General of New Spain, 1765-1771* (Berkeley: University of California Press, 1916), *passim*; Haring, *Spanish Empire*, pp. 247-249; Lynch, *Bourbon Spain*, p. 363; Brading, *Miners and Merchants*, pp. 143-165, 261; Parry, *Spanish Seaborne Empire*, p. 312; Parry, *Trade and Dominion*, pp. 133-134, 293-295.

22. Lang, *Conquest and Commerce*, p. 95; Richards, *Precious Metals*, p. 405.

23. Lynch, *Bourbon Spain*, pp. 312-316.

24. Priestley, *José de Gálvez*, pp. 25-29; Brading, *Miners and Merchants*, pp. 114-116; Lynch, *Bourbon Spain,* pp. 352-353; Vicens Vives, *Economic History of Spain,* pp. 578-579.

25. Hamilton, *War and Prices*, p. 67; Vicens Vives, *Economic History of Spain*, pp. 584.

26. Lynch, *Bourbon Spain*, pp. 348-349.

27. Buchanan Parker Thomson, *Spain: Forgotten Ally of the American Revolution* (North Quincy, Mass.: Christopher Publishing House, 1976), pp. 51, 73; Lynch, *Bourbon Spain*, pp. 315-321.

28. Nathan Miller, *Sea of Glory: The Continental Navy Fights for Independence, 1775-1783* (New York, David McKay, 1974), pp. 480-482; Thomson, *Spain*, p. 108; Kennedy, *Rise and Fall of British Naval Mastery*, pp. 107-116; Reynolds, *Command of the Sea*, pp. 261-265.

29. Vicens Vives, *Economic History of Spain*, pp. 585-597; Lynch,

Bourbon Spain, p. 326; Kindleberger, *Financial History of Western Europe*, p. 146.

30. Vicens Vives, *Economic History of Spain*, pp. 578-579; Parry, *Trade and Dominion*, pp. 278-279; Schurz, *Manila Galleon*, pp. 412-413.

31. Davis, *Rise of Atlantic Economies*, p. 175; Wallerstein, *Modern World-System*, vol. II, pp. 112, 276; Pradeau, *Numismatic History of Mexico*, p. 63; Attman, *American Bullion in the European World Trade, passim.*

32. Vilar, *History of Gold and Money*, p. 264; Wallerstein, *Modern World-System*, vol. II, p. 273; Parry, *Trade and Dominion*, pp. 65-67; Smith, *Creating a World Economy*, pp. 182-184.

33. McLachlan, *Trade and Peace*, p. 13; Parry, *Trade and Dominion*, pp. 37-38.

34. John J. McCusker, *Money and Exchange in Europe and America, 1600-1775: A Handbook* (Chapel Hill: University of North Carolina Press, 1972), p. 7; Edwin J. Perkins, *The Economy of Colonial America* (New York: Columbia University Press, 1980), pp. 163-183; Cribb, *Coin Atlas*, pp. 266-267; Shaw, *History of Currency*, p. 247; Parry, *Trade and Dominion*, pp. 50-51; Smith, *Creating a World Economy*, p. 173.

35. Parry, *Trade and Dominion*, pp. 81-86; Furber, *Rival Empires of Trade*, pp. 127-133, 175-176; Fairbank, *China*, pp. 195-196; Spence, *Search for Modern China*, p. 129.

36. Michael Greenberg, *British Trade and the Opening of China, 1800-1842* (Cambridge: Cambridge University Press, 1951), pp. 6-9; Wolf, *Europe and the People Without History*, p. 257; Spence, *Search for Modern China*, pp. 87-88, 121-122.

37. Israel, *Dutch Primacy*, pp. 77-78; Attman, *Bullion Flow between Europe and the East*, p. 42; Attman, *American Bullion in European World Trade, passim*; Pares, *War and Trade*, pp. 132-133, 142; Potter, *Treasure Diver's Guide*, p. 367.

38. James D. Tracy, ed., *The Rise of Merchant Empires: Long Distance Trade in the Early Modern Period, 1350-1750* (New York: Cambridge University Press, 1990), pp. 224-254; Richards, *Precious Metals*, pp. 397-404; Attman, *American Bullion in European World Trade, passim*; Morineau, *Incroyables gazettes, passim.*

Chapter 6. Rediscovery, 1791-Present

1. A. Barton Hepburn, *A History of Currency in the United States* (New York: Macmillan, 1924), pp. 36-43; Shaw, *History of Currency*, pp. 247-253; McCusker, *Money and Exchange*, p. 3.

2. Hepburn, *History of Currency*, p. 46.

3. John Kenneth Galbraith, *Money: Whence It Came, Where It Went* (Boston: Houghton Mifflin, 1975), p. 35; Seaby, *Story of British Coinage*, pp. 140-141; Cribb, *Money*, p. 71; Kindleberger, *Financial History of Western Europe*, pp. 60-61.

4. John Lynch, *The Spanish American Revolutions, 1808-1826* (London: Weidenfeld and Nicolson, 1973), pp. 280-284; Parry, *Trade and Dominion*, pp. 191-192, 199-200.

5. Schurz, *Manila Galleon*, p. 60; Parry, *Trade and Dominion*, pp. 189-193.

6. Cribb, *Coin Atlas*, pp. 301-306; Doty, *Money*, p. 197.

7. Cribb, *Coin Atlas*, pp. 293-294.

8. John King Fairbank, *Trade and Diplomacy on the China Coast: The Opening of the Treaty Ports, 1842-1854* (Cambridge, Mass.: Harvard University Press, 1969), *passim*; Greenberg, *British Trade and the Opening of China*, *passim*; Spence, *Search for Modern China*, pp. 149, 156; Fairbank, *China*, pp. 199-201; Yang, *Money and Credit in China*, pp. 48-50; Cribb, *Coin Atlas*, pp. 204-205.

9. Kindleberger, *Financial History of Western Europe*, pp. 62-68; Vilar, *History of Gold and Money*, pp. 321-331, 343.

10. Robert F. Burgess, *Sunken Treasure: Six Who Found Fortunes* (New York: Dodd, Mead & Co., 1988), pp. 22-34; Potter, *Treasure Diver's Guide*, pp. 221-223; Bass, *Ships and Shipwrecks*, pp. 99-103.

11. Teddy Tucker, *Treasure Diving with Teddy Tucker*, Ford Baxter and Hans W. Hannau, eds. (Hamilton, Bermuda: Buccaneer Publishing House, 1964), *passim*; Potter, *Treasure Diver's Guide*, pp. 280-283.

12. Robert Sténuit, *Treasures of the Armada*, translated by Francine Barker (New York: E.P. Dutton, 1973), *passim*; Colin Martin, *Full Fathom Five: The Wrecks of the Spanish Armada* (New York: Viking, 1975), *passim*; Potter, *Treasure Divers of Vigo Bay*, *passim*; Potter, *Treasure Diver's Guide*, pp. 343-344.

13. Kip Wagner, *Pieces of Eight: Recovering the Riches of a Lost Spanish Treasure Fleet* (New York: E.P. Dutton, 1966), *passim*; Burgess, *Sunken Treasure*, pp. 114-116; Burgess and Clausen, *Gold, Galleons, and Archaeology*, pp. 83-108; Bass, *Ships and Shipwrecks*, pp. 95-96; Potter, *Treasure Diver's Guide*, pp. 235-259.

14. Arnold and Weddle, *Nautical Archaeology of Padre Island*, pp. xiii-xiv; Bass, *Ships and Shipwrecks*, pp. 53, 89.

15. Burgess, *Sunken Treasure*, pp. 149-170.

16. G. Lee Tippin and Herbert Humphreys, Jr., *In Search of the Golden Madonna: The Treasure Finders of the RV Beacon* (Canton, Ohio: Daring Books, 1989), *passim*; Burgess, *Sunken Treasure*, p. 323.

17. John Grissim, *The Lost Treasure of the Concepción* (New York: William Morrow & Co., 1980), *passim*; Burgess, *Sunken Treasure*, pp. 190-211; Earle, *Treasure of the Concepción*, pp. 228-238; Bass, *Ships and Shipwrecks*, pp. 94-95.

18. R. Duncan Mathewson III, *Treasure of the Atocha* (New York: Pisces Books, 1986), *passim*; Lyon, *Search for the Atocha*; Burgess, *Sunken Treasure*, pp. 276-307; Bass, *Ships and Shipwrecks*, pp. 92-94.

19. Potter, *Treasure Diver's Guide, pp. 367, 425.*

Recommendations for further reading

General

Attman, Artur. *American Bullion in the European World Trade, 1600-1800.* Goteborg: Kungl. Vetenskaps-och Vitterhets-Samhallet, 1986.

Attman, Artur. *The Bullion Flow Between Europe and the East, 1000-1750.* Goteborg: Kungl. Vetenskaps-och Vitterhets-Samhallet, 1981.

Bass, George F., ed. *A History of Seafaring Based on Underwater Archaeology.* London: Thames and Hudson, 1972.

Braudel, Fernand. *The Mediterranean and the Mediterranean World in the Age of Philip II.* 2 vols. Translated by Sian Reynolds. New York: Harper and Row, 1972-1973.

Cribb, Joe, et. al. *The Coin Atlas: The World of Coinage from Its Origins to the Present Day.* New York: Facts on File, 1990.

Cribb, Joe, ed. *Money: From Cowrie Shells to Credit Cards.* London: British Museum Publications, 1986.

Davies, R. Trevor. *The Golden Century of Spain, 1501-1621.* New York: Harper & Row, 1937.

Davis, Ralph. *The Rise of the Atlantic Economies.* Ithaca: Cornell University Press, 1973.

Diffie, Bailey W. *Latin American Civilization: Colonial Period.* New York: Octagon Books, 1967.

Dominquez Ortiz, Antonio. *The Golden Age of Spain, 1516-1659.* Translated by James Casey. New York: Basic Books, 1971.

Doty, Richard. *Money of the World.* New York: Grosset & Dunlap, 1978.

Elliott, J.H. *Imperial Spain, 1469-1716.* New York: St. Martin's, 1964.

Fagg, John Edwin. *Latin America: A General History.* 3d ed. New York: Macmillan, 1977.

Fuentes, Carlos. *The Buried Mirror: Reflections on Spain and the New World.* New York: Houghton Mifflin, 1992

Gibson, Charles. *Spain in America.* New York: Harper & Row, 1966.

Gray, Colin S., and Barnett, Roger M., eds. *Seapower and Strategy.* Annapolis: Naval Institute Press, 1989.

Haring, C.H. *The Spanish Empire in America.* New York: Harcourt Brace & World, 1947.

Kamen, Henry. *Spain 1469-1714: A Society in Conflict.* London: Longman, 1983.

Kellenbenz, Hermann, ed. *Precious Metals in the Age of Expansion.* Stuttgart: Klett-Cotta, 1981.

Kindleberger, Charles P. *A Financial History of Western Europe.* London: George Allen & Unwin, 1984.

Koenigsberger, H.G. *The Habsburgs and Europe.* Ithaca: Cornell University Press, 1971.

Lang, James. *Conquest and Commerce: Spain and England in the Americas.* New York: Academic Press, 1975.

Lynch, John. *Spain under the Habsburgs.* 2d ed. 2 vols. New York: New York University Press, 1981.

McAlister, Lyle N. *Spain and Portugal in the New World, 1492-1700.* Minneapolis: University of Minnesota Press, 1984.

Marshall, Michael W. *Ocean Traders: From the Portuguese to the Present Day.* New York: Facts on File, 1990.

Marx, Robert F. *The Treasure Fleets of the Spanish Main.* Cleveland: World Publishing Co., 1968.

Means, P.A. *The Spanish Main, Focus of Envy, 1492-1700.* New York: Charles Scribner's Sons, 1935.

Merriman, Roger B. *The Rise of the Spanish Empire in the Old World and the New.* 4 vols. New York: Macmillan, 1918-1934.

Miskimin, Harry A. *The Economy of Later Renaissance Europe, 1460-1600.* Cambridge: Cambridge University Press, 1977.

Newton, A.P. *The European Nations in the West Indies, 1493-1688.* New York: Barnes and Noble, 1933.

Padfield, Peter. *Tide of Empires: Decisive Naval Campaigns in the Rise of the West.* 2 vols. London: Routledge & Kegan Paul, 1979-1982.

Parry, J.H. *The Discovery of the Sea.* Berkeley: University of California Press, 1981.

Parry, J.H. *The Establishment of the European Hegemony, 1415-1715: Trade and Exploration in the Age of the Renaissance.* 3d ed. New York: Harper and Row, 1966.

Parry, J.H. *The Spanish Seaborne Empire.* New York: Knopf, 1966.

Peterson, Mendel. *The Funnel of Gold: The Trials of the Spanish Treasure Fleets.* Boston: Little Brown, 1975.

Pick, Franz and Sedillot, Rene. *All the Monies of the World: A Chronicle of Currency Values.* New York: Pick Publishing Co., 1971.

Potter, E.B. and Nimitz, Chester W., eds. *Sea Power: A Naval History.* Englewood Cliffs, N.J.: Prentice Hall, 1960.

Pradeau, Alberto F. *Numismatic History of Mexico from the Pre-Columbian Epoch to 1823.* New York: Sanford J. Durst, 1978.

Reynolds, Clark G. *Command of the Sea: The History and Strategy of Maritime Empires.* New York: William Morrow, 1974.

Reynolds, Robert L. *Europe Emerges: Transition Toward an Industrial World-Wide Society, 600-1750.* Madison: University of Wisconsin Press, 1961.

Richards, J.F., ed. *Precious Metals in the Later Medieval and Early Modern Worlds.* Durham, N.C.: Carolina Academic Press, 1983.

Schurz, W.L. *The Manila Galleon.* New York: E.P. Dutton, 1959.

Shaw, W.A. *The History of Currency, 1252-1896.* 2d ed. New York: G.P. Putnam's Sons, 1896. Reprint. New York: Augustus M. Kelley, 1967.

Smith, Alan K. *Creating a World Economy: Merchant Capital, Colonialism, and World Trade 1400-1825.* Boulder: Westview Press, 1991.

Smith, Robert S. *The Spanish Guild Merchant: A History of the Consulado, 1250-1700.* Durham, N.C.: Duke University Press, 1940.

Spooner, Frank C. *The International Economy and Monetary Movements in France, 1493-1725.* Cambridge, Mass.: Harvard University Press, 1972.

Tracy, James D., ed. *The Political Economy of Merchant Empires: State Power and World Trade, 1350-1750.* New York: Cambridge University Press, 1991.

Tracy, James D., ed. *The Rise of Merchant Empires: Long Distance Trade in the Early Modern World, 1350-1750.* New York: Cambridge University Press, 1990.

Vicens Vives, Jaime. *An Economic History of Spain.* Translated by Frances M. Lopez-Morillas. Princeton: Princeton University Press, 1969.

Vilar, Pierre. *A History of Gold and Money, 1450-1920.* Translated by Judith White. London: NLB, 1976.

Wallerstein, Immanuel. *The Modern World-System.* 3 vols. New York: Academic Press, 1974-1989.

Wolf, Eric. *Europe and the People Without History.* Berkeley: University of California Press, 1982.

Wright, J. Leitch, Jr. *Anglo-Spanish Rivalry in North America.* Athens, Ga.: University of Georgia Press, 1971.

Chapter 1. Conquest, 1492-1544

Brandi, Karl. *The Emperor Charles V: The Growth and Destiny of a Man and of a World Empire.* Translated by C.V. Wedgwood. London: Jonathan Cape, 1939.

Cipolla, Carlo M. *Guns, Sails, and Empires: Technological Innovation and the Early Phases of European Expansion, 1400-1700.* New York: Minerva Press, 1965.

Columbus, Christopher. *The Log of Christopher Columbus.* Translated by Robert H. Fuson. Camden, Maine: International Marine Publishing, 1987.

Ehrenberg, Richard. *Capital and Finance in the Age of the Renaissance.* Translated by H.M. Lucas. New York: Harcourt Brace, 1928.

Folmer, Henry. *Franco-Spanish Rivalry in North America, 1524-1673.* Glendale: A.H. Clarke Co., 1953.

Hemming, John. *The Conquest of the Incas.* New York: Harcourt Brace Jovanovich, 1970.

Hemming, John. *The Search for El Dorado.* New York: E.P. Dutton, 1978.

Kirkpatrick, F.A. *The Spanish Conquistadores.* London: Adam and Charles Black, 1934.

MacKay, Angus. *Money, Prices, and Politics in Fifteenth Century Castile.* London: Royal Historical Society, 1981.

Morison, Samuel Eliot. *Admiral of the Ocean Sea: A Life of Christopher Columbus.* Boston: Little, Brown and Co., 1942.

Parry, J.H. *The Age of Reconnaissance.* Cleveland: World Publishing Co., 1963.

Parry, J.H. *The Discovery of the Sea.* Berkeley: University of California Press, 1981.

Pike, Ruth. *Enterprise and Adventure: The Genoese in Seville and the Opening of the New World.* Ithaca: Cornell University Press, 1966.

Prescott, William H. *History of the Conquest of Mexico* and *History of the Conquest of Peru.* New York: Modern Library, 1930.

Sauer, Carl O. *The Early Spanish Main.* Berkeley: University of California Press, 1966.

Wright, Louis B. *Gold, Glory, and the Gospel: The Adventurous Lives and Times of the Renaissance Explorers.* New York: Atheneum, 1970.

Chapter 2. Consolidation, 1545-1579

Andrews, Kenneth R. *Trade, Plunder, and Settlement: Maritime Enterprise and the Genesis of the British Empire, 1480-1630.* Cambridge: Cambridge University Press, 1984.

Bakewell, Peter J. *Silver Mining and Society in Colonial Mexico: Zacatecas,*

1546-1700. Cambridge: Cambridge University Press, 1971.

Barrientos, Bartolomé de. *Pedro Menéndez de Avilés, Founder of Florida*. Translated by Anthony Kerrigan. Gainesville: University of Florida Press, 1965.

Hamilton, Earl J. *American Treasure and the Price Revolution in Spain, 1501-1650*. Cambridge, Mass.: Harvard University Press, 1934. Reprint. New York: Octagon Books, 1970.

Haring, C.H. *Trade and Navigation Between Spain and the Indies in the Time of the Hapsburgs*. Gloucester, Mass.: P. Smith, 1964.

Hoffman, Paul E. *The Spanish Crown and the Defense of the Caribbean, 1535-1585*. Baton Rouge: Louisiana State University Press, 1980.

Kirsch, Peter. *The Galleon: The Great Ships of the Armada Era*. Annapolis: Naval Institute Press, 1990.

Lyon, Eugene. *The Enterprise of Florida: Pedro Menéndez de Avilés and the Spanish Conquest of 1565-1568*. Gainesville: University Presses of Florida, 1976.

Manucy, Albert. *Menéndez: Pedro Menéndez de Avilés, Captain General of the Ocean Sea*. Sarasota: Pineapple Press, 1992).

Miller, Helen Hill. *Captains from Devon: The Great Elizabethan Seafarers Who Won the Ocean for England*. Chapel Hill: Algonquin Books, 1985.

Parker, Geoffrey. *Philip II*. Boston: Little, Brown, 1978.

Powell, Philip Wayne. *Soldiers, Indians, and Silver: The Northwest Advance of New Spain, 1550-1600*. Berkeley: University of California Press, 1969.

Sugden, John. *Sir Francis Drake*. New York: Henry Holt and Co., 1991.

Unger, Richard W., ed. *Cogs, Caravels, and Galleons: The Sailing Ship, 1000-1650*. Annapolis: Naval Institute Press, 1993.

Weddle, Robert S. *Spanish Sea: The Gulf of Mexico in North American Discovery, 1550-1685*. College Station, Texas: Texas A&M University Press, 1985.

Whitaker, Arthur Preston. *The Huancavélica Mercury Mine*. Westport, Conn.: Greenwood Press, 1941.

Zimmerman, Arthur F. *Francisco de Toledo, Fifth Viceroy of Peru*. Caldwell, Ohio: Caxton Printers, 1938.

Chapter 3. Ascendancy, 1580-1620

Arzans de Orsuna y Vela, Bartolomé. *Tales of Potosí*. Translated by Frances M. Lopez-Morillas. Providence: Brown University Press, 1975.

Fernandez-Armesto, Felipe. *The Spanish Armada: The Experience of War in 1588*. Oxford: Oxford University Press, 1988.

Graham, Winston. *The Spanish Armadas*. London: Collins, 1987.

Hanke, Lewis. *The Imperial City of Potosi*. The Hague: Martinus Nijhoff, 1956.

Parker, Geoffrey. *The Army of Flanders and the Spanish Road, 1567-1659: The Logistics of Spanish Victory and Defeat in the Low Countries' Wars*, rev. ed. Cambridge: Cambridge University Press, 1990.

Phillips, Carla Rahn. *Six Galleons for the King of Spain: Imperial Defense in the Early Seventeenth Century*. Baltimore: Johns Hopkins University Press, 1986.

Pike, Ruth. *Aristocrats and Traders: Sevillian Society in the Sixteenth Century*. Ithaca: Cornell University Press, 1972.

Spote, Oskar H.K. *The Spanish Lake*. Minneapolis: University of Minnesota Press, 1979.

Thompson, I.A.A. *War and Government in Habsburg Spain, 1560-1620*. London: Athlone, 1976.

Chapter 4. Decline, 1621-1715

Andrien, Kenneth J. *Crisis and Decline: The Viceroyalty of Peru in the Seventeenth Century*. Albuquerque: University of New Mexico Press, 1985.

Boyajian, James C. *Portuguese Bankers at the Court of Spain, 1626-1650*. New Brunswick, N.J.: Rutgers University Press, 1983.

Bakewell, Peter J. *Silver and Entrepreneurship in Seventeenth-Century Potosi: The Life and Times of Antonio Lopez de Quiroga*. Albuquerque: University of New Mexico Press, 1988.

Bradley, Peter T. *The Lure of Peru: Maritime Intrusion into the South Sea, 1598-1701*. New York: St. Martin's, 1989.

Crouse, N.M. *The French Struggle for the West Indies, 1665-1713*. New York: Columbia University Press, 1943. Reprint. New York: Octagon Books, 1966.

Davies, R. Trevor. *Spain in Decline, 1621-1700*. London: Macmillan, 1965.

Earle, Peter. *The Treasure of the Concepción: The Wreck of the Almiranta*. New York: Viking Press, 1980.

Goslinga, Cornelis C. *The Dutch in the Caribbean and the Wild Coast, 1580-1680*. Gainesville: University of Florida Press, 1971.

Hamilton, Earl J. *War and Prices in Spain, 1651-1800*. Cambridge, Mass.: Harvard University Press, 1947.

Haring, C.H. *The Buccaneers in the West Indies in the XVII Century*. Hamden, Conn.: Archon Books, 1966.

Israel, Jonathan I. *Dutch Primacy in World Trade, 1585-1740*. Oxford: Clarendon Press, 1989.

Israel, Jonathan I. *The Dutch Republic and the Hispanic World, 1606-61*. Oxford: Clarendon Press, 1982.

Kamen, Henry. *Spain in the Later Seventeenth Century, 1665-1700*. London: Longman, 1986.

Kamen, Henry. *The War Succession in Spain, 1700-15*. Bloomington: Indiana University Press, 1969.

McLachlan, Joan. *Trade and Peace with Old Spain, 1667-1750*. Cambridge: Cambridge University Press, 1940.

Marx, Robert F. *The Capture of the Treasure Fleet: The Story of Piet Heyn*. New York: McKay, 1977.

Stradling, R.A. *Europe and the Decline of Spain: A Study of the Spanish System, 1580-1720*. London: George Allen & Unwin, 1981.

Chapter 5. Recovery, 1716-1790

Brading, D.A. *Miners and Merchants in Bourbon Mexico, 1763-1810*. Cambridge: Cambridge University Press, 1971.

Lynch, John. *Bourbon Spain, 1700-1808*. Oxford: Basil Blackwood, 1989.

McCusker, John J. *Money and Exchange in Europe and America, 1600-1775: A Handbook*. Chapel Hill: University of North Carolina Press, 1978.

McNeill, John R. *Atlantic Empires of France and Spain: Louisbourg and Havana, 1700-1763*. Chapel Hill: University of North Carolina Press, 1985.

Pares, Richard. *War and Trade in the West Indies, 1739-63*. London: Oxford University Press, 1936.

Parry, J.H. *Trade and Dominion: The European Overseas Empires in the Eighteenth Century*. London: Weidenfeld and Nicolson, 1971.

Priestley, Herbert I. *José de Gálvez, Visitor-General of New Spain, 1765-1771*. Berkeley: University of California Press, 1916.

Walker, Geoffrey J. *Spanish Politics and Imperial Trade, 1707-1789*. Bloomington: Indiana University Press, 1979.

Chapter 6. Rediscovery, 1791-Present

Arnold, J. Barto, and Weddle, Robert S. *The Nautical Archaeology of Padre Island: The Spanish Shipwrecks of 1554*. New York: Academic Press, 1978.

Bass, George F., ed. *Ships and Shipwrecks of the Americas: A History Based on Underwater Archaeology*. New York: Thames and Hudson, 1988.

Burgess, Robert F. and Clausen, Carl J. *Gold, Galleons, and Archaeology*. New York: Bobbs-Merrill, 1976.

Burgess, Robert F. *Sunken Treasure: Six Who Found Fortunes*. New York: Dodd, Mead & Co., 1988.

Grissim, John. *The Lost Treasure of the Concepción*. New York: William Morrow, 1980.

Hepburn, A. Barton. *A History of Currency in the United States*. rev. ed. New York: Macmillan, 1924.

Horner, David L. *The Treasure Galleons: Clues to Millions in Sunken Gold and Silver*. Port Salerno, Fla.: Florida Classics Library, 1990.

Lyon, Eugene. *The Search for the Atocha*. New York: Harper and Row, 1979.

Martin, Colin. *Full Fathom Five: The Wrecks of the Spanish Armada*. New York: Viking, 1975.

Marx, Robert F. *Shipwrecks in the Americas*. Rev. ed. New York: Dover Publications, 1987.

Marx, Robert F. *The Underwater Dig: An Introduction to Marine Archaeology*. New York: Henry Z. Walck, 1975.

Mathewson, R. Duncan III. *Treasure of the Atocha*. New York: E.P. Dutton, 1986.

Meylach, Martin. *Diving to a Flash of Gold*. Port Salerno: Florida Classics Library, 1986.

Potter, John S. Jr. *The Treasure Diver's Guide*. rev. ed. Garden City: Doubleday, 1972. Reprint. Port Salerno: Florida Classics Library, 1988.

Sténuit, Robert. *Treasures of the Armada*. Translated by Francine Barker. New York: E.P. Dutton, 1973.

Wagner, Kip. *Pieces of Eight: Recovering the Riches of a Lost Spanish Treasure Fleet*. New York: E.P. Dutton, 1966.

Index

Hamilton, Alexander (1755-1804), 194
Havana, 46, 53-**54**, 56, 91, 120, **174**, 179
Hawkins, John (1532-1595), 73-74, 86-89, **88**, 93, 95, 98, 102
Herrera, Juan de (1530-1597), 85
Heyn, Piet (1577-1629), **120**-123, 220
Holy Roman Empire, 8, 25-27, 71, 117-118
Howard, Charles (1536-1624), 94-95, 103
Huancavelica, 39, 135, 177
Humphreys, Herbert, 213-215, 223-224

Incas, 13, 21-22
India, 10-11, 128, 147, 175, 182, 185
Institute of Nautical Archaeology, 213, 224
Italy, 4-5, 25-27, 44, 60, 118, 126, 158

Jamaica, 128, 131, 166, 178
Jefferson, Thomas (1743-1826), 194
Juros, 29-30, 69, 72, 107, 145, 225

Kelso, Kip, 208-209

Latin America. See Spain
Legazpi, Miguel López de (1510-1572), 65, 76
Lepanto, Battle of (1571), 70
Lima, 21
Lisbon, 93, 98
Louis XIV (1638-1715), 130-132, 141, 152, 157-158
Low Countries, 4, 25, 44, 60, 70-71, 86, 158
Lyon, Eugene, 216-217

Magellan, Ferdinand (1480-1521), 15, 24, 50
Manila, 65, 69, 105, 151, 174-175
Manila galleons, 65-69, 76, 92, 111, 139, 156, 169-170, 175, 180, 196, 220
Maravillas, Nuestra Señora de las, 41, 128, 140, 213-215
Marx, Robert, 213, 224
Matanzas Bay, Battle of (1628), 120-123, **122-123**
Mathewson, Duncan, 216
McKee, Arthur, 205-207, 215, 220, 223
Medina del Campo, fairs, 9, 107
Medina Sidonia, Duke of (1549-1615), 91, 94
Mendoza, Antonio de (1492-1552), 32
Menéndez de Avilés, Pedro (1519-1574), 46-47, 55-57, 62-64, 76

Mercantilism, 33-34, 111, 131-132, 175-176
Mercury, 38-39, 43, 56, 93, 121, 135, 165, 176
Mexico, 196-197, 215-216
Mexico City, 18-19, 43, 50, 181
Milan, 25
Mining, 37-40, 43, 135-136, 176
Minorca, 156, 158, 175, 178-180
Mints, 76, 166, 177-178
  Bogotá, 138
  Mexico City, 19-20, 32, 43, 166-167, 181
  Potosí, 37-42, **39**, 80-81, 135-137, 166, 196
  Seville, 62-63, 84
Mita, 38, 135-136
Moctezuma (1466-1520), 17, 19
Money. See Currency
Morgan, Henry (1635-1688), 130-131
Morris, Robert (1734-1806), 194
Muiscas, 23, 202

Napoleonic Wars, 196
Nestares Marín, Francisco de, 136
Netherlands. See United Provinces
New Granada, 23-24, 43, 53, 82, 137-138, 196
New Spain, 16-21, 32, 43, 50, 65, 81-82, 137, 176, 181, 196
Newton, Isaac (1642-1727), 153
Nombre de Dios, 53, 75, 91, 102-103
North Carolina, 89, 91, 166, 220

Olivares, Duke of (1587-1645), 118-119, 126
Opium, 185, 198-199
Oquendo, Antonio de (1577-1640), 124-125
Orellana, Francisco de (1511-1546), 23
Ottoman Empire, 10, 25-27, 70, 86, 182, 188
Oxenham, John, 75

Padre Island, 61, 212, 223
Panama, 15-16, 51-53, 74-75, 167
Panama City, 51, 53, 131, 141, 168-169
Paper money, 11, 146-147, 179, 182-183
Paris, Peace of (1763), 175
Parma, Duke of (1545-1592), 89-90, 94-95
Patiño, José (1666-1736), 164
Penn, William (1621-1670), 127
Peru, 21-22, 37-42, 51, 75-76, 80-81, 135-137, 165, 169, 176-177, 196